Hiking
New York

by
Rhonda & George Ostertag

FALCON®

Falcon® Publishing, Inc.
Helena, Montana

A FALCON GUIDE

Falcon® Publishing is continually expanding its list of recreational guide-books. All books include detailed descriptions, accurate maps, and all information necessary for enjoyable trips. You can order extra copies of this book and get information and prices for other Falcon® books by writing Falcon, P.O. Box 1718, Helena, MT 59624, or by calling toll-free 1-800-582-2665. Also, please ask for a copy of our current catalog. Visit our website at www.Falcon.com or contact us by e-mail at falcon@falcon.com.

All black-and-white photos by authors.
Cover photo: by Peter Cole, New England Stock Photo.

Library of Congress Cataloging-in-Publication Data

Ostertag, Rhonda, 1957-
    Hiking New York / by Rhonda & George Ostertag.
        p.   cm.
    "A Falcon guide"—T.p. verso.
    ISBN 1-56044-396-0 (pbk.)
    1. Hiking—New York (State)—Guidebooks. 2. Trails—New York (State)—Guidebooks. 3. New York (State)—Guidebooks.
    I. Ostertag, George, 1957- II. Title.
    GV199.42.N65078 1996
    796.5'1'09747—dc20   96-26273
                                             CIP

CAUTION

Outdoor recreational activities are by their very nature potentially hazard-ous. All participants in such activities must assume responsibility for their own actions and safety. The information contained in this guidebook cannot replace sound judgment and good decision-making skills, which help reduce exposure, nor does the scope of this book allow for the disclosure of all the potential hazards and risks involved in such activities.

Learn as much as possible about the outdoor recreational activities in which you participate, prepare for the unexpected, and be cautious. The reward will be a safer and more enjoyable experience.

 Text pages printed on recycled paper.

CONTENTS

CONTENTS

CONTENTS

ACKNOWLEDGMENTS

We would like to acknowledge the trail associations and individual volunteers who blaze and maintain the trails, the preservationists who work to save New York State's prized natural and cultural areas, and the many landowners who have allowed for the state trail system to grow and endure. We would like to thank the individuals who helped with our research and volunteered their ideas or faces to this book, and we would like to thank our east and west coast base camps for freeing us to do our work.

OVERVIEW MAP — LOCATION OF HIKES

A. Thousand Islands-Seaway
B. The Adirondacks
C. Niagara Frontier
D. Chautauqua-Allegheny
E. Finger Lakes
F. Central-Leatherstocking
G. Capital-Saratoga
H. Catskills
I. Hudson Valley
J. Long Island

MAP LEGEND

Interstate	(210)	Wetland	
U.S. Highway	(101)	Campground	▲
State or County Road	(2)	Picnic Area	
Paved Road	▷	Trail Shelter	△
Gravel Road	▷	Bridge	)(
Unimproved Road	========▷	Building	■
Trailhead/Parking	(P)	Gazebo	●
Described Trail	～～～	Mine/Quarry	✕
Alternate Trail	～～～	Viewpoint	⊙
Brook	～～～	Point of Interest	★
River		Powerline	•—•—•—•
Body of Water		Lookout Tower	
Summit/Elevation	2,477ft.	Railroad	+++++
Waterfall		Scale	0 0.5 1 Miles
Dam	▬	Spring	

INTRODUCTION

New York State extends a premier outdoor playground, featuring thousands of miles of trail ranging from short nature walks to lengthy canal and rail trails to outstanding rugged wilderness hikes. Pacing off these routes, hikers discover a winning diversity of landscape, a seemingly limitless natural offering, and a rich geologic and cultural history that indelibly etch New York State in the journal of one's memory.

The trails described in this book explore many of the state's premier parks, forests, mountains, gorges, flatlands, swamps, beaches, and private reserves. Hikers will travel past dazzling waterfalls and daunting cliffs, bag summits and tag valley floors, but mostly they will get to know New York. Although some of this treasury is well known, great expanses remain little tapped.

This guidebook features a statewide sampling of nature walks, day-length hikes, and backpacking trips (where available), a collection to challenge, excite, and engage. Despite the East's early settlement, New York still revels in open spaces and untarnished vistas.

If the New York trail system has but one failing, it would be the design of its peak trails. Many charge straight at the summit, creating run-off channels and broad erosion scars. Hikers should take a role at the forefront of conservation and support, rather than thwart, the land management agencies in their efforts to re-route and improve these trails. Switchbacks, contours, and other design features help retain the integrity of the land. Our

Eastern hardwood forest.

adventure should not come at the price of the land or the enjoyment of future generations.

Weather

For the most part, New York offers three-season hiking, with many hiking trails serving dual roles as winter cross-country ski routes and snowshoe trails. Spring and fall offer a preferred mix of mild temperatures and low humidity. Summers can bring extremes in both categories, as well as dramatic afternoon thunder and lightning storms.

Like much of the East, New York endures a tormenting mosquito and black fly season. Less troublesome in dry years, the insects can attain unbearable numbers in wet years. June through much of July, insects may keep hikers at bay, especially in the Adirondacks and in New York's lowlands and swamp country. Wildflower devotees learn to wear netting and a smelly armor of insect repellent.

Terrain

The advance and retreat of four glacial masses over a period of two million years sculpted the face of New York State, gouging north-south lakes, scouring valleys, and depositing rock debris.

The state boasts a diversity of terrain and habitat that can inspire and fulfill for a lifetime. The coastal influence and pine barren habitat of Long Island, the highlands and valley plain of the Hudson River, the beauty and

East Branch Ausable River, Adirondack Mountain Reserve.

folklore of the Catskills, the quartzite ledges of the Shawangunks, the finger-gouged lakes and east-west gorges of the Finger Lakes Region, the flat ridges and V-shaped valleys of the Allegany Hills, the Great Lakes and Saint Lawrence River country, and the prized peak-and-lake terrain of Adirondack Park spread a buffet suitable for the gods.

Outcrop vistas, grand waterfalls, clear-coursing streams, lakes, beaver ponds, marshes, rolling hardwood forests, alpine stands of fir and spruce, and meadow and desert plains season the journey. Hikers stumble upon the paths of past presidents and literary giants, soldiers and farmers. The sparks of independence and the tide of the Industrial Revolution brush the terrain.

Land Ownership

While this book concentrates primarily on public land offerings, trails across private, trust, and conservancy lands extend one's hiking opportunity. Hikers assume full responsibility for their own well-being when they cross onto private lands; they also consent to heed posted rules. Keep to the trail, leave gates as they were found, and police your own actions as well as those of any trail illiterates who may have passed before you. "Pack it in, pack it out."

The text will indicate if and where a trail traverses private land. Occasionally, land ownership changes or a landowner may withdraw the privilege of through-travel; respect such closures. Privately operated resorts or reserves may charge fees or suggest donations.

The Nature Conservancy (TNC), a nonprofit organization devoted to the protection of biodiversity, opens its trails to the public for hiking, nature study, and photography. Please note that straying from the trail, hiking with pets, collecting, smoking, picnicking, camping, building fires, swimming, and bicycle riding are forbidden activities.

With a mission to conserve and preserve the land, its habitats and inhabitants, TNC extends hiking privileges only where and when they are compatible with this primary objective. Donations help defray the cost both of maintaining existing preserves and acquiring new ones.

A separate nonprofit entity in the Shawangunks, Mohonk Preserve, similarly protects in perpetuity a tract of prized land in its natural form. This preserve offers hiking and like pursuits, and has its own rules and fees.

Trails traversing lands managed by state, county, and federal agencies comprise the core of this book. Of the state operated properties, state park sites (overseen by the New York State Office of Parks, Recreation and Historic Preservation) typically show greater grooming and development and possess more facilities, although the trails may not necessarily reflect the same level of civility. Some are overgrown and poorly marked. At most state parks, expect to pay a seasonal entrance fee. Many hikers find the New York State Empire Pass, an annual day-use pass, easily pays for itself.

The New York State Department of Environmental Conservation (DEC) manages the vast acreage of state-owned lands. State forests account for much of New York's open space; these lands provide planted stands and woods for selective harvests and multiple-use recreation. Backcountry shelters and privies, trail registers, and parking lots are the basic facilities. The state forest preserves found at Adirondack Park and in the Catskills feature vast expanses of protected woodlands closed to harvest and other revenue-making enterprises but open to various recreational pursuits. Wildlife management areas primarily promote and sustain waterfowl and wildlife populations, with hunting and fishing, bird watching, and hiking being compatible recreations. Multiple-use areas serve a gamut of year-round recreational users.

Trail Markings

Most of the trailbeds throughout New York are worn rather than cut into existence. With the predominance of deciduous forest, some manner of trail blazing, either paint, diamond, or disk markers, guides hikers along these routes. A double-blazing pattern typically warns of a change in direction. Often the top blaze is offset to the right or left to indicate the direction of the turn.

As the intervals between blazes can vary greatly, familiarize yourself with the blazing frequency. An uncommonly long lapse between blazes may indicate that you have strayed off course. Autumn hikers need to be especially alert, as leaves conceal the tracked path.

The DEC uses color-coded and user-coded disks to mark its routes. In several areas the agency offers independent trail systems for foot, horse, and mountain bike use.

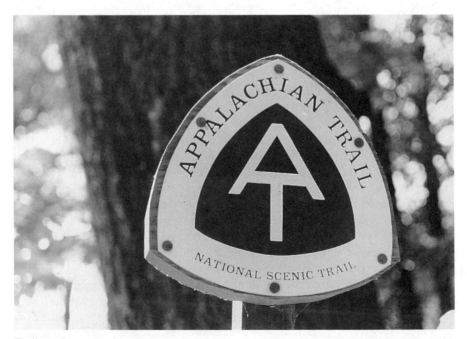

Trail marker.

Several fine long-distance routes crisscross the state, including the white Appalachian Trail, the blue Northville-Placid Trail, the yellow- or white-blazed Finger Lakes Trail, the aqua Long Path, and the orange Conservation Trail. On some private lands, blaze patterns may exist for one-directional travel only; consult a mapboard or flier before plotting your course. Cairns and stakes are other manners of marking a route.

The Volunteer Component

Devoted, energetic volunteers and established hiking organizations, such as the New York-New Jersey Trail Conference, the Adirondack Mountain Club (ADK), the Appalachian Mountain Club (AMC), the Finger Lakes Trail Conference (FLTC), and the Long Island Greenbelt Trail Conference, keep the New York State trail system maintained, promoted, and growing. Hikers should support these groups through membership as well as through the purchase of their maps and materials. Typically, the maps produced and sold by the volunteer organizations hold the most current information on the lay of the trail, land ownership, shelters and facilities, and obstacles.

Hikers likewise owe an enormous thanks to the legion of private landowners who allow trails to cross their lands. Many trails would slip from existence without their cooperation.

HOW TO USE THIS GUIDE

We have structured the book to aid in the trail selection process. First, to ease page flipping for trail comparisons, we have grouped the trails according to ten commonly accepted geographic regions. Second, a summary table heads each write-up, presenting the trail at a glance for a quick measure of its overall interest. Information bullets sketch the trail, its general location, specialness, length, elevation change, difficulty, maps, special requirements or concerns, season, and a source for more information.

At the end of the summary, find detailed directions to the trailhead. Turn to Appendix D for the complete address and phone number for each named information source.

"The hike" component of the text describes the progress of the trail, drawing attention to special features and alerting readers to obstacles and potentially confusing junctions. Mentions of habitat changes, seasonal surprises, sidelights, and discoveries flesh out the tour. Where appropriate, for a balanced view we have mentioned flaws and disappointments.

The maps included within the text are not intended to replace more detailed agency maps, road maps, state atlases, and/or topographic maps, but they do indicate the lay of the trail and its attractions to help readers visualize the tour.

Fungi at Tug Hill State Forest.

Azalea blooms, Mianus River Gorge Preserve.

An Explanation of Summary Table Terms

Distance measures for the trails represent pedometer readings. Backpacking excursions—sometimes dictated by distance, sometimes by attraction—are left to the hiker's judgment and the rules of the appropriate managing agency, landowner, or private trust.

The subjective classification of "easy," "moderate," or "strenuous" takes into consideration overall distance, elevation change (the diffcrence between the elevation extremcs), cumulative elevation (how rolling a trail is), trail surface, obstacles, ease of following, and its relative difficulty to the other hikes in the book.

We deliberately excluded estimated hiking times, as personal health and physical condition, party size, the interest of the trail, weather, and a trail's condition all influence time on the trail. Gain a sense of your personal capabilities and hiking style, and judge the time yourself based on the distance, the elevation change, the difficulty rating, and what you glean from the text. Customize the hikes to fit your needs; you need not continue just because a description does, nor must you stop where it stops. Interlocking loops, side trails, and alternative destinations await.

OUTDOOR PRIMER

Whether wilderness trekking brings about a revitalizing experience or turns into an ordeal depends largely on one's preparation. Naturc does not come without some inherent risks and discomforts, but learning to anticipate and mitigate the downsides smoothens the way to great outdoor fun.

Preparation

Ten essentials. Outdoor experts have assembled a list of "ten essentials," the cornerstone to safe backcountry travel. These are (1) extra food, (2) extra clothing, (3) sunglasses, (4) knife, (5) candle or chemical fuel to ignite wet wood, (6) dry matches, (7) first-aid kit and manual, (8) flashlight with bulb and batteries, (9) maps for the trip, and (10) compass.

Dress. The amount and the types of clothing worn and carried on a hike depend on the length of the outing, the weather conditions, and one's personal comfort. Layering is key to comfort; select items that can serve more than one purpose. A long-sleeved shirt may be layered for warmth, lends sun protection, hinders mosquitos, and protects against ticks. A lightweight raincoat may double as a windbreaker. Choose wool for cold, wet, or changeable weather conditions; it retains heat even when wet. Choose cotton for dry summer days. For their weight, hats are invaluable for shielding eyes, face, and top of the head and for preserving body heat.

Footgear. While sneakers may be passable for nature walks, boots give comfort and protection on long hikes and uneven terrain. Sock layering, with a light undersock worn next to the foot and a second wool sock worn atop, helps prevent rubbing, cushions the sole, and allows for the absorption of perspiration. Avoid socks with a large cotton content, as they are cold when wet and slow to dry.

Food. Pack plenty, as hiking demands a lot of energy. Pack foods that will not spoil, bruise, or break apart in the pack. Maximize the energy value for the weight, particularly when backpacking. Food fends off fatigue, a major contributor to accidents on the trail.

Equipment. The quantity and variety depend on the length and nature of the hike and on the season, but a good pack for transporting the gear is essential. A day pack with padded straps, a reinforced bottom, and side pockets for water bottles works for most short outings. For overnight outings, select a backpack that has a good frame and balance and supports the weight without taxing hips, shoulders, or neck.

As backpacks represent a major investment, newcomers should first try renting a backpack. One cannot evaluate a pack in the store with only a few sandbags for weight. A trail test delivers a better comfort reading, plus it demonstrates how well the unit packs with one's personal gear. Most good backpacking stores with a rental program will allow the charge of one rental to be applied to the purchase price of a new pack; ask the manager. Appendix A offers a checklist of other commonly carried items.

Map and Compass. All hikers should become familiar with maps and know how to read them in conjunction with a compass. Maps provide an orientation to an area, suggest alternative routes, and aid in the planning and preparation for the journey.

Become familiar with the United States Geological Survey (USGS) topographic maps. While most of these quads for New York State are too dated to show the lay of the trail, they still provide information about the steepness and flatness of the terrain, whether a site is treed or open, waterways, and the works of man. The USGS offers two sizes: the 7.5-minute and 15-minute series.

New York State Department of Transportation (DOT) maps, based on the USGS 7.5-minute series, provide the same information but lack color to indicate vegetation.

Remember that true north does not equal magnetic north. For New York State the declination is about 14 degrees west. Search the map border for the declination.

Taking to the Trails

Pacing yourself. Adopt a steady, comfortable hiking rhythm, take in the surroundings, and schedule short rests at regular intervals to guard against exhaustion.

Crossing streams. Cross at the widest part of a watercourse, where the current is slower and the water more shallow. Sandy bottoms suggest a barefoot crossing; fast, cold waters and rocky bottoms require the surer footing of boots.

Shed your socks before mounting a boot-clad wade. That way, once across, you will have a dry sock layer to help protect and keep your feet warm in the wet boots; wool socks show their thermal value. The discomfort of hiking in wet boots is minor compared to the alternative dunking. For frequent stream crossings or for hiking streambeds, lightweight sneakers earn their portage.

Hiking cross-country. For safe cross-country travel, one must have good map and compass skills, good survival skills, and good common sense. Steep terrain, heavy brush, and downfalls physically and mentally tax hikers, increasing the potential for injury. This, of all hiking, should not be attempted alone. Even know-how and preparation cannot fully overcome the unpredictability of nature and human fallibility.

Hiking with children. For young children, choose simple destinations and do not insist on reaching any particular site. Allow for the difference in attention span and energy level. Enjoy the passing, and share and encourage children's natural curiosity, but come prepared for sun, mosquitos, and poison ivy. Discuss what to do should you become separated; even small ones should carry some essential items: a sweater, water jug, and food.

A Wilderness Ethic

Trails. Keep to the path. Shortcutting, skirting puddles, and walking two abreast all contribute to erosion and the degradation of trails. Report any damage.

Permits and Registration. In a few areas, land agencies issue trail or camp permits to help monitor and manage the trails and minimize over-use. Check under the heading of "special requirements" in the trail summary table. On DEC lands, single-site stays of longer than three days and camping parties that exceed ten in number require permits. To protect the integrity of the wild, keep your party size small.

The DEC has an extensive trailhead registration program. Take the time to sign in and out and comment on the condition of the trail and its markings. The collected information figures into the allotment of funds for trail improvement and expansion.

Pets. Owners should strictly adhere to posted rules for pets. Controlling your animal on a leash is not just a courtesy reserved for times when other hikers are present; it is a responsibility to protect the wildlife and ground-cover at all times.

Camping. Low-impact camping should be everyone's goal. Select an established campsite and do not alter the ground cover, bring in logs for benches, bang nails into trees, or dig drainage channels around the tent. The clues that a hiker passed this way should be minimal.

Where no pre-established campsite exists, select a site at least 200 feet from the water and well removed from any trail. Avoid delicate meadow and alpine environments, and do not degrade lakeshore, waterfall, overlook, or other prized sites with a camp.

Chautauqua Creek.

Red eft, Allegany State Park.

Reduce comforts (as opposed to necessities). Carry a backpacker's stove for cooking; when a campfire is unavoidable, keep it small. Snags and live trees should never be cut.

Sanitation. For human waste disposal, select a site well away from the trail and at least 300 feet from any water body. Dig a hole 8 inches deep in which to bury the waste. This biologically active layer of soil holds organisms that can quickly decompose organic matter. If the ground prohibits digging a hole of the specified size, dig as deep as possible and cover well with gravel, bark, and leaves.

Use tissue sparingly, and for shorter excursions, carry a zip-seal plastic bag for packing out soiled tissue. Burying often results in the tissue becoming nest-building material for rodents, or unsightly garbage scattered by salt-seeking deer.

Litter. "Pack it in, pack it out." This includes aluminum foil, cans, orange peels, peanut shells, cigarette butts, and disposable diapers. For nature to reclaim an orange peel takes six months, a filter-tip cigarette butt ten to twelve years. Disposable diapers have become an incredible nuisance and a contaminant in the wild. Burying is not a solution.

Washing. Washing of self or dishes should be done well away from the lake or stream. Carry wash water to a rocky site and use biodegradable suds sparingly. Despite their benefits and ecological-sounding name, these soaps still present a threat to water.

Safety

Water. Water is the preferred refreshment; carry a safe quantity from home on all excursions, as wilderness sources dry up or may become fouled. Know that caffeine and alcohol are diuretics which dehydrate and weaken you.

Treat water taken from wilderness sources when it is to be used for drinking or washing foods or eating utensils. *Giardia lamblia*, a water-borne protozoan, which causes stomach and intestinal discomfort, finds a home in even the most remote, clear streams. Bring water to a full boil for at least five minutes. Water purification systems that remove both debris and harmful organisms offer a satisfactory alternative to boiling. As these filters come in varying degrees of sophistication, make certain the selected system strains out harmful organisms. Iodine tablets offer less protection, and no protection against Giardia, and are not considered safe for pregnant women.

Getting Lost. Prior to departure, notify a responsible party of your intended destination, route, and time of return. Then keep to it and notify them upon your return.

If lost, sit down and try to think calmly. No immediate danger exists, as long as one has packed properly and followed the notification procedure. If hiking with a group, stay together. Short outward searches for the trail, returning to an agreed-upon, marked location if unsuccessful, is generally considered safe. If near a watercourse, following it downstream typically delivers a place of habitation or a roadway where help may be sought. Aimless wandering is a mistake.

Blowing a whistle or making loud noises in sets of three may summon help. If late in the day, prepare for night and try to conserve energy. Unless one has good cross-country navigational skills, efforts are best spent conserving energy and aiding rescuers by staying put and hanging out bright-colored clothing.

Hypothermia. This dramatic cooling of the body occurs when heat loss surpasses body-heat generation. Cold, wet, and windy weather command respect. Attending to the Ten Essentials, eating properly, avoiding fatigue, and being alert to the symptoms of sluggishness, clumsiness, and incoherence among party members remain the best protection. Should a party member display such symptoms, stop and get that member dry and warm. Dry clothing, shared body heat, and hot fluids all help.

Heat Exhaustion. Strenuous exercise combined with summer sun can lead to heat exhaustion, an over-taxation of the body's heat regulatory system. Wearing a hat, drinking plenty of water, eating properly (including salty snacks), and avoiding fatigue are safeguards.

Poison ivy and poison sumac. The best way to avoid contact with these and other skin irritating plants is to learn what they look like and in what environments they grow. Consult a good plant identification book. Vaccines and creams have yet to conquer these irritating plant oils. If you suspect you have come in contact with one of these plants, rinse off as soon as possible and avoid scratching, as it spreads the oils.

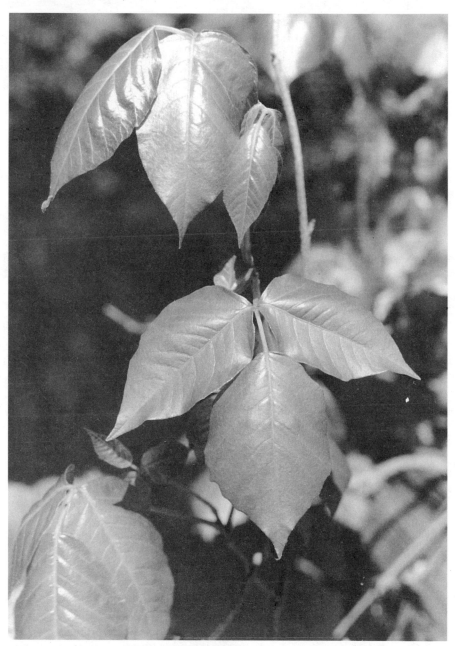

Poison ivy, Bashakill Wildlife Management Area.

Ticks, stings, and bites. Again the best defense is knowledge. Learn about the habits and habitats of snakes, bees, wasps, ticks, and other "menaces" of the wild and how to deal with the injuries they may cause. Also become aware of any personal allergies and sensitivities you or a party member might have.

Lyme disease, transmitted by the tiny deer tick, has become a serious concern in the East, but it need not deter you from the outdoors. Hikers come into contact with these ticks amid grasses and shrubs; the ticks do not drop from trees. Wear light-colored long pants and long-sleeved shirts, and keep your layers tucked into one another. This will help you identify any ticks and keep them on the outside of your garments. While hiking, make frequent checks for the unwanted hitchhiker. Once at home, shower and search skin surfaces thoroughly and launder hiking clothes directly.

Should a tick become attached to the skin, remove it by drawing evenly on the body, disinfect the bite with alcohol, and monitor over the next few weeks. Look for a red bull's-eye swelling at the site of the bite; also be alert to inexplicable muscle pain, tiredness, or flu symptoms. Consult a physician immediately should any of these warnings occur.

Bears. The black bears in the East represent more nuisance than threat. Use common sense; do not store food near camp, and especially not in the tent. If clothes pick up cooking smells, suspend them along with the food from an isolated overhanging branch well away from camp. Sweet-smelling creams or lotions should be avoided.

Hunting. While most public lands open to hunters do not prohibit hiking during hunting season and few have any record of conflict, we would still advise fall hikers to point their boots toward lands and trails where hunting is not allowed. If you hike where hunting occurs, wear bright orange clothing and keep to the trail.

Trailhead Precautions. Unattended hiker vehicles are vulnerable to clouting, but the following steps can minimize the risk:

Whenever possible, park away from the trailhead at a nearby campground or other facility.

Do not leave valuables. Place keys and wallet in a button-secured pocket or remote, secure compartment in the pack where they will not be disturbed until your return.

Do not leave any visible invitations; stash everything in the trunk, and be sure any exposed item advertises it has no value.

Be suspicious of loiterers and do not volunteer the details of your outing.

Be cautious about the information you supply at the trailhead register. Withhold information such as license plate number and duration of stay, until you are safely back at the trailhead.

Backcountry travel includes unavoidable risks that every traveler assumes and must be aware of and respect. The fact that a trail or an area is described in this book is not a representation that it will be safe for you. For while the book attempts to alert users to safe methods and warn of potential dangers, it is limited. Time, nature, use, and abuse can quickly alter the face of a trail. Let independent judgment and common sense be your guide.

For more detailed information about outdoor preparedness, consult a good instructional book or enroll in a class on outdoor etiquette, procedure, and safety. Even the outdoor veteran can benefit from a refresher.

THOUSAND ISLANDS-SEAWAY REGION

This Upstate New York region features an exciting terrain at the Canadian border uniting Thousand Islands, the St. Lawrence River Seaway, the eastern shore of Lake Ontario, and the low-lying forests west of the Adirondacks. The hikes visit exciting gorge and gulf features, racing waters, a pristine beach, an island splendor, and a unique "alvar" habitat. Vistas applaud lake, river, and Canadian shore. The changeable weather associated with the Great Lakes brings an added intensity to this rich and varied stage.

1 STONE VALLEY TRAIL

General description: This moderately difficult wooded trail rounds an exciting 3.2-mile stretch of the Raquette River.
General location: In the towns of Colton, Parishville, and Pierrepont.
Special attractions: Waterfalls, rapids, chutes, scoured potholes, gorges, islands, and overhanging cliffs; hemlock-beech forest; cathedral pines; tannery ruin.
Length: 7.8-mile loop.
Elevation: The rolling trail shows a 200-foot elevation change.
Difficulty: Moderate.
Maps: "Stone Valley: A Cooperative Recreation Area" pamphlet sponsored by Niagara Mohawk Power Corporation (generally available at the trailhead registers or from the St. Lawrence County Planning Office).
Special requirements: Be alert to the possibility of rapidly rising water. In winter, expect icy spots, and some risky stretches where an icy slip could land you in the river.
Season and hours: Year-round, but best spring through fall; 24 hours a day.
For information: Saint Lawrence County Planning Department.

Finding the trailhead: From the intersection of New York 56 and New York 68 at the southern end of the hamlet of Colton, go north on NY 56 for 3.6 miles and turn right (east) on Browns Bridge Road/Saint Lawrence County 24. Go 0.5 mile and turn right to reach the northwest trailhead parking lot near the powerhouse in 0.1 mile; this site offers the best parking. Find additional access in Colton at the Raquette River bridge.

The hike: From the northwest trailhead off Browns Bridge Road, the trail travels lands owned by Niagara Mohawk Power, Saint Lawrence County, and the town of Colton. Arrows, blue trail markers, and small plaques explaining the geologic and cultural history of the area mark the route. Be cautious where the path is canted and eroded and on log crossings.

Follow the marked service road leaving the southwest corner of the parking lot. In 0.1 mile turn left, finding the trail register and brochures. Round the site of the Niagara Mohawk Powerhouse and turn south away from the facility, following service roads and grassy tracks. The trail passes through open woods, bramble-shrub clearings, and plantations. Wildflowers spangle the way, while deer tracks riddle the soft dirt.

Be alert for a marker pointing hikers left along an old woods road at 0.6 mile. The path descends and rounds toward the river, crossing a drainage where some creative stepping may be needed in addition to the corduroys to escape getting wet.

Raquette River.

STONE VALLEY TRAIL

At a mile the trail forks; bear right. In a few feet a sign on the left indicates "O'Malley Brook Overlook." This 0.5-mile round-trip side tour travels a pine-maple slope overlooking a series of beaver dams on a river tributary before reaching a Raquette River overlook and beach. Across the river you will see 15-foot O'Malley Brook Falls. The side trail ends, swinging a small loop on the river flat.

Past this overlook spur, the true river hike begins, rolling along the wooded slope for a grand upstream tour. Where hikers first meet the tannin-colored river, it flows broad and slow, coursing between rock and fern banks.

Upstream it cuts a more volatile figure as the trail undulates between shore level and 100 feet above the stormy water.

At 2 miles bypass "Lucy's Hole" or "the Gut," a deep pool with a brightly painted geometric design adorning the rock of the far shore. The song of the river follows the trail as it draws away from the waterway.

Past three moss-mantled boulders make a steep ascent and descent to reach the lower end of "The Narrows." Here, long bedrock fingers squeeze the water into channels of river fury. Upstream 15- to 18-foot falls, tilted bedrock slabs, worn chutes, and potholes capture the imagination. Side drainages arriving as waterfalls add to the bonanza. Above "The Tub" (a 12-foot-diameter river pothole hidden by a stone lip), another set of falls dazzles the eye, dropping 25 feet over a 100-foot distance.

As the Raquette River becomes gorgelike nearing the power company dam, the trail veers away from the river, climbing above the stone ruins of a tannery. Cross the footbridge over a penstock (a water conduit) and turn left on the dirt road, entering Colton near the town museum (3.75 miles).

For the loop, cross the road bridge over the Raquette River and take the first left, following a paved road past the Colton Fire Department. At the road's end (4 miles), find a small parking lot. Here two mill stones recognize the site's hydropower history and usher hikers back onto the foot trail. River angles and the orientation of the bedrock present an entirely new perspective for the return downstream journey.

From a small ridge, the trail angles downhill, skirting a soggy meadow bottomland, which separates the path from the river. At the upcoming intersection with a woods road, turn left. At 4.4 miles, the trail curves right, edging a bedrock slab at the river. In the rock, steel anchor pins harken back to the nineteenth century when lumberjacks floated the logs to downstream mills.

By 4.6 miles the trail rolls alongside the river; side trails branch right to Lenny Road. At 4.8 miles, view several large potholes riddling the bedrock ridge that forms The Tub; spring floods transform this rock into a roaring cataract of churning stones. The east shore path grows canted, more rootbound, and less civilized than it was for its first mile, and chutes and channels characterize the waterway.

Departing The Narrows (5.2 miles), the trail makes a steep uphill charge, remaining along the upper slope to 5.6 miles, where it plunges back to the river. East shore plaques identify marble outcrops (common in the Adirondack lowland), glacial erratics, and fossils.

Past Lucy's Hole, additional deep pools characterize the next 0.1 mile. Frog, hummingbird, toad, and a grouse forge an acquaintance. At 6 miles comes the next uphill charge. Where the trail next descends, cross O'Malley Brook as it cascades beneath the cathedral pines.

From the O'Malley Brook footbridge, cross a woods flat on a dirt road to pick up the trail on the left. The trail now hugs or travels a terrace 50 feet above the river. At 6.6 miles stands an aspen gnawed half-through by beaver. Deciduous trees offer shade, and throughout easy river access exists.

The foot trail comes to an end at Lenny Road at 7.1 miles. Go left on Lenny Road to Browns Bridge Road, turning left to cross the river. Again turn left to close loop at the trailhead parking lot at 7.8 miles.

2   WELLESLEY ISLAND STATE PARK

Overview

Wellesley Island State Park introduces the beauty of the Thousand Islands to the land-locked traveler. Once farmed, this island shows mixed deciduous woods, abandoned field and pasture, rocky shores, and hilltop knolls. Panoramas take in the Saint Lawrence River, Thousand Islands, and Canadian shore.

In the southwestern portion of the park, a 600-acre peninsula and nature preserve holds 10 miles of interlocking trail, welcoming short excursions. The featured hike for this park, the Round-the-Peninsula Trail, links several of the named paths for a first-rate depiction of the island, its terrain, and locale.

St. Lawrence River, Wellesley Island State Park.

WELLESLEY ISLAND STATE PARK

General description: This rolling tour travels the perimeter of the peninsula, serving up outstanding Saint Lawrence River-Thousand Islands views.
General location: On the Saint Lawrence River.
Special attractions: Vistas, fishing, steep cliffs and knolls, beaver ponds, glacial potholes, wildflowers, nature center.
Length: 4.4 miles round trip.
Elevation: The trail shows about a 100-foot elevation change.
Difficulty: Easy.
Maps: Welcome to Minna Anthony Common Nature Center brochure.
Special requirements: Fee access to park.
Season and hours: Spring through fall, dawn to dusk.
For information: New York State Parks, Thousand Islands Region.

Finding the trailhead: From Watertown, go north on Interstate 81 for 26 miles and take exit 51 for Wellesley Island State Park (after the Thousand Islands Toll Bridge). Following the signs, turn right in 0.1 mile, and again turn right on Jefferson County 100 in another 0.5 mile. Go 0.5 mile more and turn right onto Cross Island Road. The park entrance is in 1.6 miles. Follow the signs to the nature center for the trails.

The hike: The Round-the-Peninsula Trail unites five shorter interlocking nature trails that tour the peninsula. Enjoy views of Eel Bay, The Narrows, South Bay, and the islands of the United States and Canada. In turn, mixed forest, oak-grassland, wetland, and field frame the journey.

Follow signs for Eel Bay Trail, rounding the west side of the Minna Anthony Common Nature Center (museum) via the paved Friendship Trail, an interpretive trail with raised-letter plaques. Past the geology wall comprised of rocks found in the Saint Lawrence Valley, bear left. Maple, hickory, ash, aspen, birch, and mixed oaks overlace the trail and filter looks at Eel Bay. At 0.1 mile, go right; Eel Bay Trail begins at the end of the pavement, crossing over the North Field Loop Trail.

The trail travels a bluff 50 feet above the bay, passing through tall woods with a full canopy. A jeweled lighting dances off Eel Bay as the Saint Lawrence River spreads away big, wild, and blue, bustling with recreation and transportation vessels.

At 0.5 mile the trail curves left, descending to Sand Cove. Here the Sand Cove Trail arrives on the left, and the peninsula tour continues straight. To the right lies the cove with a thin sandy beach edged by box elder and willow.

The trail then rolls uphill, traveling a semi-open bench above the water; outcrops sloping to the water prove popular with anglers and daydreamers. More views await where the trail travels atop a 70-foot cliff at 0.8 mile. Stairs again draw travelers closer to the bay and the clear, rocky-bottomed water. Where hilltop Rocky Knob Overlook comes into view, a spur trail to the right descends to the glacial potholes. The upper pothole measures 3 feet wide and 15 feet deep; the lower one about a third that size.

The peninsula tour resumes following The Narrows Trail, with an early look at the watery channel separating Wellesley Island and Murray Isle. Where the trail tops out after a rocky ascent, a detour left finds Rocky Knob Overlook. The site holds benches and locator boards, pointing out the Thousand Islands neighborhood, including Mosquito, Big Gull, and Little Gull islands, Eel Bay, and the Canadian islands to the north.

At 1.25 miles, an outcrop offers an open view of The Narrows; stairs then descend the slope. Bear right, keeping to The Narrows Trail, which rolls up and over the next hill. Where the trail next bottoms out, a 100-foot spur heads right to a shoreline outcrop offering a farewell look at The Narrows.

Before long, the trail parallels South Bay, passing amid an oak-grassland. At the 1.9-mile junction, the Pond Spillway Trail heads left, adding a pond visit; the Round-the-Peninsula tour continues straight on the South Bay Trail.

For the pond detour, ascend along the outlet ditch. At 2 miles lies the small round pond and the 0.4-mile trail encircling it. Counterclockwise, the trail travels the open grassy bank. Drowned snags, a marshy edge, and perhaps an irritable beaver sounding its alarm with a thunderous beat of the tail add to a tour. Gases percolate up through the waters. As the trail skirts a smaller lily pond, it curves left past picnic tables and a usable privy. A blind offers looks at the beaver lodge before the loop ends. Grouse, frog, porcupine, and kingfisher are other possible encounters.

The South Bay Trail offers a wider path, advancing with mild undulations, touring a wooded plateau 15 feet above the water. Opportunities to shorten the loop branch away to the left; stay on the South Bay Trail for the full tour. At 3.1 miles, wooden steps descend to a viewing dock overlooking a mosaic of open water, lily pads, and cattail marsh. In 1995 the stairs were in disrepair; be watchful of your step.

Ahead, the Round-the-Peninsula Tour turns left, now following the East Bay Trail through moister woods. The path straight ahead soon leaves the park. Deer commonly crisscross paths with hikers as the East Bay Trail steadily ascends to 3.5 miles, where it tops out and curves left, rolling and meandering but trending downhill. Maple, oak, and white pine dominate the forest mix.

While this section of trail is newer and less tracked, red disks with central white arrows point the way. At 3.75 miles, the trail overlooks a large snag marsh parted by a boardwalk. The trail then dips and crosses side-by-side logs over a drainage, coming to a T-junction. Here a 100-foot detour to the right adds a visit to the previously admired wetland pond. The boardwalk journeys to a central dry island amid the shallow pond, where beaver lodges, open water, buttonbush, duckweed, cattails, and snags create a rich stage.

En route to the museum, the trail crosses a boardwalk to follow a wider more defined trail. At 4.25 miles, bypass North Field Loop and traverse a field. The next junction offers an opportunity to visit yet another beaver swamp, a 0.5-mile round-trip detour to the right. Ahead, the East Bay Trail forks; conclude the hike by going right to the parking lot or left to the museum.

3 CHAUMONT BARRENS PRESERVE

Overview

At this Nature Conservancy preserve, discover the unusual habitat of a rare alvar landscape—an austere barren with a naturally occurring linear-vegetation scheme. In North America only a pocketful of alvar sites occupy an arc swinging from northwest Jefferson County in New York through Ontario, Canada and into northern Michigan. Chaumont Barrens represents the premier site in New York State.

This harsh landscape holds a textured mosaic of tufted grassland, juniper-shrub flats, evergreens, mixed deciduous woods, and cracked bedrock. Aerial photographs best reveal the site's odd linear vegetation pattern. Intense glaciation, recurring cycles of flood and drought, and strong winds together shape this severe but intriguing land.

General description: An easy self-guiding loop examines the mystery and beauty of this globally significant habitat.
General location: 14.5 miles northwest of Watertown, off Jefferson County 125.

Limestone fissures, Chaumont Barrens Preserve.

CHAUMONT BARRENS PRESERVE

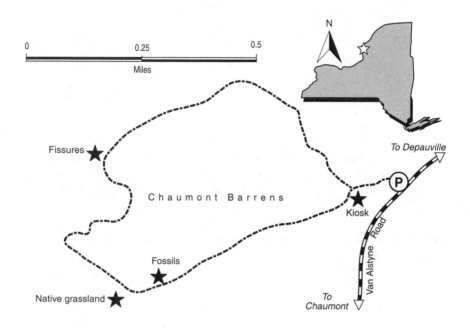

Special attractions: Limestone bedrock fissures, marine fossils, rare native grasslands, rubbly moss gardens, shrub savannas, spring and autumn wild-flowers, bird watching.

Length: 2-mile loop.

Elevation: Travel is virtually flat.

Difficulty: Easy.

Maps: Preserve brochure.

Special requirements: Keep to the trail, using stepping stones where available, and beware of cracks, fissures, and hidden holes. Leave pets at home, and obey The Nature Conservancy's (TNC's) rules and closures that protect this fragile treasure. Summer temperatures may reach extreme highs, so carry water.

Season and hours: Early May through mid-fall, dawn to dusk. Exact dates depend on the flooding cycle.

For information: The Nature Conservancy, Central and Western New York Office.

Finding the trailhead: From Interstate 81 at Watertown, take exit 47/Coffeen Street, and follow New York 12F west for 2 miles. Turn right (north) on Paddy Hill Road/NY 12E crossing over the river and turning left, staying on NY 12E all the way to the village of Chaumont (8.4 miles from the NY 12F junction). In Chaumont, take the first right on Morris Track Road/Jefferson County 125, go 3 miles, and turn left on unsigned Van Alstyne Road, just beyond a small cemetery on the right. A board with an arrow indicating Chaumont Barrens points out the turn. Preserve entrance and parking are on the left in 1.1 miles; closures are posted at the parking lot.

The hike: An excellent brochure helps visitors identify the habitats and the plant and animal life found at the preserve. The simple 2-mile loop suggests a slow, respectful tour.

The trail starts to the left of the Chaumont Barrens sign, passing through a juniper flat and a pine-hickory corridor and alongside early examples of limestone fracturing (4 to 6 inches wide and 1.5 feet deep) before reaching the interpretive kiosk at 0.1 mile. Here hikers find panels describing the preserve habitats, trail brochures, and the start of the loop. A left begins a clockwise tour.

The trail is mostly open, passing through a complex of juniper, shrub, and grassland dotted by oak, pine, hickory, and a few snags. A varied tapestry of texture, layers, and color addresses the eye, while the clicking of summer insects entertains the ear.

At 0.5 mile the trail skirts a glacial erratic; at 0.7 mile the limestone bedrock comprising the trail reveals long, segmented fossils, those of a predatory cephalopod, a primitive marine animal. Elsewhere, corals and wormhole fossils may be spied. Just ahead, hikers overlook a rare remnant 10-acre prairie grassland, with sketchy tufts of native grasses, sedges, and wildflowers; some of these plants occur nowhere else in New York.

The trail then briefly travels a mixed woods of cedar, spruce, and aspen before crossing the Calcareous Barrens, with open, fractured bedrock, boulders, grasses, juniper, and runty cedar. Another native grassland sweeps away to the far right, as one overlooks the barren. The trail then returns to woods. In places, hikers might notice where trees sprout in a line along the fissures, hinting at the linear arrangement seen from the air.

Scarlet tanager, hawk, warbler, deer, toad, and snake may divert the eye. Foxes find the more remote fissures suitable for dens. At 1.2 miles, the trail crosses a broad, block-fractured bedrock plate. Again, worm borrows and other fossils can be detected; milkweed and wild rose grow from the cracks. Habitat changes occur in quick succession. Open hickory-deciduous woods yield to grassy flats, which yield to shrubs, which yield to shady woods.

At 1.6 miles, an old dirt road advances the loop, passing from an open cedar-deciduous woods through a shrub and wildflower grassland, bringing the loop to a close at the kiosk. Return to the parking lot as you came (2 miles).

4   INMAN GULF HIKING AND NATURE TRAILS

General description: Three nature and hiking trails line up end-to-end for a single rim tour, overlooking 5 miles of Inman Gulf.
General location: About 10 miles south of Watertown.
Special attractions: Sheer shale walls, a waterfall, the ancient river drainage, diverse forests, wildflowers, fall foliage, interpretive plaques, wildlife.
Length: 5.5 miles one way (11 miles round trip).
Elevation: The trail shows about a 200-foot elevation change.
Difficulty: Easy.
Maps: Inman Gulf trail flier.
Special requirements: Beware of unstable edge; keep to trail.
Season and hours: Spring through fall, dawn to dusk.
For information: New York State Department of Environmental Conservation, Region 6.
Finding the trailhead: From the intersection of New York 177 and U.S. Highway 11, go east on NY 177 for 6.4 miles and turn north onto Lowe Road at Tremaines Corners. In 1.4 miles, bear left and continue 0.2 mile more to Williams Road/Old State Road. There turn east (right) on Williams Road, going another 0.2 mile to reach parking area 1, with space for a half dozen vehicles. Four additional parking lots lie farther east along Williams Road, offering opportunities to shorten the tour or find alternative starting points.

Mushrooms, Tug Hill State Forest.

The hike: Inman Gulf extends 9.6 miles between Barnes Corners and the Sandy Creek confluence in Rodman. Sidewinding through its depths, Gulf Stream alternately displays sections of riffles and still, black pools. A west-to-east (upstream) tour along the south rim offers a restful woods walk, with overlooks of the impressive chasm that measures 250 feet deep. Trail disks, paint blazes, and cairns at various places mark the tour.

The yellow-marked Oak Rim Trail launches the hike, journeying north from parking area 1 through a pine-deciduous forest; jewelweed replaces the woods flora in the moister pockets. At 0.3 mile reach the gulf rim, snaring a quick, restricted look at Inman Gulf. A better view lies just ahead, where a bench seat serves the best up-canyon view of the entire tour. This banner look presents the fluted cliffs and steep wooded walls of Inman Gulf meeting in a "V," with the back rim peeking through the pointed gap. Wooden plaques identify the trees along the route.

Next, with a rock-hopping crossing, follow a drainage downstream. In a steep cataract, Cascade Falls plummets over tiered rock and races into the gulf. At 0.7 mile pass beneath an ancient red oak, reaching a broad, tree-framed down-canyon view. A congestion of thin-trunked deciduous trees enfolds the tour, as it bypasses yet another prized vista and bench. Views prove particularly stirring when the gulf dons fall color.

Ahead, tread carefully where an open, crumbling shale nose protrudes into the gulf. As the tour progresses, views across the gulf and into its twisting belly urge travelers onward. Hemlocks often claim the rim, oaks cling to the cliff's edge, and mixed deciduous trees fill the gulf. As the trail drifts away from the rim, follow a drainage, descending amid ash, maple, black cherry, and pine to cross a footbridge.

At the bridge (0.9 mile), hikers may continue straight ahead or take the red-marked Chickadee Loop, a 0.2-mile side tour that returns to the Oak Rim Trail east of the bridge. Chickadee Loop ascends a small side ridge and point for a gulf vista that showcases a tight downstream bend and the steep shale cliff of the north wall.

Where Chickadee Loop rejoins the main (yellow) trail, hikers again have an option of either following the main trail or taking another side tour, the blue-marked Joe's Ridge Trail that heads left. This 0.3-mile side loop passes through a natural mineral lick, where deer commonly gather, to ascend yet another thin pull-apart ridge (perhaps isolated by the ancient Gulf Stream). This side tour likewise offers a front row seat to Inman Gulf, while the main trail gets lost in the cheap seats.

The rim-hugging tour resumes with stolen glances through the hemlock boughs and later through the branchwork of oak, beech, and aspen. At an open utility-corridor (2.25 mile), find an unobstructed look at the gulf. Cross the width of this clearing to continue the rim tour; turn right and hike out the corridor to reach Williams Rd. and parking area 2.

The rim tour shows gentle gradients, while brightly colored mushrooms and virtually colorless Indian pipe sprinkle the forest floor. At 2.9 miles the

INMAN GULF HIKING AND NATURE TRAILS

red-marked John Young Nature Trail replaces the Oak Rim Trail as host for the tour. Steep plunging cliffs give admirers a sinking-stomach thrill.

At 3.3 miles pass through a depression formed in the Ice Age, when the Gulf Stream flowed near the top of the forest. Gulf views grow more teasing. To the right a bench swing invites the unburdening of the pack for a quiet communication with the forest. Aspens fill out the canopy, and a spongy forest floor soothes travelers. Interpretive plaques come more often, where the trail travels away from the rim.

At 3.9 miles the blue-marked Inman Gulf Glide brings home the tour. It briefly follows an overgrown woods road, crossing a drainage to return to the rim. A plush green vegetation claims the southern wall. At 4.4 miles a tree-framed look at Rainbow Falls halts travelers. Rainbow Falls is a 60- to 80-foot white veil spilling from a treed drainage on the north wall. When full, the falls rages. Deer, owl, toad, and raven offer surprise encounters.

At 4.7 miles a terrace below the trail distances hikers from the gulf. Where deciduous trees again win dominance, pass within 15 feet of the rim. At 5 miles curve away from the gulf, passing through mature, planted white and red pine. Here round-trip hikers may choose to turn around. Jewelweed, brambles, and berries along with ash and dogwood frame the trail to its exit at parking area 5 (5.5 miles).

5 LAKEVIEW NATURAL BEACH HIKE

General description: This hike offers a relaxing stroll along a limited-access natural barrier beach on Lake Ontario.
General location: 20 miles southwest of Watertown.
Special attractions: Natural, white-sand beach and spit; protected vegetated dunes; Floodwood Pond; seabirds.
Length: 6.5 miles round trip.
Elevation: The flat trail travels at an elevation of 250 feet.
Difficulty: Easy.
Maps: None.
Special requirements: No swimming, picnicking, camping, fires, or radios. Access the natural beach via Southwick Beach State Park, a fee area.
Season and hours: Spring through fall.
For information: New York State Department of Environmental Conservation, Region 6.
Finding the trailhead: From Interstate 81, take exit 40 and go west on New York 193 for Southwick Beach State Park, reaching the entrance in 8.3 miles. For a beach hike alone and better parking, start at the state park's beach parking lot. For an inland start, follow the Nature Trail south from the Southwick Beach entrance station.

The hike: Ideal for exercise or daydreaming, this tour travels the northern 3-mile spit of Lakeview Wildlife Management Area (WMA); the more remote southern spit is inaccessible, save by boat.

The tour begins heading south from the bathhouse and concession building at Southwick Beach State Park. In the 1920s, this beach bustled with bathhouses, a midway, dance hall, rollercoaster, and ballfield. Today, a much quieter developed beach for swimming and sunbathing abuts the natural spit of the WMA.

The compressed fine-grained sand creates a wonderful avenue for strolling. Wave-deposited lines of duckweed and tiny mussel shells embellish the strand. Mornings, the cottonwood trees that shade the campground above the beach toss long, extended shadows over the sand.

At 0.25 mile, leave the developed state park and find a sign for the Lakeview Wildlife Management Area-Natural Beach Area. A low berm or flattish dune backs the beach; cottonwoods still claim the back swale. At 0.5 mile a boardwalk traverses the dune, marking the arrival of the Nature Trail.

A rhythmic lapping and the tranquil, blue water provide a soothing backdrop for the tour. Storms rolling across the Great Lakes churn out a much more exciting stage. A low, flat lake terrain sweeps away to the horizon, as treed shorelines curve away north and south. Across the broad blue expanse, a power plant spews steam.

Bonaparte gulls bob in the shallows and race along shore, as terns cut and dive in sharp, clean movements, retrieving silvery fish. By 0.75 mile,

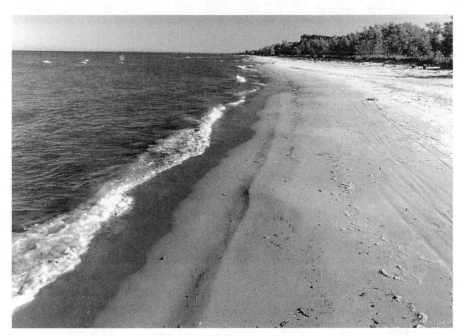
Lakeview Natural Beach.

the dunes grade higher, showing larger, more rolling humps stabilized by trees and vegetation. Some reach 30 feet high, but the dunes show little loose sand other than that on the low seaward brow and between the discreet bunches of dune grass. At times, small yellow beetles cling to everything, including the hiker who lingers too long.

Fish carcasses picked bare by gulls and the occasional flotsam from a boat or a wayward balloon alone mar the clean wilderness strand. Makeshift wind shelters dot the beach.

At 3.1 miles, travelers meet the river outlet of Floodwood Pond; across the outlet lies the inaccessible southern spit. Driftwood-strewn sands and beachgoing red-winged blackbirds precede the outlet and pond. Tiny cottonwoods take root amid the weathered gray wood, while bird tracks reveal a dizzying pattern of search.

Hikers may extend the tour upstream along the outlet, reaching the mouth of the pond at 3.25 miles. Large reed beds characterize Floodwood Pond. At this point, the hike must be reversed; return as you came.

For hikers who opt to start along the Nature Trail, the path heads south, bypassing an abandoned orchard, impressive beech trees amid a hardwood grove, and a small waterfall at the Filmore Brook crossing. It then turns right (west) and arrives at the beach via the boardwalk. Ask rangers about the trail's condition before starting; beware of poison ivy.

LAKEVIEW NATURAL BEACH

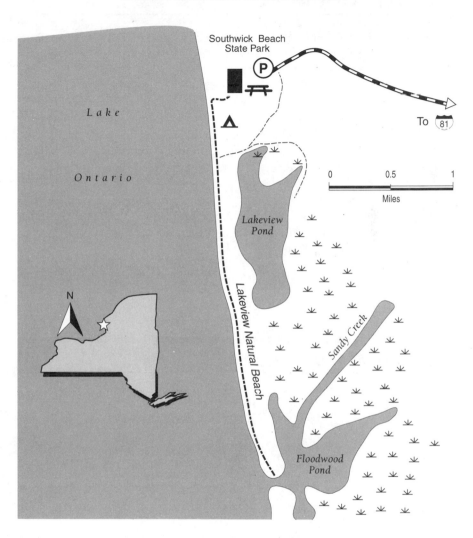

Southwick Beach
State Park

P

To 81

L a k e

O n t a r i o

0   0.5   1

Miles

*Lakeview
Pond*

Sandy Creek

N

Lakeview Natural Beach

*Floodwood
Pond*

THE ADIRONDACKS

For seekers of chiseled mountains, remote wooded valleys, crystalline streams, enticing lakes, and expansive views, the Adirondacks answer the quest. Occupying the eastern two-thirds of Upstate New York, 6-million-acre Adirondack Park provides a much needed and sought-after outlet for challenge and adventure, renewal and escape. Two visitor information centers, one at Paul Smiths, the other at Newcomb, launch travelers on their way.

The Adirondack High Peaks Region, encompassing all of the peaks over 4,000 feet in elevation, receives the greatest amount of boot traffic, but superb trails explore the entire region. Venture to pristine lakes for fishing or swimming; inspiring streams, cascades, and waterfalls; wildflower-dotted beaver meadows; whisper-quiet forests; and stirring vistas of the region's lake-forest tapestry. From virtually every corner, visitors can admire the majestic High Peaks, and the region's northern locale treats visitors to one of the showiest fall color changes to be had.

6 EVERTON FALLS PRESERVE

Overview

This 530-acre preserve of The Nature Conservancy (TNC) protects a 1.5-mile stretch of the East Branch St. Regis River, including Everton Falls. The preserve also incorporates the site of an 1800s timber town that cut itself out of existence. Hints at what once was the timber hamlet of Everton include a nature-reclaimed logging railroad, a river crib pier, and the renewing forest of red spruce, balsam fir, and hardwoods.

General description: A lightly traveled self-guiding nature trail introduces the tree species, understory vegetation, and forest succession occurring at this isolated north-central Adirondack site.
General location: Along Red Tavern Road, 7 miles west of New York 30 and 7 miles east of the village of St. Regis Falls.
Special attractions: 18-foot river falls marked by Precambrian rock ledges, conifer-hardwood forest, beaver pond, 10 miles of canoeable water upstream from falls.
Length: 1.25 miles round trip, with falls spur.

Hobblebush.

EVERTON FALLS PRESERVE

Elevation: The trail shows an elevation change under 100 feet.

Difficulty: Easy.

Maps: Hardwoods Trail brochure (available at trailhead or from the Adirondack Nature Conservancy office).

Special requirements: Obey posted TNC rules.

Season and hours: Spring through fall, dawn to dusk.

For information: Adirondack Nature Conservancy.

Finding the trailhead: From the New York 30 - Franklin County 14 (Red Tavern Road) junction (17 miles north of Paul Smiths), go west on County Road 14 toward St. Regis Falls. In 7.4 miles, find the easternmost trailhead (the Hardwoods Trail) on the north side of Red Tavern Road, with a canoe access located 0.1 mile west of here on the south side of the road. Locate the falls spur 0.2 mile farther west on the south side of the road, nearly opposite a northbound seasonal dirt road (Everton Road). Be alert to odometer readings, as trails are minimally marked. Small roadside turnouts serve each access.

The hike: The Hardwoods Nature Trail journeys north from a roadside trail post, rolling from wooded hollow to wooded hollow, bypassing a beaver pond near its start. Numbered disks corresponding to the nature trail brochure and diamond markers with The Nature Conservancy's oak emblem help point the way.

The trail initially follows a grassy bed through a young forest of birch, maple, and conifer. Finely spun hammock-shaped webs drape between the tall weeds, while mosses, Canada Mayflower, oxalis, and clintonia dress the forest floor green. The beaver marsh shows a ring of open water around a soggy island and a snag perimeter. A few aquatic plants patch the pond's surface.

Frogs, toads, woodpeckers, and deer introduce surprise on this rich multistory-forest tour. Fern patches and the blooms and berries of the hobblebush hold seasonal interest.

Where the trail dips to the second hollow, it travels a segment of the old Everton logging railroad. Time and greenery have softened the raised railbed. A clearing where the trail nears Everton Road (a dirt road) indicates the old timber hamlet abandoned in 1890. Return as you came for a 1-mile round trip or turn left, descend Everton Road, and angle right across Red Tavern Road to add a visit to Everton Falls.

On the south side of Red Tavern Road, a 200-foot trail descends to an outcrop overlooking the upper cascades and top of this roiling, chaotic river falls. Working one's way downstream along the bank unveils the biggest drop, accounting for some 8 feet of the overall 18-foot waterfall.

The river itself enchants, steeped nearly black with tannin, swirling around boulders and over ledges. Meadow banks and overhanging limbs of birch, maple, and fir complete the postcard image. Bubbles churned by the falls ride the black river downstream, while kingfishers noisily sound their passing. Return as you came.

7 GRASS RIVER WILD FOREST HIKE

General description: Trail fragments travel both shores of this wild river, overlooking a waterfall, deep pools, rapids, and cascades; a single bridge links the fragments.

General location: 15 miles south of Canton.

Special attractions: Waterfall, picturesque river, mixed forest, wildlife, solitude, colorful fall foliage.

Length: 5.25 miles round trip.

Elevation: The trail shows about a 100-foot elevation change.

Difficulty: Easy.

Maps: None. Look for mapboard where trail enters state land.

Special requirements: An easement through private property accesses this trail; respect the private landowner's rights.

Season and hours: Spring through fall.

For information: New York State Department of Environmental Conservation (DEC), Region 6.

Finding the trailhead: From Cranberry Lake Village, go west on New York 3 for 19.9 miles. There turn north toward DeGrasse on Saint Lawrence County 27 (DeGrasse Fine Road). Bear right in 0.8 mile, go another 7.6 miles and turn right at a T-junction in DeGrasse, remaining on County 27. Go 4.3 miles from DeGrasse to find the DEC sign for Grass River Wild Forest on the left. Park along the road shoulder away from the gate.

The hike: This hike incorporates the walkable designated trails that presently explore Grass River and its enfolding forest preserve.

Round the gate and hike west through private property, keeping to the dirt truck trail for 0.2 mile. The wooded lane offers a pleasant stroll with blue jays, squirrels, and grouse as co-travelers. Where yellow DEC blazes replace the orange ones of the private landowner, look right for the mapboard, which indicates existing and proposed routes.

Continue west on the road, touring amid transition woods and magnificent conifers, coming to a Y-junction at 0.4 mile; either way leads to the river. A right on the truck trail followed by a quick left on the foot trail leads to the pool at the base of the falls. Go left at the fork to add an upstream and side view of Lampson Falls.

Where the left option, in turn, forks (0.5 mile), the main foot trail turns right (downstream). The path ahead quickly dead-ends where the river flows broad, black, and deep above the falls. To continue downstream, pass through an herb and forb clearing, entering the woods, where a well-tracked footpath descends the east bank. The 60-foot plunge of Lampson Falls churns and sheets over an outcrop measuring 60 feet wide, spilling to a black pool.

Where the trail bottoms out at a small boardwalk (0.6 mile), the two river-access routes merge. Mount the reinforced steps, ascending the steep

Lampson Falls, Grass River Wild Forest.

slope to the north. Midway uphill, turn left to round an outcrop for a frontal view of the falls and the continuation of the river trail; atop the rise lies a scenic white pine flat, campfire ring, and privy.

On the outcrop point, find the first red marker and an end to the confusion of footpaths that accompany the falls. Here Grass River glides over bedrock reaching a second black pool. Pine, maple, and hemlock bring spotty shade, while poison ivy pushes up amid the rock.

The trail rolls, alternately traversing the river-plain meadow and hemlock-deciduous shore. Hobblebush, fern, sarsaparilla, whorled aster, clintonia, oxalis, and bunchberry bring a burst of green. Spurs branch to shore.

A quiet-flowing river hosts the tour from the falls to the hiker bridge (1.5 miles), where a scenic rock island parts the river, launching riffles. At the bridge the truck trail from 0.4 mile arrives on the right, and an informal trail continues north (downstream) along the east shore. Future plans call to develop this trail, extending the hike north to Harper's Falls on the North Branch Grass River.

To continue the hike though, cross to the west shore. Here DEC trails branch in both directions. The yellow-marked trail to the left (upstream), follows an overgrown and cobble-riddled woods road for 0.1 mile, halting at a beaver pond. To continue farther south requires an adventuresome spirit, as a series of these ponds dictate bushwhacking bypasses. Snag-pierced, with cattails, marsh islands, and a central beaver lodge, the pond still merits a side trip.

GRASS RIVER WILD FOREST HIKE

Backtrack to the bridge and hike the west shore downstream, still following yellow DEC trail markers. Rock outcrops replace the meadow plain, narrowing the waterway and shaping rapids, as the river shakes off the mute voice from upstream.

This little-traveled route offers a relaxing stroll amid hemlock, white pine, black cherry, birch, and maple. By 2 miles, the river reassumes its robe of composure, and small sandy beaches mark the shore. Where steep outcrops push the trail inland, expect a few rough spots. Back-to-back attractions of an 8-foot cascade and a hairpin river turn engage travelers.

At 2.5 miles the traveled path and marked trail briefly divide; for ease of travel, stay the tracked route along shore. Exciting rapids passing through outcrop fingers signal the end of the west shore tour; private lands lie downstream. In late August, the birds begin to flock, and the tips of the maples flash a showy orange and red.

Return upstream to the bridge at 3.9 miles. Here hikers may opt to retrace the east shore route or hike the truck trail south to the junction at 0.4-mile, both equidistant. From the junction, turn east to return to the vehicle.

---

8 *FLOODWOOD LOOP*

General description: This easy woodland loop in the Adirondack lakes region strings together prized canoe waters.

General location: 17 miles northeast of the hamlet Tupper Lake.

Special attractions: A network of glacial ponds, with rock and pine-clad islands; mature conifer-deciduous woods; water lilies bloom in mid-July to August; loons, osprey, heron, frogs, and fish.

Length: 7.7-mile loop, plus another mile of canoe-carry spurs.

Elevation: The rolling tour shows a 100-foot elevation change.

Difficulty: Easy.

Middle Lake, Adirondack Park.

Maps: Adirondack Mountain Club, Adirondack Northern Region map.
Special requirements: None.
Season and hours: Spring through fall.
For information: New York State Department of Environmental Conservation, Region 5.
Finding the trailhead: From Tupper Lake, travel east on New York 3 East/New York 30 North to the split-off in 5.3 miles. There take NY 30 north for 8.6 miles and turn left (west) on Floodwood Road, bearing left at the fork. The eastern trailhead lies 2.1 miles west of NY 30, the western trailhead 3 miles west. The final 2.3 miles are unpaved; the western trailhead has better turnout parking.

The hike: By taking full advantage of the canoe carries, this hike visits the shore of seven large ponds and the waters of Fish Creek. Orange and yellow snowmobile markers point the way. The final 0.9 mile is on Floodwood Road.

Head south from the western trailhead. Beech, birch, maple, and hemlock overlace the cushiony path, while ferns, hobblebush, oxalis, and club moss decorate the floor. A mild gradient, diffused lighting, and scenic snags and logs all contribute to the relaxation of this counterclockwise tour.

As the trail descends to a footbridge crossing, it presents a quick peek at Middle Pond. At the 0.5-mile mark, T-junction, find the first canoe carry heading left to Middle Pond in 0.1 mile; the loop journeys right. Here Middle Pond presents a charming forest-rimmed crescent, a conifer-clad island, and vast mats of lily pads. Approach quietly as turtles sun on the logs.

The loop resumes bypassing an enormous, mossy boulder coming to the second canoe carry at 0.8 mile. Go right 250 feet to view Floodwood Pond.

The loop trail then drifts from shore, exploring an engaging woods, where logs ease the crossing of Middle Pond outlet. At 1.6 miles, sphagnum moss claims a typically soggy site. Past a campsite overlooking the steep bank of Floodwood Pond, bear left for the loop; side paths branch to shore.

At the marked junction for Floodwood Passage Bridge, detour right; straight continues the loop. Aspen and pine frame the way to the lengthy bridge spanning the Floodwood-Little Square ponds passage. Log-riddled and flowing with aquatic plants, the tranquil, muddy-bottomed stream hosts schools of fish and the occasional canoe. Otter Hollow Trail travels the opposite shore; for Floodwood Loop alone, return to the junction and go right.

From the loop at 2.4 miles, look across Floodwood Passage to see a couple of beaver lodges. At a point on Little Square Pond, a campsite and privy serve both land and water travelers. A marshy peninsula and lily-pad shallows lend character to the long rectangular pond; berry bushes and sheep laurel adorn the shore. At a camp flat and fire ring at 2.6 miles, bear right. Trail markers disappear for a spell, but the path remains good.

Hemlocks weave in and out of the mix, bringing richer shade, as the trail flattens for the next 1.5 miles. At a three-pronged junction at 3.9 miles, a right turn yields a boardwalk access to Fish Creek; straight leads

FLOODWOOD LOOP

To Floodwood
Pond

P

Floodwood Road

To 30

Middle Pond

N

Floodwood
Pond

Polliwog
Pond

Little
Polliwog
Pond

Floodwood
Passage
Bridge

Horseshoe
Pond

Otter Hollow
Trail

Little Square Pond

Follensby
Clear Pond

Fish Creek

Copperas
Pond

To Fish Creek
Campground

0	0.5	1

Miles

to Fish Creek Campground; and left leads to Follensby Clear Pond and the loop. Fish Creek reveals a broad, slow, marshy-sided water, with sheep laurel, cranberry, and pitcher plants along shore.

En route to Follensby Clear Pond, quickly come upon another trail intersection. To the left lies the loop; to the right, a second trail journeys south to Fish Creek Campground. The canoe carry straight ahead leads to Follensby Clear Pond, a huge water body, with rounded peninsular shores and islands. Conifers dominate its skyline; motorboats disturb its calm.

From the intersection the loop swings north for the return leg, traversing low glacial ridges. In places, snags open up the cathedral. The deep blue ahead belongs to Horseshoe Pond.

At 4.9 miles the trail dips to a spruce bog before resuming its rolling tour through mixed woods. At 5.3 miles, come within striking distance of Horseshoe Pond, but no formal access exists until the footbridge for Little Polliwog Pond outlet. North of the outlet bridge lies a junction. A left finds not-so-tiny Little Polliwog Pond, with a marshy far end and jail-like look to the rim of pine snags.

Northbound, the loop travels the ridge between Little Polliwog and Polliwog ponds, reaching the canoe carry between the two at 6.25 miles. To the left lies an open-water look at Little Polliwog Pond; to the right a beautiful hemlock avenue ushers hikers to Polliwog Pond, a much larger water body.

At 6.65 miles, a drowned 20-foot segment of the loop proves tricky to skirt. At the 7.2-mile junction, a spur to the right leads to an isolated arm of Polliwog Pond; the loop continues left, coming to a fork in 0.2 mile. Straight leads to an open-water view of Middle Pond, while a right leads to Floodwood Rd. (7.8 miles). Turn left on this lightly-used dirt road to close the loop at 8.7 miles.

9 JENKINS MOUNTAIN TRAIL

General description: This newly opened trail explores forest, glade, and glacial drift before attaining a summit vista.
General location: Paul Smiths Visitor Interpretive Center, 15 miles northwest of the village of Saranac Lake off New York 30.
Special attractions: Vistas, mixed forests, meadow openings, beaver pond, wildlife sightings, fall foliage.
Length: 8.2 miles round trip.
Elevation: The trail climbs 800 feet to a summit elevation of 2,477 feet.
Difficulty: Moderate.
Maps: Paul Smiths Visitor Interpretive Center (VIC) Trail System flier.

Special requirements: An experimental permit system limits travel to Jenkins Mountain to twenty hikers per day. Half the permits may be reserved, half are available on a first-come, first-served basis. Inquire at Paul Smiths VIC.

Season and hours: Summer and fall only; during the wet season, the trail remains closed to protect the bed from damaging wear and erosion. Center hours: 9 a.m. to 5 p.m. daily, except Thanksgiving and Christmas days (June 1 through September, the center stays open until 7 p.m.).

For information: Paul Smiths VIC.

Finding the trailhead: From the New York 30/New York 86 junction (26 miles north of the hamlet of Tupper Lake, 13 miles west of Saranac Lake), go north on NY 30 for 0.9 mile and turn left (west) to enter Paul Smiths VIC.

The hikes: Paul Smiths VIC boasts a fine collection of nature trails, but for those with an appetite for a greater challenge and a quest to get above it all, the site's Jenkins Mountain Trail may better fill your time.

Uphill from the parking lots, this blue-blazed trail follows the gated service road west off the VIC entrance road for 1.75 miles. The road offers a good walking surface and mild grade with stepped ascents. Maple, beech, birch, and the occasional conifer weave a semi-full canopy; hobblebush and brambles claim the road shoulder.

Jenkins Mountain view, Paul Smiths VIC.

JENKINS MOUNTAIN TRAIL

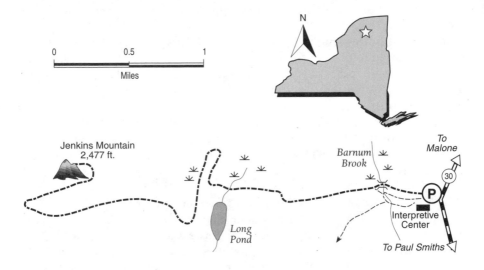

Locator boards for cross-country skiers and 0.5-mile incremental markers assist hikers. At 0.4 mile, the route crosses over Barnum Brook; to the right the brook shows a snag-pierced marsh. The path heading left along the brook's west shore leads to Barnum Brook Trail; keep to Jenkins Mountain Road. After a mile, small meadows and wetlands open up the corridor, and a dogged beaver thwarts trail managers with its attempts to flood the road.

Past a privy, a foot trail replaces the service road, traversing a glacial-drift ridge that parts a fern glade from a beaver pond. Beech, maple, and birch cover the ridge. The beaver lodge, a neatly constructed dam, and the north summit of Jenkins Mountain contribute to the view.

Round the point of the glade and continue advancing along and over similar low glacial ridges. Sarsaparilla, fern, and club moss accent the rock-studded forest floor. A few black cherry trees appear amid the forest ranks. After crossing a small drainage, the trail enters a long straight-away at the base of Jenkins Mountain. Deer, songbirds, woodpeckers, and fingertip-sized toads divert attention. The distant wail of a coyote may slow strides.

At 3.25 miles, the trail ascends fairly steeply, taking a switchback passing between boulders and outcrop ledges. Where the trail hugs the line of Jenkins Mountain Ridge, the grade moderates. Stepping stones assist travel through a small jewelweed meadow.

Just beyond the 4-mile marker, the summit outcrop presents a 180-degree southwest panorama with tower-topped Saint Regis Mountain claiming center stage. The Adirondack high peaks, Long and Black ponds in the valley bottom, and a rolling wooded expanse complete the view. Fog may lift from the ponds and paint the drainages between the mountains, enhancing the view. Return as you came for an 8.2 mile round trip.

10 PAUL SMITHS VISITOR INTERPRETIVE CENTER NATURE TRAILS

Overview

One of two visitor interpretive centers serving travelers to New York State's 6-million-acre Adirondack Park (the other is Newcomb), Paul Smiths itself suggests one lace on the hiking boots to check out the site's five superb nature trails. Seasonally, the nation's first Native Species Butterfly House offers a detour.

General description: Five easy interlocking interpretive trails travel mature mixed forest, tree plantation, and wetland habitats.
General location: 15 miles northwest of the village of Saranac Lake off New York 30.
Special attractions: Bird watching, diverse forests, insect-eating plants, nature discovery.
Length: The trails range between 0.6 and 1.2 miles in length.
Elevation: Less than 100 feet.
Difficulty: Easy.
Maps: Paul Smiths Visitor Interpretive Center (VIC) Trail System flier.
Special requirements: None.
Season and hours: Spring through fall for hiking. Center hours: 9 a.m. to 5 p.m. daily, except Thanksgiving and Christmas days (June 1 through September, center stays open until 7 p.m.).
For information: Paul Smiths VIC.
Finding the trailhead: From the New York 30/New York 86 junction (26 miles north of the hamlet of Tupper Lake, 13 miles west of Saranac Lake), go north on NY 30 for 0.9 mile and turn left (west) to enter Paul Smiths VIC.

The hikes: The nature trails may be toured independently or woven together for longer loops. They travel over wood shaving or improved earthen beds, with boardwalks, observation decks, and interpretive panels adding to the tour.

Starting at the gazebo to the right of the VIC's entry walk, **Barnum Brook Trail** a 0.6-mile barrier-free loop travels wide earthen trail and a handsome boardwalk and bridge spanning the grassy-shored water of Barnum Brook. A dial-a-tree identification wheel and species identification tags introduce a stunning woods of big pines, maple, birch, black cherry, beech, red spruce, and balsam fir. Observation decks overlooking Heron Marsh and the mirror black outlet pool of Barnum Brook win over travelers. Quotes from Theodore Roosevelt bridge time and the sentiments of naturalists.

From the loop's midpoint, hikers may access the 1.2-mile **Forest Ecology Trail**, which edges Heron Marsh, touring mixed conifer-deciduous woods,

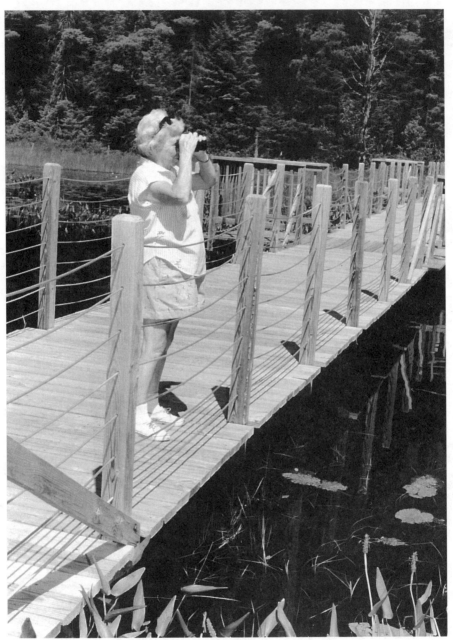

Heron Marsh boardwalk, Paul Smiths VIC.

PAUL SMITHS VISITOR INTERPRETIVE CENTER NATURE TRAILS

offering an overlook. Interpretive plaques introduce geology, habitat, and natural processes. A marsh boardwalk traversing bog and fen habitats wins praise. Initially, tamaracks line the walk; elsewhere, sphagnum moss, alder, sedges, cattail, heath, and insect-eating bladderwort, pitcher plant, and sundew engage botanists and photographers. The ecology trail ends at a T-junction. Here, a connector trail journeys right to the **Silviculture Trail**; going left finds the VIC and remaining nature trails.

Out the back door of the VIC, the **Heron Marsh Trail,** an 0.8-mile loop, offers an alternative launch pad for the Paul Smiths nature trail system. A counterclockwise tour takes visitors along the shore of extensive Heron Marsh, while side loops and spurs lead to marsh vantages and an observation platform. Birders travel with scopes, binoculars, and identification books. An ascent through mature mixed conifer and young deciduous woods returns one to the center.

Forming a figure-eight with the Heron Marsh Trail, the 0.6-mile **Shingle Mill Falls Trail** rolls along the wooded rim of the open water of Heron Marsh. A long bridge across the wetland neck may either begin or end the tour; cow lilies, arrowhead, and cattail-sedge islands contribute to the view. At the bridge near Heron Marsh Dam, hikers overlook Shingle Mill Falls. Spilling over a natural bedrock sill, the falls powered early-day mills. Bittern, heron, osprey, and a variety of ducks number among the winged sightings. Beaver-girdled trees dot the shore.

The most remote of the nature trail loops, the 1-mile **Silviculture Trail** can be reached only by traveling parts of at least two other nature trails, along with a connector spur. The circuit passes through mixed-age conifer and deciduous forests and plantations of red and white pine and Norway spruce. Plaques explain the forest management practices witnessed along the way; a gazebo marks the midway point.

---

11 *POKE-O-MOONSHINE TRAIL*

General description: This hike climbs an eastern Adirondack peak, passing through mixed woods and topping outcrops, before reaching the rocky summit and fire tower.

General location: Some 7 miles south of Keeseville off US Highway 9.

Special attractions: Granite-gneiss cliffs, mixed forest, lean-to, fire tower, and Lake Champlain-High Peaks views.

Length: 2.4 miles round trip.

Elevation: The trail ascends 1,300 feet to a summit elevation of 2,180 feet.

Difficulty: Moderate.

Maps: Adirondack Mountain Club, Adirondack Eastern Region map.

Special requirements: Day-use or campground fee charged; hikers may avoid this fee by parking along the road shoulder of US 9 outside the no-parking zone that abuts the state campground.

Season and hours: Late spring through fall.

For information: New York State Department of Environmental Conservation, Region 5.

Finding the trailhead: From the junction of New York 9N and U.S. Highway 9/New York 22 in Keeseville, go south on US 9 for 7.2 miles, turning west to enter Poke-O-Moonshine State Campground. From Interstate 87, take exit 33 and go south on US 9 for 3.1 miles to reach the campground. The trail heads west near site 14 at the south end of the campground.

The hike: This sometimes steep, eroded trail scales the wooded flank of Poke-O-Moonshine Mountain, which owes its peculiar name to a dichotomous profile of fractured cliff and summit rock slabs. To the Algonquin Indians these features suggested a descriptive name, combining the words Pohqui, meaning "broken," and Moosie, meaning "smooth." Through general use the name corrupted into being "Poke-O-Moonshine." Peregrine falcons and rock climbers coexist in this rocky realm.

The trail charges steeply up the mostly shady slope, cloaked in sugar maple, birch, and beech. Oaks rise among the bigger trees—rare interlopers in the Adirondacks. Side trails branch away, rounding below the cliffs to the right. Sarsaparilla and a few fern dot the rock-studded forest floor. Although boots have broadened the trail, the slope retains much of its soil.

At 0.2 mile veer left at the base of a cliff, topping a ledge for an early view of the highway corridor below and the ridges stretching east to Vermont. White pine, hemlock, striped maple, and oak prefer these rockier reaches. A variety of bird whistles, pipes, and caws draws attention from the roadway drone.

The trail now stays inland from the edge of the cliff and so should hikers. The effects of weathering combined with a canted surface can steal one's footing. The trail narrows, exhibiting a more moderate grade. Soon it follows a drainage crowded with nettles, trillium, and red-flowering raspberry. As the drainage steepens, so does the trail.

At 0.6 mile a formidable cliff rises beyond the trees to the right. In a saddle clearing, a rock fireplace and old foundation hint at the one-time lookout cabin. Skirt the site to the left to reach the present overnight lean-to and privy. The trail to the fire tower bears right at the ruins, ascending the eroded, spring-soaked slope. Infrequent red markers point the way.

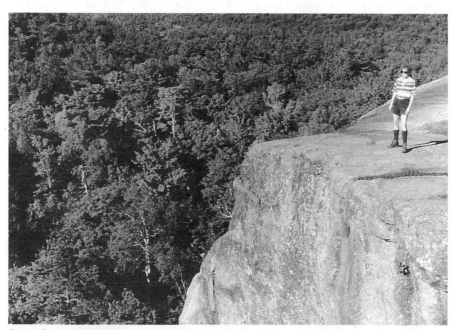

Poke-O-Moonshine Mountain summit outcrop, Adirondack Park.

POKE-O-MOONSHINE TRAIL

N

Poke-O-Moonshine Mountain
2,180 ft.

To Keeseville

P

Poke-O-
Moonshine
Campground and
Day Use Area

87

9

Lookout
cabin ruins

To 9

0   0.25   0.5

Miles

To Lake
George

Just above the saddle, come upon a bald outcrop sloping up to the left. It affords fine views west of ski-run streaked Whiteface Mountain, as well as a ragged skyline of rounded and conical peaks. For overnight hikers staying at the lean-to, the outcrop proves ideal for stargazing, especially during the annual Perseid meteor showers, which peak in early August.

Additional outcrops follow, but they neither improve upon nor significantly alter the view. The trail advances via brief ups and level stretches. At 0.95 mile, top and follow the ridge to the right. After cutting through a corridor of low-stature white birch and striped maple, come out on the summit outcrop at the tower.

The abandoned fire tower, while showing early signs of disrepair, remains open to the public; ascend at your own risk. It puts travelers five flights up for a full 360-degree view. The long, shimmery platter and dark treed islands of Lake Champlain dominate the view to the east-northeast; Whiteface Mountain rises to the west. Smaller lakes, rural flats, and the ridge and cliffs of Poke-O-Moonshine Mountain complete the panorama. Below the tower, mountain ash joins the tapestry of green.

Should the tower eventually close, the bald summit slab still warrants the journey, adding dimension and drama to the eastern view overlooking the peak's plunging cliffs and broken rock tiers. Lichen and mineral leaching streak the cliffs green, orange, and black. When ready to surrender the view, return as you came.

General description: This demanding all-day or overnight hike arriving from the north offers the shortest approach to Mount Marcy, at 5,344 feet the highest point in New York State.

General location: Adirondack High Peaks, 12 miles southeast of Lake Placid.

Special attractions: Spectacular High Peaks panorama, rare arctic alpine habitat, wildlife, scenic brooks, lake, lean-tos, visitor information center.

Length: 14.8 miles round trip.

Elevation: The trail shows a 3,200-foot elevation change.

Difficulty: Strenuous.

Maps: Trails in the High Peaks pamphlet; Adirondack Mountain Club, Adirondack High Peak Region map.

Special requirements: Adirondak Loj charges for parking; its lots sometimes fill in summer. Expect a rock scramble for the final 0.5 mile to the summit. Come prepared for chill winds and cool summit temperatures, and be alert to weather changes. Camp only at the lean-tos or designated tent sites, properly storing food away from bears. Camping and fires above 4,000 feet are prohibited. Find privies near the camp areas.

Season and hours: Year-round, spring through fall for hiking.

For information: New York State Department of Environmental Conservation, Region 5.

Finding the trailhead: From the junction of New York 73 and New York 86 in the village of Lake Placid, go east on NY 73 for 3.2 miles and turn right (south) on Adirondak Loj Road. Go 5 miles to reach the entrance station for the Loj. Find the trailhead at the opposite end of the lower parking lot from the High Peaks Visitor Information Center.

The hike: From the register, follow the wide, well-trampled blue-marked trail, passing through a mixed conifer-deciduous forest, crossing over the Mr. Van Ski Trail. Over the years, improvements have reduced the mire and erosion that once characterized the Van Hoevenberg Trail. Reinforced steps, footplanks, levees, and stepping stones number among the changes.

Passing through a stand of planted pines, cross the footbridge over Heart Lake outlet, followed soon after by the footbridge over MacIntyre Brook. At 0.5 mile enter state land and wilderness. Despite the popularity of this hiker highway, wildlife sightings still reward the early morning traveler. Owl, deer, bat, and even a pine marten may surprise you.

At the 1-mile junction bear left, staying on the blue trail; the yellow trail leads to Algonquin Peak. Maple, birch, small beech, hobblebush, and striped maple enfold the tour. In another mile, ascend along rushing Marcy Brook, sequestered deep in a draw; here campsites occupy the woods of balsam fir and birch.

At 2.2 miles cross scenic wooden Marcy Dam. From it, campers typically suspend their foodstuffs, but the bears do at times come out winners. Cross-pond views feature Mount Colden; Avalanche, Phelp, and Table mountains; and the slope of Wright Peak and Algonquin. Over the shoulder looms Whales Tail Mountain. Six lean-tos and a ranger station bring bustle to the Marcy Dam area.

Bear right from the dam, following the blue markers along the shore. In 500 feet, go left for Mount Marcy; to the right lies the trail to Avalanche Lake and Lake Colden.

Following the rocky terrain of Phelps Brook upstream, find the high-water bridge at 2.5 miles; during low-water, cross 500 feet upstream via the rocky streambed itself. The tour continues upstream on the opposite shore, but Phelps Brook slips from sight. From the junction with the red Phelps Mountain Trail, continue forward; dense spruce and fir narrow the corridor.

At 3.5 miles cross a bridge back over Phelps Brook, finding a steeper climb and larger rocks. Shortly the trail turns away from the brook, while a winter-use trail continues upstream. Small-stature trees weave an open cathedral. Stone steps and short log ladders add to the trail.

Bypassing an area of designated camp flats, cross Marcy Brook (4.4 miles) upstream from Indian Falls. Upon crossing, take an immediate right on the foot trail heading downstream. In 100 feet, exit onto a broad outcrop plane washed by the brook. From the head of Indian Falls, where the water

Mount Marcy summit view, Adirondack Park.

VAN HOEVENBERG TRAIL

spills through a cliff fissure, find a striking look at Algonquin and the MacIntyre Range.

Resume the hike to Marcy, continuing away from the creek, skirting campsites. At the junction at the 3,600-foot elevation, bear left with the blue disks, temporarily enjoying a more relaxed grade. Bunchberry, moss, and whorled aster carpet the ground. Corduroys cross a spring-muddied area to reach a steep rocky ascent with stones aligned as stairs. Overhead, the clouds whip past.

In a high meadow, find the first view of imposing Mount Marcy. A better view follows, capturing the ridge to Little Marcy, silver snags amid the fir mantle, an open summit outcrop, and tiny hikers winding skyward. This eye-opener also alerts hikers to the hefty climb still ahead. At the 5.8-mile junction, to the left lies Keene Valley; go right for Marcy.

Canted exposed outcrop alternates with corduroy as the trail draws into an alpine opening with boulder seating addressing Mount Marcy. With the climb, views build, previewing the summit attraction. At the saddle junction at 6.4 miles, bear right; yellow paint blazes and the occasional cairn point out this final leg to the summit.

En route views suggest a breather; close-by Haystack proves particularly arresting. An arctic-alpine habitat claims the upper reaches of Marcy, so keep to the prescribed route, now a rock scramble to the top. From the summit plaque (7.4 miles), one last scramble tags the ultimate high point. The view is nothing less than glorious, humbling onlookers. During summer months, a steward watches over Marcy, educating hikers about this sensitive site and its habitat.

The first recorded ascent came in 1837. To the Indians the mountain was known as "Tahawus" or "Cloud Splitter," an apt name. Views sweep the regal MacIntyre Range, the ridges north to Canada, the Green Mountains of Vermont, lakes Champlain and Placid, Boreas Ponds, and Lake Tear-of-the-Clouds, the highest lake source of the Hudson River. The Hudson-Saint Lawrence River Divide passes over the top of Mount Marcy; crystals and lichen adorn the rock. Return as you came.

General description: Within a private Adirondack reserve, this rolling tour travels the east and west shores of a pristine river drainage, with side trips to an overlook and waterfall.

General location: 19 miles southeast of Lake Placid.

Special attractions: Old-growth hemlocks, overlooks and valley floor vistas, scenic river and side brooks, waterfalls.

Length: 9.1 miles round trip, including side trips (10.5 miles with the road distance to and from the trailhead parking).

Elevation: The trail travels between 1,350 and 2,700 feet in elevation, with the high point at Indian Head.

Difficulty: Moderate to strenuous.

Maps: Adirondack Mountain Club, Adirondack High Peaks Region map.

Special requirements: All hikers entering the reserve must register. No pets, fires, camping, or bicycles on Lake Road, and only reserve members may fish or swim. The reserve has protected this site since 1897, so do your part. Visitors must park away from Ausable Club and not block the area road with shuttle drop-offs and pick-ups.

Season and hours: Spring through fall, daylight hours.

For information: Adirondack Trail Improvement Society; New York State Department of Environmental Conservation, Region 5.

Finding the trailhead: From Keene Valley, go south on New York 73 East for 2.8 miles and turn right (west) on an unmarked gravel road opposite the marked trailhead for Roaring Brook Trail to Giant Mountain. Find trail parking lots on the left in 0.1 mile and in 0.2 mile. As these lots often fill, hikers may need to use the Roaring Brook turnout or park along the shoulder of NY 73.

Hike west on the unlabeled road (surface later changes to pavement) to reach Ausable Club (0.5 mile). Turn left and descend the road between the tennis courts. Hike past member parking to reach the register and watchman's hut at 0.7 mile.

The hike: For an east-west tour, hike the dirt road past the watchman's hut and round the rustic wooden gate to Adirondack Mountain Reserve. In 100 feet turn right, following the Ladies Mile Trail, marked by a tiny wooden sign; keep an eye out for it. This footpath travels hemlock-beech woods, crosses small drainages, and bypasses a woodshed coming to a loop junction (0.2 mile); go right to reach and follow the river upstream. Orange "ATIS" (Adirondack Trail Improvement Society) markers point the way.

The East Branch is a clean-coursing mountain water, reflecting the hues of the rocks it bathes. Upstream, the river reveals a variety of personalities. At 0.4 mile, as the Ladies Mile Trail loops left, continue

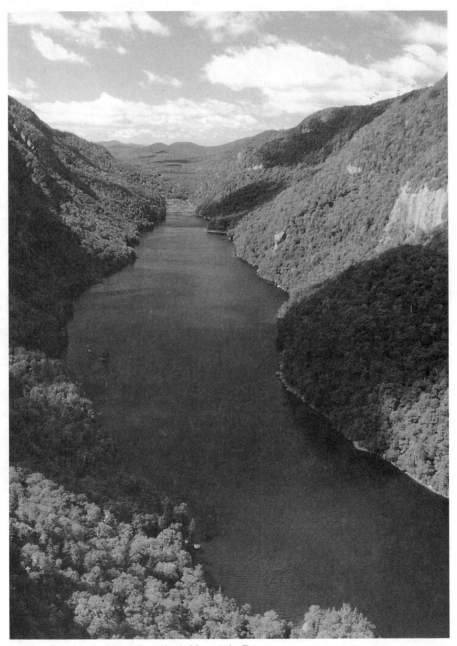

Lower Ausable Lake, Adirondack Mountain Reserve.

straight to reach the river trails in 500 feet. Keep to the east shore for a clockwise tour; a footbridge spans the East Branch to West River Trail.

Along the elevated bank, hemlock and hardwood enfold the tour, and a few mossy stones stud the trail. Periodically, the trail veers away from and above the river. At 0.75 mile, young spruce rise amid the forest. Cross the footbridge over gravelly Gill Brook, and turn left following this side brook upstream to another reserve road and trail junction.

Cross the road and ascend amid a high-canopy forest of maple and beech. The trail rounds below an isolated outcrop, offering views of Wolfjaw Mountain, and travels an old-growth hemlock plateau, drawing some 200 feet above the river. From the plateau, travel the slope's rim before making a quick difficult descent of the steep wooded flank.

Along the lower slope, find an overlook of a double river falls at 1.8 miles. In a pinched gorge the upper 20-foot falls feeds a lower 6-foot falls, with a surging channel between and a dark pool at the exodus. Where the trail returns to the elevated river bank, look for a pair of room-sized boulders. At the 2.2-mile junction bear right keeping to the east bank; to the left lies the main reserve road. Briefly the trail parallels a blue pipe drawing river water for the club.

At 2.3 miles bear left for the East River Trail; the path to the right finds a river bridge to Beaver Meadow Falls. The rolling tour now overlooks the meadow shore and gray cliff of the west bank; upstream views feature the irregular skyline of Sawteeth and the Gothics. A railing eases descent where erosion and outcrops have made this a split-level trail.

Beaver Meadow soon claims the river bottom, braiding the stream. At 2.8 miles lies Bullock Dam, a plank-topped single log stretched the length of the river. Despite the infrequency of the ATIS markers, the trail remains easy to follow. Birch and spruce line the route.

At 3.3 miles Leach Bridge crosses the river below the dam at the outlet of Lower Ausable Lake. The lake waters and boathouse are closed to the general public, and shore access is limited to the marked trails. Cross the bridge for the loop. To visit Indian Head for a lofty vantage, remain on the east shore, ascend sharply left, turn right near a storage shed, and ascend 50 yards on gravel road to come out on the main reserve road (3.4 miles).

Go left on the main reserve road for 500 feet, finding the marked trail to Indian Head on the right. Where a spur descends to the private boathouse area, stay left contouring and switching back up the rocky deciduous-clad slope. At 3.6 miles, a 115-foot spur heads right to Gothics Window, a tree-framed look at the rugged Gothics and high-peak amphitheater. The main trail continues climbing, with short ladder segments overcoming the steepest stretches.

At a three-way junction on the ridge (4.1 miles), go right 0.1 mile, topping Indian Head, a broad, flat outcrop with a spectacular view surpassed only by the view from the Indian's brow below. Nippletop, Colvin, the beautiful curved platters of Upper and Lower Ausable lakes, Sawteeth, the Gothics, and

EAST BRANCH AUSABLE RIVER LOOP

Wolfjaws comprise the pristine stage. The view honors the forward-thinking reserve members from the 1890s, who protected this raw beauty.

Return to Leach Bridge (5.1 miles) and cross the river, viewing the rock profile of Indian Head and the Mount Colvin-Sawteeth gateway at the head of Lower Ausable Lake. Turn left at the west shore junction, adding a 0.5-mile round trip spur to Rainbow Falls. At the dam, bear right and shortly after, again bear right to find sheer cliffs, the 150-foot misty shower of Rainbow Falls, and a green-filled box canyon. When sun touches the mist, a rainbow spectrum autographs the picture. Return to Leach Bridge to follow the West River Trail downstream (5.6 miles).

Bypass the trail to Lost Lookout for a demanding shoreline hike removed from the river, weaving in and out and stepping up and over the rocks below the cliffs. A spruce-hardwood complex shades the tour. The trail briefly eases, crossing a beech flat and raised dike. Views east span the alder meadow to Bear Den-Dial Mountain ridge. Next cross a couple of drainages and bypass a ladder ascent to the Gothics to reach Beaver Meadow Falls alongside the trail (6.8 miles). This attractive 80- to 100-foot falls splashes over a tiered cliff, broadening at the base.

Cross the brook downhill from the falls for an easier tour. Deciduous trees dominate with a few interlopers. Find a different perspective on the double falls of the East Branch before drawing away from the river into a realm of old-growth hemlock.

Stay on the West River Trail, crossing a paired-log bridge over a pretty brook with a 10-foot falls spilling through a slot in the rocks. A forest gap offers a look at Noonmark, and the 7.5-mile vista presents a limited look at Noonmark-Dial ridge. Descend the steep ridge, remaining above the river, which is also dropping.

Where the trail bottoms out, veer left coming to a junction (8 miles). Downhill to the right lies Canyon Bridge, the largest of the river foot-bridges; stay on the West River Trail. Spurs branch left to Pyramid Brook and a falls mostly swallowed by the rocks. To see the falls, make a 0.4-mile round-trip detour; for this description, forgo the side trip.

Downstream, the trail again travels at river level, bypassing yet another river bridge. The West River Trail now merges with the Nature Trail (brochures available at the watchman's hut); tags identify the vegetation. Three-hundred-year-old hemlocks grace the tour, which now rolls along a side channel of the river.

Cross the river bridge at 9 miles, turn left (downstream), and veer right into the woods. Amid a developed area, cross over a drainage and continue gently up, closing the loop at the watchman's hut (9.1 miles). Ascend through the grounds of Ausable Club and turn right to return to the car.

General description: This grueling boulder-and-mud obstacle course passes through typical Adirondack splendor: mixed forests, pristine waters, and inspiring views. Beware though, the loop includes the notoriously difficult Cold Brook Pass.

General location: MacIntyre Mountain Range, Adirondack Park.

Special attractions: Wallface Cliff and High Peaks views, chill-blue lakes and crystalline brooks, challenge and adventure, springboard to Mount Marcy and other peak/lake destinations.

Length: 15.9-mile loop.

Elevation: The trail travels between 1,800 and 3,840 feet in elevation, with the high point found at Cold Brook Pass.

Difficulty: Strenuous backpack; extremely strenuous day hike.

Maps: Adirondack Mountain Club, Adirondack High Peaks map.

Special requirements: Steely determination, stamina, a sure foot, and good backcountry skills. Avoid during high water.

Season and hours: Best in summer and fall.

For information: New York State Department of Environmental Conservation, Region 5.

Finding the trailhead: From the New York 30 - New York 28N junction in Long Lake, go east on NY 28N for 18 miles. There turn left on Essex County Road 2 (seasonally maintained), bearing left at the intersection in 0.4 mile. In another 0.8 mile, turn left on County 25 toward Tahawus, following the road to where it dead-ends at Upper Works Trailhead (another 9.5 miles). As trailhead parking and the beginning and ending trail miles represent state easements on private land, keep to the trail.

The hike: Take the cabled-off gravel road next to the trail register, following the Upper Hudson River upstream crossing over it at 0.25 mile. Cedar, spruce, birch, and beech frame the corridor; a beaver pond lies beyond the trees to the left. At the 0.4-mile loop junction, go left for a clockwise tour, following yellow disk markers. Still traveling logging roads, bear right at 0.75 mile.

With a descent come tree-filtered glimpses of Henderson Lake. The trail now crosses a brook, and travels worn log corduroys and soggy road stretches. At 1.5 miles, bear right traveling the slope above Indian Pass Brook coming to a junction; for the loop continue straight ahead. Red disks now point the way to Indian Pass. A few big spruce, fir, and snags weave amid the deciduous trees; hobblebush, clintonia, sarsaparilla, and ferns dress the forest floor.

Journey past brookside Henderson Lean-to, following a well-traveled though minimally marked footpath. Where the trail exits a small brushy

Trail ladder near Summit Rock, Adirondack Park.

INDIAN PASS-LAKE COLDEN LOOP

passage, a sign points upstream (right) to a bridge crossing. In another 200 feet bear left to cross the attractive three-plank-wide bridge.

The gentle-grade trail turns left (downstream), before veering into woods, where it becomes more root-bound and rocky, with boot-swallowing organic muds slowing progress. At 2.7 miles, bypass the Wallface Lean-to and privy to parallel Indian Pass Brook upstream along the west shore, stone-hopping side brooks at regular intervals. Jewelweed and dogwood dot the banks.

By 3.7 miles, the cliff of Wallface looms beyond the leaves, as conifers wane from the mix. Below a camp flat on the west shore comes the crossing of Indian Pass Brook. The trail now weaves and ascends amid gigantic boulders, some the size of barns, others with cavelike overhangs.

At 4 miles, the red trail turns right, charging at an angle up the slope; keep an eye out for markers. A wooden ladder provides a leg up as the trail briefly rounds to the back side of the bouldery slope.

At the base of a second ladder (4.3 miles), uneven-sized logs braced against a split boulder offer the intrepid explorer a means to scale the rock for a stirring view of Wallface. Rival, more accessible views lie but a minute away at Summit Rock.

Wallface, a much-sought Adirondack landmark, presents a Western profile with sheer cliffs, broken ledges, and spire-topped conifers. From Summit Rock, views also span the southern drainage of Indian Pass Brook, toward Henderson Lake and Mountain.

The trail ahead remains extremely rugged and steep, bypassing camp flats and crossing brooks, allowing you to snare a look at a 100-foot side waterfall. At 4.9 miles, ease down a steep rock crease for a rock-hopping tour amid the rushing water of the Indian Pass Brook. Here the trail and northern brook drainage are generally one and the same. In this tailbone-cracking terrain, give full attention to the rocks.

Where a footpath again follows the east shore of Indian Pass Brook, find a trail junction at 5.5 miles and turn right, following the yellow-marked trail to Lake Colden. After an uphill plod, dip back down to follow a side brook upstream. Again rocks and conifer-birch woods characterize travel. Brook crossings tie together the trail fragments, showcasing crystalline waters, falls, cascades, and deep pools. For brief periods the trail departs the brook, passing amid woods.

At 6.4 miles climb steeply to cross the next brook over, traversing a conifer-birch forest where Iroquois Peak may be glimpsed. After topping Cold Brook Pass (7.2 miles), the trail flattens, giving way to a plank boardwalk across wet pockets and meadow openings, serving up looks at mounts Marcy and Colden. Blue gentian dots the meadow.

Before long, a demanding rock-hopping and oozing-mud descent advances the loop; the young trees trailside provide an anchor for the slip-sliding traveler. At 8.25 miles comes a crossing of Cold Brook—another Adirondack classic beauty comprised of chutes, cascades, and siren pools. Again, sections of rocky-brook travel stitch together the trail segments.

By 8.6 miles, the trail's steep character subsides, giving way to a rolling tour. At the junction in 8.9 miles, follow the blue trail to the right, crossing a footbridge and traveling atop stones, pallets, and hewn logs to round the Lake Colden shore. Cross-lake views find Mount Colden with its sheet-like cliff and rocky crest. Length-of-the-lake views present a picturesque mountain gateway shaped by Mount Colden and Avalanche Mountain.

Near the end of the lake, a pair of prized lean-tos, occupy a treed point. At Lake Colden Dam (9.4 miles), go straight for the loop; a detour to the dam adds a grand farewell lake view.

Red markers again lead the way, with logs aiding passage through a beaver-grown wetland. At the footbridge, look downstream and find the wetland-meadow corner of Flowed Lands Lake, with views of the blue platter reserved for later. Conifer and birch again claim the way.

The route remains rolling, rocky, rooted, and muddy; flattish stones brought in by trail crews aid hopscotch travel. At 10.6 miles, cross an old diversion channel, coming to a junction with two Calamity lean-tos and a picturesque view of the open water and rimming marsh of Flowed Lands Lake. Go right for the loop.

At the alder rim of Calamity Pond (10.9 miles), a path to the right leads to the 6-foot-tall marble monument honoring David Henderson, who helped open up the Adirondacks and who died on this site in an accidental shooting in 1845. The loop resumes left with more mud, stone, and plank crossings and with a meadow crossing at 11.2 miles. Maples reappear, as the moderate-grade trail descends parallel to but away from Calamity Brook.

At 12.5 miles, turn right, cross Calamity Brook on a suspension bridge, and continue following the brook downstream through a deciduous-conifer forest. At 12.8 miles, a couple of scenic camp flats lie to the left, the last ones before private land.

The trail improves as it follows a well-drained road bed. After 13.25 miles, travel is on private land; keep to the marked trail. At 14 miles go left again crossing Calamity Brook via footbridge to travel a wide logging-road easement to close the loop at 15.5 miles, to return to the trailhead 15.9 miles.

15 *NORTHVILLE-PLACID TRAIL*

General description: This difficult long-distance route through the rugged splendor of the Adirondacks takes an average of two to three weeks to hike.
General location: From Northville to Lake Placid.
Special attractions: Wilderness solitude; lakes, rivers, and brooks; colorful fall foliage; spur trails to ponds and peaks.
Length: 132 miles one way; 121.1 miles one way, forgoing the southern road miles and starting at Upper Benson.
Elevation: From its southern terminus at Upper Benson, the trail travels from an elevation of 1,300 feet to a high of 3,000 feet at Central Plateau (4.6 miles south of Long Lake). It ends at 2,000 feet at Averyville Road in the north.
Difficulty: Strenuous.
Maps: Adirondack Mountain Club, Northville-Placid Trail map.
Special requirements: Hikers need to work out the logistics of getting adequate food and supplies, plan what to do in case of an emergency, and arrange for transportation at the end of the trail. Expect rocky, difficult conditions; strong map and compass skills ease travel.
Season and hours: Late spring through fall.
For information: New York State Department of Environmental Conservation, Region 5.
Finding the trailhead: From Northville, go 4.1 miles north on New York 30 and turn west on Northville-Lake Placid Trail (Hamilton County 6), a

Northville-Placid Trail, Adirondack Park.

paved road. Following the signs in 5.6 miles, turn right on a dirt road and quickly take a second right. In 0.6 mile near Trailhead Lodge, turn left on Godfrey Road to reach the trail register in 0.5 mile; parking precedes it on the right. Find the northern terminus at the junction of Averyville and Old Military roads. Reach the junction by going south on Old Military Road from NY 86 or west on Averyville Road from the village of Lake Placid.

The hike: Built in 1922 by the Adirondack Mountain Club, this blue-marked trail receives regular maintenance from New York State's Department of Environmental Conservation (DEC). The southern two-thirds of the trail rolls to obtain a top elevation of 3,008 feet at Central Plateau, south of Long Lake, the largest water body on the tour. The northern portion twists through valleys parting trailless high peaks to end at Averyville Road near Lake Placid.

Much of the tour passes through low- and middle-elevation forests, showing easy to moderate climbs. The route typically travels along drainages, past lakes, and over low passes. Expect more rugged conditions while passing through the wilderness interior.

The trail traverses public lands for the most part. Where it crosses private lands, some logging may be witnessed; keep to the trail and respect the posted rules of private landowners. Passage is along foot trail and old logging tote roads; spurs represent opportunities to view other ponds or to ascend peaks for vistas. Otherwise, one's admiration of the Adirondack Mountains comes by way of gaps in the tree cover.

While some thirty lean-tos lie along or just off the trail, offering convenient, dry overnight waysides, a tent remains standard equipment. As lean-tos cannot be reserved, chancing that you will be the first to arrive and claim the lean-to for the night is both unwise and an unnecessary wilderness risk. Secure a camping permit from the area ranger if your group number exceeds ten if you plan to use the same campsite for more than three nights.

Three primary crossroads, NY 8 near Piseco, NY 28 at Lake Durant (near Blue Mountain Lake), and NY 28N near Long Lake, break the route into four disproportionate segments. From Upper Benson to NY 8 covers 24.2 miles; from NY 8 to NY 28 covers 45.2 miles; from NY 28 to NY 28N covers 14.8 miles; and from NY 28N to the intersection of Averyville and Old Military roads covers a distance of 36.9 miles. These primary routes, along with some secondary crossroads suggest likely resupply or exit points.

The first quarter of the tour shows gentle ups and downs, crossing branches of the Sacandaga River and numerous brooks and creeks. Beaver ponds, lakes, and meadows punctuate travel through the mostly deciduous woods of the Southern Adirondack foothills. The lakes tend to support trout.

A series of large wild lakes and virgin forests in the popular Spruce Lake-West Canada Lakes-Cedar Lakes area highlight the second leg of the tour. The remote lakes, while enchanting in beauty, remain quiet, stilled by acid rain. Scoured clean, the lakes show not a ripple nor a dragon fly. Only the mournful call of a loon breaks the silence.

This long wild stretch of the Northville-Placid Trail provides unrivaled escape from the concerns of a workaday world. Pristine West Canada Lakes Wilderness Area remained untouched, until this trail opened its gates. The picturesque spruce-hardwood forests captivate travelers. Cedar River Road, a dirt access road within Moose River Recreation Area, offers another resupply or exit point.

Along the third segment of the tour hikers find a rolling woods excursion that takes them past several lakes before claiming the high point of the tour and dipping to NY 28N. Views still remain limited.

A 6-mile tour along the eastern shore of Long Lake launches the final leg of the journey; a half-dozen lean-tos dot the shore of this popular destination. Land ownership along the lake is mixed; the trail travels primarily public lands, skirting private parcels.

From Long Lake, pass through forest to reach Cold River, an exciting, crystalline Adirondack waterway guiding travelers upstream into the High Peaks area. The trail then passes lakes, following Roaring Brook and Moose Creek (side drainages of the Cold River) upstream and over a pass entering the Upper Chubb River drainage.

Reached by a short spur 5.5 miles from the finish line, Wanika Falls puts a sterling imprint on the tour. Find the last lean-to along the waterfall spur, just below the falls.

NORTHVILLE-PLACID TRAIL

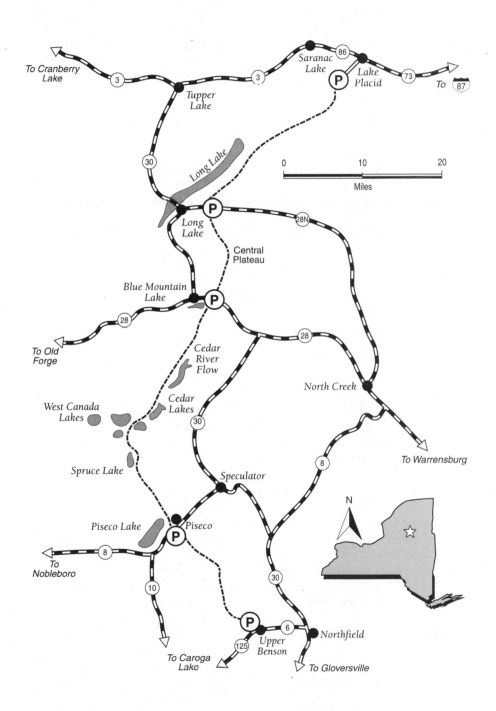

Wildlife sightings, wildflowers, autumn hues, and clues to the past all contribute to a lifetime memory of hiking the Northville-Placid Trail.

As the spatial constraints of this book limit the detail of this description, through-trail travelers and hikers planning short excursions along the Northville-Placid Trail should contact the DEC for its brochure, *The Northville-Placid Trail*, which offers a concise point-to-point synopsis of the trail. Also, entire books have been devoted to this premier hiking trail; consult the bookshelves of your local library, bookstore, or backpacker/outfitter store.

16   BLUE MOUNTAIN TRAIL

General description: A quick, steep summit ascent reaches a fire tower for a cherished 360-degree Central Adirondack view.
General location: Above the east shore of Blue Mountain Lake.
Special attractions: Sweeping vistas, spruce-fir forest, fire tower, historic Verplanck Colvin benchmark.
Length: 4 miles round trip.
Elevation: The trail travels between 2,200 feet at the trailhead and a summit elevation of 3,759 feet.
Difficulty: Moderate, with some difficult rocky stretches.
Maps: Adirondack Mountain Club, Adirondack Central Region map; Trails in the Blue Mountain Lake Region brochure.
Special requirements: None.
Season and hours: Spring through fall.
For information: New York State Department of Environmental Conservation (DEC), Region 5.
Finding the trailhead: From the intersection of New York 28, New York 30, and New York 28N in Blue Mountain Lake Village, go north on NY 30/NY 28N for 1.4 miles and turn right (east) for the marked trailhead parking lot for Blue Mountain and Tirrell Pond trails. For Blue Mountain Trail, follow the red disks along a cable-closed road at the northeast corner of the parking lot. Avoid Tirrell Pond Trail (also marked by red disks), traveling the grassy road shoulder north.

The hike: This popular, highly accessible interpretive trail ascends a peak looming above the east shore of Blue Mountain Lake, providing area newcomers with a taste of the challenge and wilderness discovery found in the Adirondacks. The DEC no longer staffs the fire tower atop Blue Mountain.

BLUE MOUNTAIN TRAIL

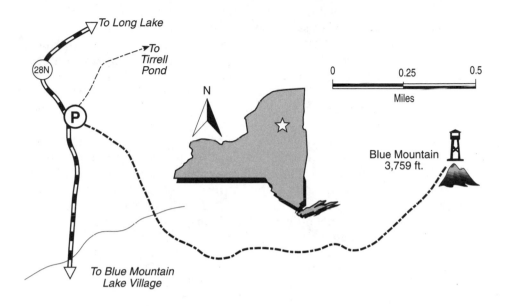

Hike 100 feet up the closed road (past the trail register) to find the box containing interpretive brochures. While normally stocked, the popularity of the trail can draw down stocks. Tall maple, black cherry, and birch frame the thin, exposed road corridor, while fern, viburnum, striped maple, and brambles fill out the woods. Numbered posts correspond to the brochure write-ups.

After 0.2 mile a rocky trail replaces the old road. Following rainstorms, its worn bed becomes a drainage; in places, side-by-side planks ease travel. Big birch trees, both yellow and white, claim the way as the trail briefly levels. Many of these birch germinated following the blowdown of 1950. Where the trail crosses a brook at 0.7 mile, look upstream to find a burgundy pool and small cascade sheeting over canted rock.

The trail briefly degrades to a wide, sharply ascending erosion channel. At times, snags open the canopy, but the trail remains semi-shaded. At the next brook crossing, both forest and trail undergo a character change. A higher-elevation forest of spruce, fir, birch, and mountain ash claims the peak, while the trail narrows, steepens, and grows more rocky.

By 0.9 mile steep rock outcrops advance the trail, while clintonia, bunchberry, oxalis, and club moss adorn the sides. After rains, this section becomes a full-fledged creek, with racing water spilling around and over the rocks. Be watchful of your footing.

In another half mile, canted bedrock offers a more moderate climb through tight stands of picturesque fir and spruce. At 2 miles tag the bald summit outcrop, topped by the five-story steel-frame observatory and radio tower. A low ring of spired spruce allows only limited looks north.

The public may ascend the fire tower, but limit numbers on the structure at any one time. Erected in 1917, the tower was restored by a volunteer committee in 1994. Summit views sweep Whiteface, Algonquin, Colden, and Marcy peaks; Blue Mountain, Eagle, Utowana, and Durant lakes; Minnow, Mud, South, and Tirrell ponds; and Blue Ridge—a bold terrain of forests, peaks, and lakes.

Other summit structures include a boarded-up cabin and concrete foundations from an old radar installation. Some ten paces north of the 35-foot fire tower, look for the original benchmark placed on the summit by Verplanck Colvin. A famous name in the New York State annals, he played a key role in opening the Adirondacks to the public. From this site in the 1870s, his men shot off bright explosions, so the Adirondack survey teams could triangulate on this peak. Return as you came.

General description: This easy trail accesses three sparkling lakes—Bennett, Middle, and Murphy—cradled in the quiet wooded beauty of the Southern Adirondacks.

General location: 9 miles north of Northville.

Special attractions: Fishing, camping, historic settlement site, loons, colorful fall foliage.

Length: 10.3 miles round trip.

Elevation: From a trailhead elevation of 940 feet, the trail tops the 1,600-foot mark while rounding Middle Lake. It then dips to Murphy Lake at 1,473 feet.

Difficulty: Easy.

Maps: Adirondack Mountain Club, Adirondack Southern Region map.

Special requirements: None.

Season and hours: Spring through fall.

For information: New York State Department of Environmental Conservation (DEC), Region 5.

Finding the trailhead: From Sacandaga Campground and Day-use (3.4 miles south of Wells), go south on New York 30 for 5 miles and turn left (east) onto Creek Road. From Northville, find the turn for Creek Road 3 miles north of the NY 30 bridge over the Sacandaga River. Find the marked trailhead on the left side of Creek Road in 2.2 miles; park on the broad road shoulder.

The hike: This trail heads north along a former roadbed, passing through a tall forest of white pine, oak, hemlock, ash, maple, birch, and aspen. Various ferns, sarsaparilla, and sugarscoop spot the understory. Past the register, ascend with a steady, moderate grade. Mossy boulders and logs add interest to the forest floor. In places, the old road is worn deep into the terrain.

By 0.3 mile hemlock, birch, and beech dominate with greenery virtually absent from the forest floor. As the incline flattens, big white pines shade the route and soften the roadway with their discarded needles. Bypass a remnant rock wall and round a barrier, which reaffirms the DEC prohibits vehicle travel save for snowmobiles. The snowmobile markers serve a dual service, guiding hikers in summer.

The trail then dips away. At 1 mile, keen-eyed travelers may discern some exposed red soil, hinting at a turn-of-the-century ferric oxide (paint pigment) mine. While trees and leaf mat have reclaimed the mining settlement, hikers still may discern unusual mounds, cellar holes, or rusting debris.

A pair of cairns on the right at 1.4 miles funnels hikers down a wide trail to Bennett Lake, a camp flat, and privy (1.5 miles). The elongated oval of Bennett Lake rests below a rolling wooded ridge. Aquatic grasses and plants adorn its shallow edge, while insect chirrs enliven the air. A small boot-compressed beach offers lake access.

MURPHY LAKE TRAIL

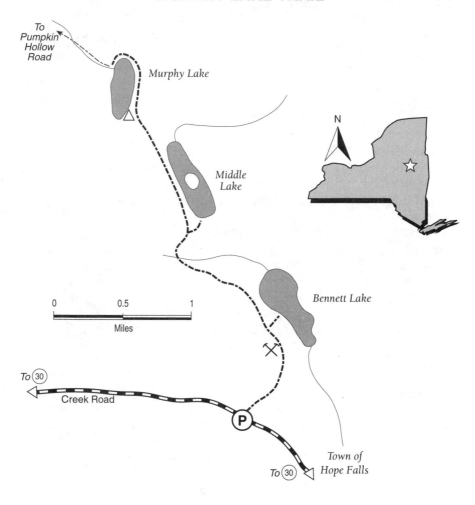

To Pumpkin Hollow Road

Murphy Lake

Middle Lake

N

Bennett Lake

0   0.5   1

Miles

To (30)

Creek Road

P

To (30)   Town of Hope Falls

A moderate, rocky ascent from the Bennett Lake basin continues the tour. Toad, red eft, gray squirrel, and grouse number among the wildlife sightings. From somewhere on the lake rises the haunting cry of a loon.

Where the trail passes between two low ridges, the comfortable earthen bed returns, and more greenery spreads beneath the trees. At 2.4 miles, skirt a mud hole to follow a small drainage; bridges span the larger run-offs.

At 2.8 miles the trail tops out. At 2.9 miles a side trail veers right, passing through a hemlock grove to reach a Middle Lake campsite. A muddy shoreline with a few logs for footing offers a lake perspective featuring a small island topped by white pines and a large central island that deceives visitor into thinking it is the far shore.

The primary trail contours the slope 200 feet above Middle Lake. Small-diameter trees choke out meaningful views, but the sparkling blue provides a grand canvas for the leafy boughs. Slowly, the trail inches toward the lake.

At 3.4 miles a second unmarked spur ventures 200 feet to the right, reaching Middle Lake and another campsite; a log-strewn, marshy shore greets hikers. Views feature the north end of the big central island and a scenic rounded hill marked by west cliffs rising to the north. Aquatic grasses, pickerelweed (arrowhead), and water lilies adorn the shallows.

The trailbed alternately shows grass, rock, and earthen stretches, as hikers continue to round Middle Lake. Prior to leaving the lake (3.8 miles), find a couple of open views.

After a wooded ascent, cross a rocky drainage and curve right to reach Murphy Lake (4.25 miles), where a lean-to overlooks an outcrop sloping to the water. The reflecting waters of Murphy Lake and the enfolding rounded tree-mantled hills with their cliff outcrops hold a signature charm, dazzling in autumn attire.

A marked foot trail continues past the lean-to, traveling counterclockwise halfway around the lake, bypassing campsites and lake accesses. The trail rolls just above shore, rounding through meadow, hemlock stand, and leafy woods. Lake coves thick with pickerelweed draw attention.

At 5.25 miles a natural rock-and-log dam at the outlet signals the end of the lakeshore tour but not the trail. A footpath descends along the outlet to a northern trailhead on Pumpkin Hollow Road 3.8 miles away. Return as you came.

18 *PHARAOH MOUNTAIN AND LAKE LOOP*

General description: This all-day or overnight tour tags the summit of Pharaoh Mountain and encircles large, deep Pharaoh Lake, touring mixed forest and wetland meadows.

General location: Eastern Adirondacks, east of Schroon Lake.

Special attractions: Summit and shore vistas, swimming and fishing lake, expansive marsh, lean-tos, solitude, fall color.

Length: 14.5 miles round trip.

Elevation: The trail shows a 1,550-foot elevation change, with the high point atop Pharaoh Mountain, elevation 2,556 feet.

Difficulty: Strenuous.

Maps: Adirondack Mountain Club, Adirondack Eastern Region map.

Special requirements: None. Find privies near most lean-tos.

Season and hours: Spring through fall.

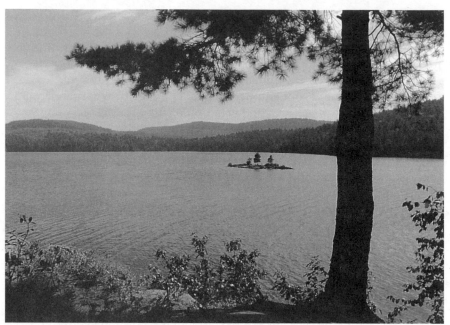
Pharaoh Lake, Adirondack Park.

For information: New York State Department of Environmental Conservation (DEC), Region 5.

Finding the trailhead: From the New York 74/New York 9 junction (0.1 mile east of New York State Interstate 87), go south on NY 9 for 0.6 mile, and turn left (east) onto Alder Meadow Road toward Schroon Lake Airport. In 2 miles, bear left on Crane Pond Road and go 1.4 miles east, reaching a parking area on the left; en route the road changes to gravel.

The road now narrows to a single dirt lane with turnouts. Drivers with conventional vehicles should go no farther than the Goose Pond Trailhead, 0.8 mile ahead. Those with four-wheel-drive vehicles generally can reach the Crane Pond Trailhead at road's end in another mile. Beware of a steep loose-sand area with moguls from spinning tires and a beaver-flooded stretch.

Should the DEC eventually opt to close this roadway into Pharaoh Lake Wilderness, park at the large turnout on Crane Pond Road and walk the final 1.8 miles to the trailhead. While adding distance, the route offers a pleasant tree-shaded tour, paralleling Alder Creek upstream. Outcrops, a dark hollow, wetland, and Alder Pond vary the tour. Look left at 1.5 miles for a yellow bypass trail to skirt the flood site.

An alternative approach would be to take the blue trail south from NY 74 near Paradox Lake, which comes out on Crane Pond Road 0.1 mile west of the trailhead; this approach adds 2.9 miles of travel each way.

PHARAOH MOUNTAIN AND LAKE LOOP

To (9)
Crane Pond Road

Alder Pond

Crane Pond

P

0   0.5   1
Miles

Oxshoe Pond

Crab Pond

Glidden Marsh

N

Pharaoh Mountain 2,556 ft.

Split Rock Bay

To Putnum Pond

Wintergreen Point

Pharaoh Lake

To Desolate Brook

To Springhill Ponds

To Mill Brook

To Whortleberry Pond

The hike: From Crane Pond Trailhead, follow the red markers across a split-level bridge over the outlet linking Crane and Alder ponds. Huge boulders punctuate the evergreen-deciduous shore. Alder Pond shows a more vegetated water with meadowy islands; both ponds draw canoeists.

Follow an old woods road into the wilderness for an easy ascent, overlooking the wooded slope of Crane Pond. Maples and fir join the hemlock-birch mix, as do 4-foot-diameter white pines. At 0.6 mile find the loop junction and bear right, staying on the red trail for a counterclockwise loop that tops Pharaoh Mountain first. Skirt an elbow pond of Glidden Marsh before passing behind a low ridge, where a foot trail replaces the woods road. Gradually, the uphill grade intensifies.

At 2.25 miles, swing right for a long angling ascent. Spruce and young fir appear, as bedrock slabs now shape a more vertical charge up Pharaoh Mountain. Aspen and mountain ash interweave the open forest. Find a preview look northwest at Desolate Swamp, Goose Pond, and Schroon Lake.

At 2.9 miles, top Pharaoh Mountain near an old mining adit. To continue the tour, head south, straight across the crown. First though, mount the summit outcrops to piece together a 270-degree view. The final puzzle piece falls into place as the trail descends.

A fantastic landscape of rolling ridges, rounded peaks, and a myriad of lakes and marshes treats the eye. Atop the western outcrop (the one to the right), one of four survey markers dates back to 1896. Early in the summit descent, detour right, topping yet another outcrop to complete the panoramic puzzle with a southern view of Pharaoh Lake, big and glistening, with rock islands, an irregular shoreline, and encompassing wilderness.

Rocks and roots complicate the steep descent, which zigs and pitches, working its way south off the mountain. Corner outcrops shape short difficult drops. Where bedrock opens up the forest, looks northeast find Treadway Mountain.

A plank walk over a wet meadow leads to the lake at 4.5 miles. Bear right, contouring and rolling along the wooded slope, crossing rocky drainages for a counterclockwise tour. At 5.4 miles detour left, following yellow markers along a peninsula to two lean-tos in 0.25 mile. The peninsula's rocky end invites swimming, fishing, daydreaming, and stargazing.

Resume the counterclockwise tour (5.9 miles); yellow disks now mark the lake loop as well. An outcrop pushes the trail up and inland. At 6.25 miles, a spur angles left to a secluded lean-to along the wooded shore. Round above the shallow, pinched outlet bay to cross a footbridge. Beaver-peeled sticks clog the brook, while frogs and mergansers commonly enliven the bay.

At the junction across the bridge, follow the yellow markers uphill to the left, soon traveling a soft woods road. Bypass a lakeside shelter at 7.1 miles and pull away from shore, passing through a corridor of spruce and reindeer lichen. At 7.5 miles, find a lean-to overlooking the lake. Past guests have christened it the "Pharaoh Hilton"; the DEC knows it by Shelter 2.

Beyond the Springhill Ponds trail junction, bear left, skirting a quiet bay to cross a hewn log bridging a peninsular island to shore. Here sits

Shelter 3, another choice site for overnight lodging and swimming. Cross back over the log to resume the loop, touring amid mixed evergreens, birch, and sheep laurel. More outcrops lure sweaty travelers lakeside; views pan to Pharaoh Mountain.

At a camp flat at 8.75 miles, turn right, ascending and rounding the steep rocky slope above a lily-pad bay. From a log bridge admire Wintergreen Point, the long, thin treed outcrop separating the main lake from the bay.

At 9.2 miles, bypass the trail heading right to Putnam Pond. In another 50 feet, turn left on a red secondary trail to reach Wintergreen Point—a 0.2-mile round-trip detour. Past Wintergreen Point the lake trail again draws away from shore, touring a deciduous woodland with hobblebush, striped maple, and young beech; follow markers.

Past Shelter 4 (10.25 mile) round Split Rock Bay, named for a distinctive offshore feature. Views southwest span Pharaoh Lake to Number 8 and Little Stevens mountains. Cross a spring-muddied area (10.7 miles), top a small ridge for a farewell look at Pharaoh Lake, and turn right, ascending away (11 miles). Find the grade steep, the terrain rocky, and the woods deciduous; yellow remains the guiding color.

Next travel the outskirts of some beaver wetlands in various states of reclamation. Rock-free stretches ease a slow descent. From the junction at the 12.7-mile mark continue straight on the yellow trail to reach the east shore of Glidden Marsh at its snag-riddled end. Ahead, lily pads, cattails, islands of grass and rock, and open water alter the marsh's appearance; Pharaoh Mountain looms to the south. Round east behind a low ridge, returning to Glidden Marsh. White pine and birch line the way.

At the blue-trail junction at 13.5 miles, continue straight for Crane Pond. Edge around Glidden Marsh, before dropping behind a ridge to round the west shore of a snag-riddled meadow basin. Cross the footbridge over the dark outlet of Glidden Marsh to close the loop (13.9 miles); turn right and return to the trailhead, 14.5 miles.

19 WHETSTONE GULF STATE PARK

Overview

Whetstone Creek cuts a 380-foot deep, 3-mile-long narrow gash into this 2,100-acre park on the eastern edge of the Tug Hill Plateau. The trail system applauds the impressive gulf feature from both rim and belly.

Whetstone Creek, Whetstone Gulf State Park.

General description: Two day hikes explore the geology and flora of Whetstone Gulf. One promises to get your feet wet.

General location: About 6 miles south Lowville.

Special attractions: Whetstone Creek, dramatic sandstone-shale cliffs, an overlook platform, fossils, falls, and wildflowers.

Length: Rim Loop, 6 miles round trip; Gorge Trail, 3 miles round trip.

Elevation: Rim Loop, 400-foot elevation change; Gorge Trail, about a 100-foot elevation change.

Difficulty: Moderate.

Maps: State park brochure.

Special requirements: Fee access to park. Hikers are to be off the trail by 6 p.m.; no one may start a hike after 3 p.m. The Gorge Trail should be reserved for times of low water.

Season and hours: Spring through fall.

For information: New York State Parks, Thousand Islands Region.

Finding the trailhead: From central Lowville, go south on New York 26 for 6.1 miles and turn northwest (right) onto West Road/Lewis County 29. Go another 0.2 mile and turn left entering the state park. Find the trailheads near the beach house/swimming area and off the picnic area road.

The hikes: The **Rim Loop** links the park's North and South trails for a circuit tour.

For a clockwise tour, start on the South Trail, which begins uphill to the left from the beach house. A steep, steady ascent on a wide earthen trail passes through pine woods with oak, maple, beech, birch, and ash. Moss, Mayflower, fern, and striped maple fill out the forest. At 0.4 mile the trail levels amid a pine plantation with a maple midstory.

After a bridge crossing of a small side brook, the trail curves right toward the gulf rim and a junction. The right leads to a lookout platform; the left continues the rim loop. Detour right descending along the rim edge, with foreboding overlooks of the steep forested slope. Respect the potential for danger, keep to the trail, and forget horseplay.

At 0.75 mile, an open look up-canyon presents the pinched wooded gulf. From the overlook platform, which juts from the rim, views span to the north wall and northeast beyond it to a pastoral valley and flattened ridges folding to the horizon.

Return to the rim junction at 1 mile and resume the loop. Hemlock, white pine, maple, and birch shade the rim-hugging trail. Openings offer cross-gulf views of the wooded slopes, tree-filled canyon bottom, and occasional dark pool. At times aspens whisper overhead.

By 1.75 miles, tree-filtered glimpses feature the dark, fluted cliffs of the north wall. Later, a short side spur to a point offers views up and out the gulf, as well as down and across. Infrequent trail disks mark the well-traveled path, while Indian pipe may enhance the tour.

WHETSTONE GULF STATE PARK

Passing through an area of small spruce and fir, the trail dips to an open view of a sheer cliff bowl where Whetstone Creek makes a hairpin turn. The cliffs now measure more than 350 feet high. The view at 2.75 miles features a 10-foot-wide falls streaming down the sheer north wall. A fast-surging Whetstone Creek announces itself below.

After a dip to cross a footbridge over a side drainage, a spur to the right leads to a long, furiously tumbling cascade on Whetstone Creek as it courses through a squeezed gorge at the head of the gulf. The cascades grade from a couple of feet high at the top to 40 feet high at the bottom. Tannin-colored water, bubbling foam, and dark weeping ledges contribute to the spectacle.

Crossing a log corduroy, the trail meets dirt Corrigan Road. Turn right, cross the bridge over Whetstone Creek, and take a quick right on the North Trail for the return. A varied woods of spruce, hemlock, birch, beech, and maple envelops the trail. By 3.5 miles, glimpse the north-wall falls and the dramatic cliffs of the opposite shore.

Past a side-creek footbridge, two razorback points protrude from the north wall meeting a treed point from the south wall, shaping the hairpin turn in the gulf. Hemlocks and deciduous trees alternately claim the route. After a drainage crossing at 4.6 miles, the descent begins.

At 5.2 miles the trail descends a thin ridge separating the gulf and a steep-sided gully. Oaks claim the gulf slope, while hemlocks fill the gully. At times the trail pitches steeply. Look toward the gulf to view the park road, picnic area, and later the manmade swimming hole. At 5.9 miles, continue straight to cross a footbridge to the swimming area parking lot, coming out downstream from the beach house to end the tour.

The **Gorge Trail** journeys upstream through the narrow gulf, criss-crossing Whetstone Creek. Since there are no footbridges, bring sneakers for wading and have some fun.

From the end of the picnic area road, pass through the barrier and cross a gravel flat to enter the deciduous wooded canyon. Thimbleberry, nightshade, Virginia creeper, and poison ivy contribute to the ground-cover. Initially a built-up bank isolates the foot trail from the creek; tadpoles shimmy through the side-water pools. At 0.2 mile comes the first of a dozen or more crossings. Avoid the false trail contouring the steep, sloughing north slope.

Whetstone Creek shows flat sandstone plates, rounded boulders, and tea-colored water, with sections of riffles, deep pools, gravel bars, and veg-etated islands. Overhanging trees, a play of shadow and light, and a tran-quil creek voice all lend to the tour's charm.

Ski-trail disks and faded blazes help mark the tour, which has a strong cross-country character, with wadings linking short snatches of trail. By 1.2 miles, steep shale slopes shoot skyward, the canyon tightens, and the water becomes more braided. Look closely at the creekbed sandstones for fossils, but no collecting. Upstream fossils show better detail, having more recently broken from the rock.

By 1.4 miles, the trail sections become so overgrown that wading proves more convenient. Here, too, the tour reaches the impressive heart of the gulf with its 380-foot-high sandstone and shale cliffs. The softer shales erode out leaving behind ledges and lips where wildflowers find root. Hikers feel antlike amid the looming cliffs. At 1.5 miles lie the stepped cascades at the foot of the canyon's hairpin turn, signaling the turnaround. Touring upstream becomes far more treacherous.

General description: A relaxing stroll through magnificent woods and meadow clearings leads to an outcrop overlooking this falls and gorge on the Independence River.

General location: About 15 miles east of Lowville.

Special attractions: Stepped falls, Independence River Wild Forest, stone ruins, beaver pond, wildflowers, wildlife.

Length: 6.5 miles round trip.

Elevation: The trail shows about a 100-foot elevation change.

Difficulty: Easy.

Maps: Crystal Dale 7.5-minute USGS quad, Number Four 15-minute USGS quad.

Special requirements: None.

Season and hours: Spring through fall.

For information: New York State Department of Environmental Conservation, Region 6.

Finding the trailhead: From New York 12/New York 26 in Lowville, turn east on River Street, which becomes Number Four Road (Lewis

Independence River, Adirondack Park.

GLEASMANS FALLS TRAIL

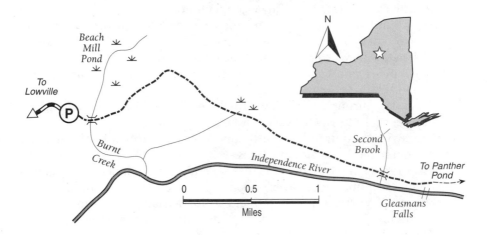

County 26), leaving town. In 4.1 miles, turn left staying on Number Four Road for another 4.8 miles. There turn right onto Erie Canal Road, go 2.5 miles and turn left on McPhilmy Road, a single-lane dirt road. In 0.2 mile, turn left on Beach Mill Road, a narrower dirt road with limited shoulder for turnouts; reduce speed. Where this road forks in 0.9 mile, stay left and go another 2 miles, reaching the trailhead at road's end.

The hike: On the west-central outskirts of the Adirondack Mountains, this trail combines easy walking through majestic woods with a satisfying destination.

Follow a closed dirt road downhill from the trailhead parking lot. In 100 feet on the right, look for an old rock foundation recalling the saw mill that once operated here. Maple, aspen, and pine frame the open corridor. Soon overlook a shrubby meadow threaded by the tannin waters of Burnt Creek, the outlet of Beach Mill Pond.

With a footbridge crossing of Burnt Creek, enter the enchantment of a rich, deep hemlock forest, with yellow disk markers pointing the way. A 4-foot-wide hiker lane parts the woods; if it were once a road, it lacks any telltale ruts or tracks. Maple and black cherry interweave the hemlock; the open midstory allows eyes to search far into the forest. Fern, viburnum, brambles, and club moss paint the understory green, attaining peak beauty when bejeweled by rain.

From 0.75 to 1 mile the trail shows a mild ascent then returns to a meditation-inducing evenness. Striped maple and beech join the ranks, along with sarsaparilla, Mayflower, and clintonia.

At 1.5 miles a beaver-grown brook has swallowed the trail's footbridge; to cross the water now, top the dam of mud and sticks. Green boughs on the drowned trees hint at the dam's newness, dark pools mirror the white pines, and scent mounds dot the shore. The trail resumes edging the "pond."

Next pass through a meadow of tall weeds, wild berries, and shrubs. Where the trail returns to woods, it becomes more rolling, still traveling the grassy bed acquired back at the meadow. The forest becomes more open, dominated by deciduous trees.

At 2.1 miles the trail dips to cross several small drainages, any one of which is susceptible to a beaver's adoption. In the meantime, the crossings remain easy, with simple step overs or log assists. At 2.3 miles, bear right, still touring an open woods but one with a woods flora.

Where the trail descends toward the Independence River, look for the path to curve left and cross Second Brook via footbridge (2.9 miles). The trail now rolls up, over, and between rock outcrops, touring a pine-deciduous forest, coming to a primitive campsite and the first rocky access to the Independence River and lower Gleasmans Falls. Here the river pulses through a gorge shaped by outcrops, cliffs, and boulders—an exciting union of cascades, deep pools, dark water, and gneiss (metamorphic rock). Pockets of fern adorn the gorge.

Continue along the north shore to top a cliff outcrop 50 feet above the rushing waters. Traverse the rim to find an open look at the uppermost falls at 3.1 miles, before again losing the angle. The upper cascade shows the greatest drop, measuring some 12 feet. Overall, the falls drops some 50 to 60 feet over a 0.2-mile distance; long, flat stretches interrupt the half-dozen stepped cascades.

While most halt at the 3.1-mile overlook, wade through the ferns of the upstream trail to reach a spur leading to a gravel bar at the head of the falls (3.25 miles). The size of the bar will depend on the water's level.

From here, the more determined can push their way downstream through shrubs, coming out on the rocks directly above the upper cascade. At times of high water, the gigantic whoosh kicks out a skin-soaking spray; be careful scrambling over the wet rocks. Downstream views of the river, gorge, and rock overhangs further add to the investment. Return as you came.

21 *MIDDLE SETTLEMENT LAKE LOOP*

General description: An all-day or overnight trek travels the forests and meadows of Ha-De-Ron-Dah Wilderness, visiting prized lakes.

General location: 6.5 miles southwest of Old Forge.

Special attractions: Lakes and ponds, mixed forest, varied wildlife sightings, overnight lean-tos.

Length: 14.25 miles round trip, including spurs to Middle Branch Lake and Grass Pond.

Elevation: The trail passes from a low point of 1,650 feet at Stony Creek to a high point of 1,900 feet at Grass Pond.

Difficulty: Moderate.

Maps: Adirondack Mountain Club, Adirondack West-Central Region map; Trails in the Old Forge-Big Moose Region brochure.

Special requirements: Good trail and map skills. Be aware that in a few places the trail markers grow scarce or disappear altogether.

Season and hours: Spring through fall.

For information: New York State Department of Environmental Conservation, Region 6.

Finding the trailhead: From Old Forge, go 6.4 miles south on New York 28 and turn right (west) at the signed easement for the trails to Ha-De-Ron-Dah

Middle Settlement Lake camp, Adirondack Park.

MIDDLE SETTLEMENT LOOP

Wilderness and Middle Settlement Lake. Go 0.5 mile north on the gravel road to find parking on the right, the arrow for the trail just beyond it on the left.

The hike: This rolling, meandering tour gathers beauty and relaxation from Ha-De-Ron-Dah Wilderness, while using a relatively new access.

Round a metal gate to travel the conservation easement across paper company land. In 250 feet, turn left to find the yellow-marked trail and register. Woody stems pop up under the boots on this fairly new trail, which employs several time-healed logging roads and crisscrosses the faint grassy beds of others. A forest of maple, birch, beech, and viburnum enfolds the tour. A single wet passage poses a seasonal problem.

At 0.75 mile, meet a narrow dirt road and follow it left for a section of fast, easy travel. Periodic postings indicate the "Wild Forest Preserve." At 1.1 miles, turn right leaving the road, following an established footpath through similar woods. At times ferns overlace the trailbed.

Cross small, braided Stony Creek and ascend to the loop junction at 1.25 miles. Go left for a clockwise tour, now passing beneath some big black cherry; mossy boulders accent the woods. The trail continues its rolling meander, crossing small brooks and soggy bottoms of sphagnum moss; hikers still must be attentive, eyeing footing and spying markers.

At 2.4 miles, descend to round the southwestern arm of Middle Settlement Lake, with cross-lake views featuring a large beaver lodge. Lily pad clusters, evergreen points, and islands lend character to the large open-water lake, while starflower and a host of mushrooms spangle the woods floor. Ruffed grouse, owl, deer, beaver, mink, toad, frog, and red eft offer possible wildlife encounters.

Cross the inlet on either of two beaver dams within easy reach of the trail. Afterward stay low to the water, before pulling away from shore and coming to a trail junction. To the left leads to Lost and Pine lakes; bear right, staying with the yellow disks, for Middle Settlement lean-to (3.2 miles).

After crossing the outlet via rocks and boot-polished logs, find the shelter atop a 7- to 10-foot-high outcrop, overlooking the main body of Middle Settlement Lake; its shimmery depths suggest a swim. For the privy, follow the red-marked trail past the huge boulders and into the woods.

From the prized lean-to, continue rounding the wooded shore, now on a well-traveled path; here the forest floor appears hummocky. Amid the gargantuan boulders at the end of the lake, find the junction at 3.5-miles. Uphill to the right lies the blue trail to NY 28 (a more established access); bear left, staying along the drainage for the loop.

At 4 miles the yellow trail passes through a soggy meadow, coming to a stone-stepping crossing (or a high-water wading) of picturesque Cedar Pond outlet with its fern-flowing banks. At 4.25 miles, glimpse Cedar Pond, a mosaic of open water and wet shrub islands and shores. Spruce, maple, and birch comprise the forest, with mixed ferns and brambles.

At the junction in 4.5 miles, the red trail straight ahead continues the loop, but detour left on the yellow trail to add a visit to Middle Branch Lake.

The detour shows more marked climbs and pitches. At the junction in 1 mile, turn left to reach the shelter, which occupies a small point overlooking the long water body of Middle Branch Lake. During rainstorms, one may pass time reading the sagas in the lean-to journal.

At 7 miles resume the clockwise loop back at the junction, now following red markers. The trail rolls through an open woods, sometimes marshy or rocky. Pretty pockets of bunchberry and club moss seduce photographers.

At 8.25 miles cross the stones over the dark-ale water of Grass Pond outlet, and in another 0.5 mile, look for a yellow trail angling left to the pond. On the detour to Grass Pond, young beech, striped maple, and viburnum frisk hikers as they pass. At 9.2 miles find a camp flat between the spruce woods and meadow shore; the main pond sweeps away to the right, requiring a bushwhacking approach.

Resume the clockwise tour of Middle Settlement Lake Loop with a tranquil woods stroll. At 10 miles, continue forward, once again on a yellow-marked trail, crossing a boardwalk through a wet bottomland near the state lands boundary. At the junction in 10.1-mile, again stay straight on the yellow trail, which is now wide, flat, and easy. To the left lies NY 28 and the popular Scusa Access. Hardwoods claim the forest.

At 11 miles, where a blue trail heads right to Middle Settlement Lake, stay on the yellow trail to bring the loop to a close; the route grows less broad and refined. Nearing a beaver pond, turn left, cross atop the earthen dam, and again turn left to travel at the wooded edge of the expansive floodplain meadow. Markers become scarce.

At 11.7 miles turn right following an overgrown woods road; the tracked trail remains visible beneath the masking ferns. While pleasantly removed from grand central station, this section of the tour requires greater attention to avoid straying off trail. Bottom areas can be soggy even in August.

Continue to follow the overgrown road bed as it curves away from the floodplain of Middle Settlement Creek. Where deciduous trees gain a stronghold, rocks and leaves interrupt the fern wadings and eventually replace the ferns. At 12.95 miles, veer right off the woods road to close the loop at 13 miles. Continue straight for Copper Lake Road, retracing the initial 1.25 miles to the trailhead.

22 *WEST CANADA LAKES WILDERNESS*

Overview

Within Moose River Recreation Area of the West-central Adirondacks, this designated wilderness represents one of the last regional wilds opened to foot travel. It sports picturesque spruce-hardwood forests, charming meadows, and large wilderness lakes. From this tour, wilderness hikers may access the trans-Adirondack Northville-Placid Trail or visit such other celebrated features as Spruce Lake and Cedar Lakes.

General description: An overnight outing or demanding all-day hike travels to the core of West Canada Lakes Wilderness, passing through conifer-deciduous forest and meadow breaks to visit three pristine lakes: Falls Pond, Brooktrout, and West.
General location: 20 miles southeast of Old Forge.
Special attractions: Wilderness forest and lakes, beaver ponds, gentian meadows, solitude, loons, fall foliage.
Length: 18.2 miles round trip, including Falls Pond detour.
Elevation: The trail shows a 550-foot elevation change.

Falls Pond, Adirondack Park.

WEST CANADA LAKES WILDERNESS

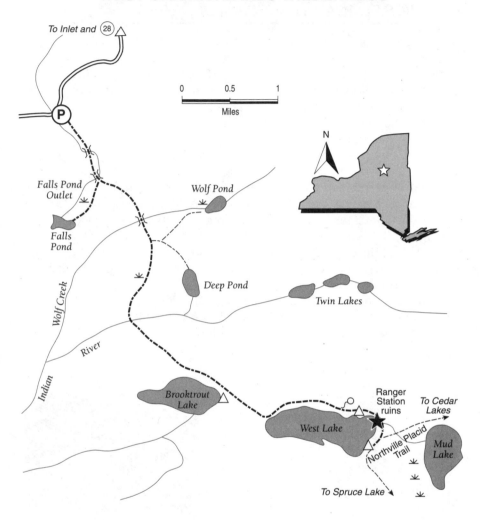

Difficulty: Moderate to strenuous.

Maps: Moose River Recreation Area brochure; Adirondack Mountain Club, Adirondack West-Central Region map.

Special requirements: Drivers entering Moose River Recreation Area must register upon entering. Several backcountry privies exist in disrepair.

Season and hours: Memorial Day weekend through fall.

For information: New York State Department of Environmental Conservation, Region 5.

Finding the trailhead: From central Inlet, go east on New York 28 for 0.8 mile and turn south on Limekiln Road for Moose River Recreation Area. Go 1.8 miles, turn left, and register for the recreation area. Continue east on the wide improved dirt road (15 miles per hour), following the signs for Otter Brook. In 11.4 miles cross over the Otter Brook bridge and follow signs to Brooktrout Lake (right). Find the trailhead on the left in 0.9 mile, and parking for a dozen vehicles.

The hike: Go around the barrier, following a retired logging road for a steady ascent, overlooking a series of beaver ponds. Young maples, small spruce, birch, and beech overlace the route, while sarsaparilla, fern, whorled aster, grasses, and bramble comprise the sides. The trail possesses a good walking surface, with a few rocky or cobbly areas.

Cross a small logging bridge at 1.2 miles, and in another 0.25 mile look for the marked Falls Pond Trail on the right. Some yellow markers point the way, as the trail tours a scenic fir-spruce woods, skirts the edge of the outlet meadow, and crosses the outcrop at the head of the meadow, returning to forest. The trail tags the lake outlet, a campsite, and an outcrop view before drawing to an end.

A mountain beauty with an irregular shoreline, Falls Pond enchants with outcrop points and islands, a fir-spruce rim, and enfolding deciduous hillsides. The morning mist and the distressful cry of an unseen loon conjure a haunting image.

Resume the wilderness hike at 2.5 miles, turning right on the main trail. Outcrops open up the trail corridor, while dense stands of low-growing spruce and fir squeeze it. By August's last days, the leaves show the onset of change, with orange, yellow, red, and maroon hues.

The trail tops out (3 miles) and slowly descends, crossing the bridge over the Wolf Lake outlet at 3.2 miles. Go 200 yards past the bridge to find the access trails to Deep and Wolf lakes on the left, offering additional exploration. Deep Lake lies 0.9 mile off trail, Wolf Lake a mile. Wetlands and beaver flooding create a soggy trek to the latter.

For this description, forgo these side excursions, keeping to the main trail as it passes over exposed bedrock (slippery when wet) and amid young deciduous trees. Per the cairn at 3.4 miles, round the lower edge of the outcrop to pick up the foot trail. Paired planks cross wet spots and delicate meadow habitats. At 3.6 miles skirt a meadow swath adorned in late summer by blue gentian and sunlit nodding cotton grass.

The trail again skirts a scenic beaver pond and meadow at 4.1 miles. Wildlife watching likewise reflects the changing of the seasons, as beavers tug leafy branches across the pond, dive, and anchor the limbs, preparing for winter.

After 4.4 miles lose all trace of the old road, as well as such niceties as the wetland footplanks, although more yellow disks mark the way. The trail rolls, generally descending to a stone crossing of Deep Lake outlet, then ascends to 5.3 miles, passing from conifer to deciduous woods.

At 5.5 miles, bypass a scenic cluster of mossy boulders and logs, keeping left touring a spruce bog. Here the trail becomes muddied both literally and figuratively; beware of impostors. Next cross over a rise where hobblebush and young beech frisk passersby to contour the wooded slope above Brooktrout Lake—a gleam in the basin. As the wilderness trail remains removed from the lakes, take advantage of all side trails to camp flats and lean-tos to admire the waters.

Find Brooktrout Lake lean-to at 6.5 miles. Side trails venture to the lake, reaching a boulder and marsh shore that prohibits travel. A fellow hiker tested the temperature and Ph factor, finding 68 degrees Fahrenheit and a Ph of 3.8. The legacy of acid rain still silences these remote prized lakes.

Pass the lean-to, bear left rounding away from the lake, following red and yellow disks. Again the trail crosses over a rise at 7.3 miles, touring above a meadow basin at the upper extent of West Lake. At a trail sign near a split boulder, find a spur to a lakeside camp. From this lake corner, views span West Lake to Pillsbury Peak.

The rolling trail now contours the forested slope above West Lake. In places, brushy growth and spruce intrude. At 8.8 miles find piped spring water. In another 0.1 mile, reach the first of two lean-tos along West Lake. Again spurs branch to the bouldery lake shore, with a pretty treed island offshore.

Continue rounding the lake to the southeast, crossing rotting foot-boards amid a wet meadow. Where the trail returns to the woods, beautiful carpets of oxalis accent the curvature of the trail. After crossing the outlet bridge and bypassing an old dump from the former rangers cabin, find a junction post amid a meadow.

Here hikers meet the blue Northville-Placid Trail. To the left leads to Cedar Lakes; go right for the second West Lake lean-to, the ending for this hike. While at the junction post, look right to a cross; a visit finds an old rock foundation, the fireplace from French Louie's cabin that previously occupied the site of the rangers cabin, and the cross inscribed "RIP West Canada Lakes Rangers Cabin Jan. 29, 1987 Age about 50 yrs. 'You did not conform.'" A trail leads past the ruins to the bouldery shore for another lake view.

Return to the junction and resume the tour to the second West Lake lean-to, bearing right at the next junction. Reach the prized lean-to at 9.6 miles. It looks out at West Lake, its bouldery shore, a string of rocks concluding at a small rock island and an attractive rolling wooded terrain. Return as you came or investigate some of the other wilderness lakes.

23 SIAMESE PONDS HIKE

General description: This easy all-day hike or backpack tours a scenic low-elevation Central Adirondack forest, parallels the East Branch Sacandaga River, and visits a large wilderness pond.

General location: 9.5 miles south of Wevertown off New York 8.

Special attractions: Historic 1800s Bakers Mills-North River Stagecoach Route, colorful fall foliage, bear, beaver, mink, otter, and grouse and other woodland creatures.

Length: 11.8 miles round trip.

Elevation: This trail shows a 500-foot elevation change. From a trailhead elevation of 1,800 feet, the trail ascends 200 feet before descending to a river elevation of 1,600 feet and ultimately climbing to Siamese Ponds at 2,118 feet.

Difficulty: Easy.

Maps: Adirondack Mountain Club; Adirondack Central Region map.

Special requirements: None.

Season and hours: Spring through fall.

For information: New York State Department of Environmental Conservation (DEC), Region 5.

Finding the trailhead: From Bakers Mills (south of Wevertown), go 3.8 miles south on NY 8; a small DEC sign marks the large gravel trailhead parking lot on the west side of the highway.

The hike: Ideal for a family backpack or a first backpack outing, this trail journeys west into Siamese Ponds Wilderness, ascending steadily and moderately along a former roadbed overlaced by young birch, aspen, and maples. The blue-disk trail markers are few in number, but little needed. In places, rocks riddle the bed. Fern, hobblebush, and sarsaparilla contribute to the woodland understory, while jewelweed accents the moist drainages.

The grade eases, as the trail parallels a small drainage upstream, crossing over the low shoulder of Eleventh Mountain (0.4 mile). Here the historic stagecoach route hosts the descent. The forest's spatial order and changing mix create visual diversity. By 1.1 mile firs and spruce fill out the complex, and black cherry trees enter the mix. Joe-pye-weed, aster, and dogwood push up in the meadow clearings.

As the stage route levels off, enjoy carefree strolling above the riparian corridor of the East Branch Sacandaga River. At 1.5 miles comes the Diamond Brook bridge crossing; budding biologists often detour to the bank, seeking tiny fry, crayfish, and mud puppies beneath the streambed rocks.

Goldenrod, brambles, and low alders contribute to the riparian meadow, which continues along the trail. At a plank bridge at 1.6 miles look for Diamond Mountain to the right. Woodland travel resumes within 100 feet of

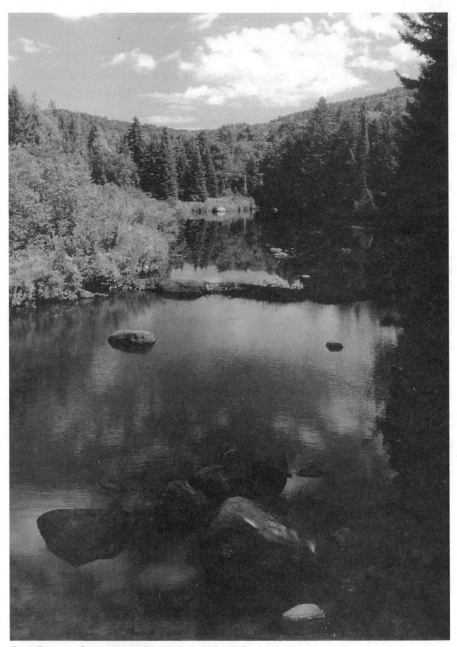

East Branch Sacandaga River, Adirondack Park.

SIAMESE PONDS HIKE

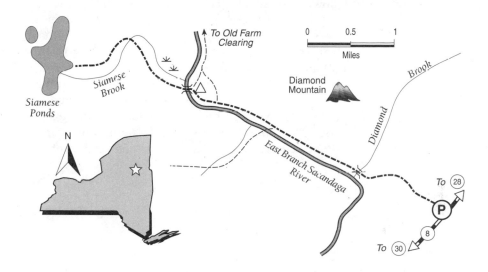

the river; birch, fir, maple, and hemlock dominate. In turn, trillium and clintonia decorate the forest floor.

At 2 miles the trail briefly tags the herb-and-forb river bank for an open look at the shallow 50-foot-wide river marked by occasional riffles, rocks, and bedrock. Its mood varies widely from times of high water to times of low water. The mild-grade earthen trail frees eyes to enjoy the setting, perhaps even to spy a bear clumsily splashing in the river.

By 2.6 miles the trail draws farther from the river, again rolling somewhat. Abandoned apple trees and a younger, more open woods announce a former farm site. Afterward, the trail drifts back toward the river.

At the 3.5-mile fork, the old stagecoach route continues to the right toward Old Farm Trailhead. To reach Siamese Ponds, bear left following a former road grade as it dips to a drainage crossing. The hike then resumes along the wooded river bench for occasional views.

At 3.9 miles a suspension bridge crosses the East Branch Sacandaga, continuing the trail to Siamese Ponds. On the east bank at the crossing site, a lopsided lean-to overlooks the water. This rain-tight lodging comes complete with table, fireplace, and functional privy. A connecting spur to the Old Farm Trail passes in front of the lean-to; avoid taking it.

From the suspension bridge find fine up and downstream views of the East Branch Sacandaga River. Leaving the bridge, continue straight ahead, as side spurs branch to camp flats and shore. The trail rolls and at 4.2 miles dips to a small run-off meadow, with a pair of hewn logs for crossing.

A rock-riddled ascent follows, but easy travel resumes, with an earthen bed and nothing more strenuous than a moderate grade. Fir, spruce, birch, hemlock, and striped and sugar maples shade the way, with fickle showings of moss, fern, hobblebush, sarsaparilla, and bunchberry.

At 4.8 miles, cross Siamese Brook atop rocks. Another rocky ascent and brief muddy stretch follow, marking the start of a more continuous ascent. By 5.4 miles a few boulders dot the slope, trees exceed 18-inches in diameter, and the trail gently rolls. A woodpecker, grouse, or red eft may divert the eye. The trail then bypasses campsites, descending to the main Siamese Pond (5.9 miles).

Shaped like an amoeba, Siamese Pond presents a bouldery-sandy beach at its point of access. Humped conifer-deciduous hills, including Hayden Mountain to the north, overlook the pond, while aquatic vegetation spots its shallow edge. To round the shore for new perspectives or to reach Upper Siamese Pond requires bushwhacking. When ready, return as you came.

24 PEAKED MOUNTAIN TRAIL

General description: This split-character trail joins an easy hike to Peaked Mountain Pond with a rugged summit ascent.
General location: Siamese Ponds Wilderness, 16 miles southeast of Indian Lake, off New York 28.
Special attractions: Lake, brook, pond, forest, and meadow habitats; summit vistas; loons, beaver, frogs, and toads.
Length: 6 miles round trip.
Elevation: The trail travels from 1,700 feet at Thirteenth Lake to a summit elevation of 2,919 feet, with 600 feet of elevation gain occurring in the final 0.3 mile.
Difficulty: Easy to pond; strenuous to summit.
Maps: Adirondack Mountain Club, Adirondack Central Region map.
Special requirements: Expect difficult footing on the summit ascent; wear boots.
Season and hours: Best in summer and fall; rain compounds the difficulty of attaining the summit.
For information: New York State Department of Environmental Conservation, Region 5.
Finding the trailhead: At the hamlet of North River on NY 28 (12 miles east of Indian Lake), turn south on Thirteenth Lake Road for Siamese Ponds Wilderness/Thirteenth Lake. Go 3.3 miles and turn right on improved-dirt Beach Road to reach the wilderness entry and trailhead parking in another 0.5 mile.

The hike: This trail holds great variety and offers a fine wilderness stroll for its first 2.7 miles. The final 0.3 mile laughs at gravity, uniting boot-skidding, steep dirt surfaces and severe bare rock inclines. For any uninitiated with the rugged nature of the Adirondacks, this summit approach shouts a loud, clear "howdy."

The hike begins on a barrier-closed road shaded by birch, beech, and fir. Pass campsites and a privy, coming to a trail register next to a primitive boat launch on Thirteenth Lake (0.1 mile). At low water, a thin rocky beach greets hikers; high water presents an alder-shrub shore. From the launch, a foot trail rounds the west shore of Thirteenth Lake, with red paint dots and disks showing the way.

For the next 0.5 mile enjoy a mildly rolling shoreline tour, seldom straying more than 25 feet from the lake's edge. Thirteenth Lake is a big, elongated water body at the base of Balm of Gilead Mountain, the saddle-shaped peak dominating cross-lake views. Canoes ply the water, while loons or mergansers suggest the raising of binoculars.

Picture-pretty birch, beech, aspen, and some towering white pines frame both trail and shore. Despite some rock studding and roots, the path remains highly passable, and lake overlooks occur at regular intervals.

At 0.6 mile, turn away from the lake following the rocky outlet of Peaked Mountain Pond upstream. Depending on flow, the upper brook may show exciting chutes, cascades, and bedrock water slides. Massive boulders loom trailside, while hemlock and birch shade the brook-hugging tour.

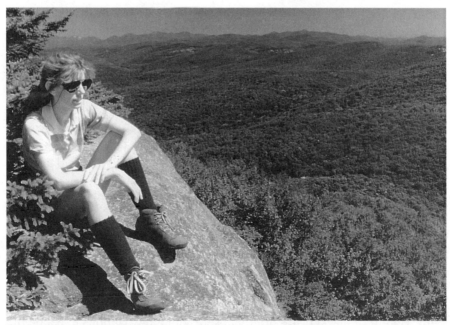

Peaked Mountain summit, Adirondack Park.

PEAKED MOUNTAIN TRAIL

At 1.2 miles the trail levels prior to a stone-stepping crossing of the brook. Ahead, small muddy drainages spot the way. At 1.4 miles, glimpse Peaked and Big Thirteenth Lake mountains. The trail then crosses over a rise, rounding an expansive grassy meadow—a classic mountain beauty edged by low alders and snuggled below Little Thirteenth Lake Mountain.

A conifer stand with a rich understory of oxalis, bunchberry, whorled aster, trillium, and clintonia gives pause before the next meadow rounding, this one below Hour Pond Mountain. Silver snags and logs, boulders, and an abandoned beaver lodge accent this grassy opening. Next, find another treed passage, coming out at an active beaver pond.

A brief, steep ascent presents Peaked Mountain Pond at 2.45 miles. At the pond, look for the main trail as it curves right for the summit ascent. A detour straight ahead finds a shoreline outcrop overlooking a thin cove severed from the main pond by a slender shrub-mantled peninsula. Continue rounding the shore to the left to attain cross-pond views of rock-crested Peaked Mountain.

The summit route takes hikers across the outlet just below the pond, passing over an old beaver dam. As the trail again turns toward shore, stay right. Here trail markers are briefly absent, but a few ribbons may cue the way. Before long, the trailbed regains definition, and the markers return.

At 2.6 miles, ascend and round the slope of Peaked Mountain, passing through a picturesque stand of paper birch. Above a meadowy pond extension, look for the trail to enter its mad summit ascent. Even being careful, hikers may find themselves up-ended, with skidding dirt, pitched slopes, and a couple of grip-defying canted outcrops. Some of the worst problem areas have been bypassed by wiser travelers, going off trail, shaping switchbacks; consider following their lead.

At the top (3 miles), easily mounted outcrops amid low-growing spruce gradually unfold a 270-degree view; looks north require more effort. Best views sweep the immediate neighborhood with Peaked Mountain Pond, the meadows, and Big and Little Thirteenth lakes, Slide, and Hour Pond mountains. Distant looks round up the Adirondack High Peaks and Vermont's Green Mountains. Ravens offer noisy commentary, while vultures drift upon the thermals.

On return, watch your footing, and as you near Peaked Mountain Pond, keep an eye out for a 2-inch-diameter garnet that studs a rock in the trail. Prior to wilderness protection, garnet mining occurred near Peaked Mountain; collecting is forbidden.

25   TONGUE MOUNTAIN RANGE LOOP

General description: This demanding loop tags five summits of the peninsular Tongue Mountain Range for unsurpassed looks at the Lake George countryside. It then dips to lake level and visits Point of Tongue, before returning along Northwest Bay.
General location: 6.5 miles northeast of Bolton Landing.
Special attractions: Spectacular lake, island, and ridge views; diverse woods; colorful autumn foliage; marsh, cliffs, and vernal pools; wildlife sightings.
Length: 14 miles round trip.
Elevation: Trail shows nearly a 1,500-foot elevation change, with the low point at Montcalm Point (Point of Tongue), the high point at Fifth Peak Lean-to (1,813 feet).
Difficulty: Strenuous; steep pitches may require hand assists.
Maps: Adirondack Mountain Club, Adirondack Eastern Region map.
Special requirements: Carry adequate drinking water, and beware— rattlesnakes live in this rugged terrain.
Season and hours: Spring through fall.
For information: New York State Department of Environmental Conservation, Region 5.
Finding the trailhead: From Interstate 87, take exit 24 and head east toward Bolton Landing. In 5 miles, turn north on New York 9N and go 4.4

miles, to find head-in parking on the east side of the highway at the old quarry pond. Find Clay Meadow Trailhead just south of the parking lot; the trail heads east.

The hike: Blue disks initially lead the way along a woods road touring a conifer plantation. Where the trail crosses a wetland boardwalk, common sightings include whitetail deer, frog, and heron. At 0.4 mile lies the loop junction; for a clockwise tour bear left (straight) toward Fifth Peak Lean-to.

Red disks now mark the steadily ascending woods road, sometimes rocky and root-bound. In 1995, a severe windstorm gleaned some of the framing hemlock, beech, and maple, opening up the passage. Where the trail grows steeper at 1.3 miles, look for it to switchback left. Now, round below mossy outcrop cliffs, traversing a scenic hemlock-birch plateau. At 1.6 miles, the ascent resumes.

At the saddle junction (1.9 miles), turn right for the loop, continuing toward Fifth Peak Lean-to, and stay right for a pleasant rolling tour to the shelter junction at 2.4 miles. A 0.5-mile round-trip detour follows yellow markers left to Fifth Peak Lean-to, where hikers find a dry overnight wayside, privy, and open outcrop for a southern Lake George vantage. Oak and hickory cloak the summit.

At 2.9 miles the primary loop journeys south along a narrow, less-used foot trail, descending a hemlock-pine slope to reach a moist deciduous bottom. Mounting Fourth Peak, top outcrops amid an old fire zone, opened up with silvered snags, sumac, aspen, and young oak; views pan south and west.

Lake George from Tongue Mountain, Adirondack Park.

TONGUE MOUNTAIN RANGE LOOP

To Ticonderoga

To Fivemile
Mountain

P

9N

To
Bolton
Landing

Fifth Peak
1,813 ft.

Tongue Mountain Range

French Point
Mountain
1,756 ft.

Northwest
Bay

Lake

George

French
Point

First Peak
1,586 ft.

N

Dock
Montcalm
Point

The Narrows

0   0.5   1

Miles

At the base of an outcrop at 3.5 miles, a trail marker on a snag points left. Briefly contour then sharply descend right, easing over rocks coming to a notch. Again climb from maple-hemlock woods to a piney crest, with overlooks of Lake George and the forested islands from South Sacrament to Floating Battery Island and with cross-lake views of Black and Erebus mountains.

After topping Third Peak at 3.9 miles, find a steep pitch before climbing to another open view. The trail then pitches, rolls, and streaks up French Point Mountain for the best views of the tour. Looks encompass French Point (a peninsula extending into Lake George), the many treed islands of The Narrows, the chain of islands stretching north, and the ridges and mountains rolling east. Open outcrops for views line up from 4.7 to 4.9 miles.

At 4.9 miles, round a small cairn atop an outcrop and descend past a vernal pool and an outcrop presenting Northwest Bay and First Peak—the final summit conquest now separated by a 400-foot elevation drop and matching gain. The trail shows a similar pitch-and-climb character, passing through oak-grassland. Where the path again overlooks the steep eastern flank, views laud the narrow lake, the dark humped ridges, and jigsaw puzzle of islands.

Beech-oak woods claim the trail where it bottoms out at 5.4 miles. Atop First Peak at 6 miles, find a 180-degree Lake George vista. The trail now hugs the east side of the ridge, passing amid oak, hickory, and ash. At 6.8 miles, two small bumps add views toward Bolton Landing.

Ahead, the tour opens up, descending amid juniper, sumac, and small cedar; looks include Montcalm Point. At 7.6 miles, snare final low-angle looks at The Narrows, then curve away west, returning to hemlock deciduous woods.

In a half mile the loop bears right, while a detour left follows blue markers to Montcalm Point (Point of Tongue). It travels the forested peninsula, by-passing a state-owned boat dock (on the left) to reach the point. Open views at both Lake George and Northwest Bay and a large outcrop call to swimmers and sunbathers as a recommended side trip.

At 8.8 miles resume the loop north, passing through a moist woodland along Northwest Bay toward Clay Meadow. The trail rolls to and from shore, rounding shallow coves and cutting points, touring muddy pockets and meadowy areas, and passing through stands of birch. Wherever the steep bank meets an abrupt lake drop-off, the urge to take a plunge overwhelms.

At 10.4 miles cross an ash swale (formerly a beaver pond). Beyond a tiny inlet flowing over a mossy boulder cliff, a canted outcrop offers swim-mers yet another lake access. At 11.25 miles the trail rolls away through mixed woods. Before long, a spur leads to a point overlooking the marshy head of Northwest Bay. Remain close to shore, with passing looks at the marsh grass, lily pads, and stands of red maple and cedar.

At the 12-mile footbridge, drift inland for a steady 0.6-mile ascent. Warblers divert attention. The trail returns once more to the marsh's edge before crossing another footbridge to close the loop at 13.6 miles. Retrace the first 0.4 mile to the trailhead and vehicle parking.

General description: This loop tops Black Mountain, the tallest mountain above Lake George, for a superb panorama of the lake region; eastern looks strain to Vermont. Ponds and beaver marshes put a stamp on the tour.

General location: East ridge of Lake George.

Special attractions: Lake, island, and ridge vistas; ponds and beaver marshes; overnight lean-tos; colorful fall foliage.

Length: 7 miles round trip.

Elevation: The trail shows a 1,046-foot elevation change between the trailhead at 1,600 feet and the closed fire tower, summit elevation 2,646 feet.

Difficulty: Moderate.

Maps: Adirondack Mountain Club, Adirondack Eastern Region map.

Special requirements: Expect some soggy trail stretches.

Season and hours: Spring through fall.

For information: New York State Department of Environmental Conservation, Region 5.

Finding the trailhead: From the junction of New York 74 and New York 22 at Ticonderoga, go 17 miles south on NY 22, turning west on Washington County 6 for Huletts Landing. In 2.5 miles turn south on Pike Brook Road, finding the gravel parking lot for the trailhead on the right in 0.8 mile.

The hike: This loop combines a fairly steep assault on the mountain with a tempered, switchbacking descent.

Lake George from Black Mountain summit.

BLACK MOUNTAIN LOOP

Red disks and snowmobile markers point the way along a fire road enclosed by maple, birch, beech, ash, viburnum, and wet meadow vegetation. At 0.25 mile continue straight; remnants of an old corduroy and flat rock placements indicate this stretch can turn to muck. At 0.6 mile, turn right following an arrow; the path ahead enters an old farmstead.

Red efts and deer number among the sightings. Aspen join the mix. Skirting the farm area, the loop travels a time-narrowed woods road through a more mature hemlock-deciduous forest. At 1 mile comes the loop junction; go right for a counterclockwise tour.

Where the marked foot trail bears left at the the fork in 1.3 miles, stay right following the snowmobile trail to avoid areas of canted outcrop, loose rock, and mire, and to avoid contributing to greater erosion. The two trails meet and part several times en route to the summit. Spruce join the mix; bunchberry, Mayflower, clintonia, and mosses adorn the sides of the route, and snags open up the canopy.

Where the snowmobile trail meets and briefly merges with the hiker trail at 2 miles, follow the shared trailbed for a couple hundred feet and turn right, returning to the red-marked hiker trail. Be careful on the ascent as run-off makes the outcrop slippery; stay to the right.

At 2.3 miles the trail comes out at the ranger's cabin and work shed, both in disrepair and scheduled for removal sometime in the future. A spur to the right leads to a picnic table and a view to the north and east, featuring the north end of Lake George, Elephant and Sugarloaf mountains, and the abandoned lookout tower atop Black Mountain.

Although the tower is closed, the outcrop nose at the tower site dishes up a grand view. Looks pan northern Lake George with Main, Harbor, and Vicars islands; Five Mile Mountain and the northern Tongue Mountain Range; and the ridges rolling east to Vermont. In fall, the spired evergreens pierce a vibrant sea of deciduous color.

For the loop return, take the trail curving west into the spruce-fir forest, as the trail reaches the tower (2.4 miles). Bypassing a shaded picnic table, begin a moderate decent. Multi-trunked birch capture the imagination, pines replace the spruce and fir, and aspen join the mix. An early view finds Black Mountain Pond, with looks building to the south. Wild raspberry, striped maple, brambles, grasses, and ferns vegetate the clearings. From an open outcrop at 3 miles, the view sweeps Lake George, Bolton Landing, The Narrows, Point of Tongue, and Shelving Rock Mountain.

The trail now descends and rounds a striated boulder cliff, snaring additional Lake George-Black Mountain Pond views. At a second outcrop vantage, the trail turns right for a switchbacking descent, entering a fuller woods of hemlock, birch, maple, and big pines.

At the base of the mountain at 3.4 miles, bear left on the yellow-disk trail for the loop; the red trail to the right leads to Black Mountain Point on Lake George in 2 miles. Be alert; although the junction is marked, rangers report several hikers unintentionally find themselves at Lake George.

The loop now travels the north shore of Black Mountain Pond, an open water with a broad meadow shore of leatherleaf and other marsh shrubs. Fish tap the surface leaving ever-widening rings. Dragonflies, kingfishers, garter snakes, and bullfrogs further enliven the stage. Where the trail crosses an outcrop at 3.7 miles, uphill to the left lies a shelter, picnic table, and privy; the loop continues straight ahead.

At 4 miles the trail crosses the inlet drainage of Round Pond, which resembles the first pond but with a broader marsh shore, pockets of phragmites (tall, feathery headed grasses), and small silvered snags. The trail stays amid the rimming hemlocks. At 4.3 miles, cross-pond views find Black Mountain.

At the 4.6-mile junction, the path to the right leads to additional ponds; for the loop, continue straight ahead, now following blue disks toward the Lapland Pond lean-to. After crossing a rocky drainage, continue straight for the loop; a detour right follows the Lapland Pond shoreline to the lean-to (0.2 mile). Perched atop an outcrop, the lean-to looks out at the lily-sprinkled pond and across its rim to Black Mountain.

Back on the loop (5 miles), follow the drainage upstream away from Lapland Pond, traveling along a soggy meadow with ash, birch, beech, and hemlock. Crossing over the drainage, the trail rounds an old beaver pond of silvered snags, wetland, and dark standing water. From the pond the trail descends mostly through hemlock woods.

At 5.75 miles, it approaches the shore of a larger snag-congested pond. From the footbridge over the outlet, views span the drowned woods to Black Mountain. The woods become more mixed as the loop draws to a close at 6 miles; retrace the first mile to the trailhead.

General description: An easy climb through rich mixed forest follows the outlet drainage to attractive Jockeybush Lake.

General location: 20 miles northwest of Gloversville.

Special attractions: Fishing, rich forest, woods flora, colorful fall foliage.

Length: 2.2 miles round trip.

Elevation: The trail shows a 250-foot elevation change.

Difficulty: Easy.

Maps: Adirondack Mountain Club, Adirondack Southern Region map.

Special requirements: Expect some soggy reaches.

Season and hours: Spring through fall.

For information: New York State Department of Environmental Conservation, Region 5.

Finding the trailhead: From the junction of New York 29A and New York 10 in the village of Caroga Lake, go north on NY 10 for 14.6 miles, passing through the village of Canada Lake and the small hamlet of Arietta. Find the marked trailhead and paved parking area on the left side of NY 10 across from a lily pond. Find the register on the left at the hike's start.

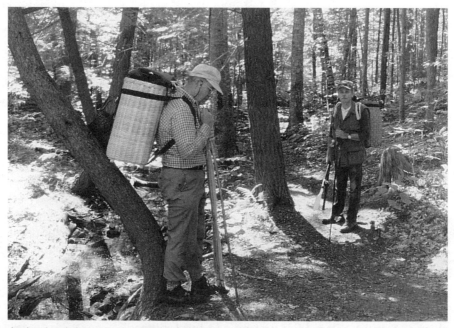

Jockeybush Lake Trail, Adirondack Park.

JOCKEYBUSH LAKE TRAIL

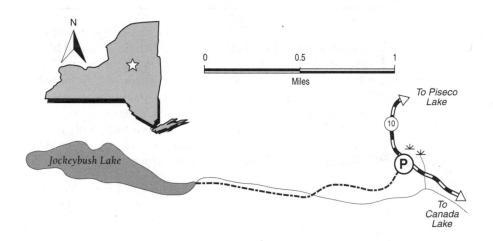

The hike: Head west ascending into the woods, following the orange snowmobile markers. A mixed age, multistory forest of white pine, hemlock, birch, black cherry, maple, and beech, along with hobblebush and fern, weaves an enchanting tour. Sunlight filters through the branches, and often a breeze lilts through the woods, contributing to the setting's charm. At 0.15 mile, pass between a pair of grand hemlocks.

At 0.3 mile cross a mud hole atop a disorganized scatter of logs from a former corduroy. The trail now travels the north shore above the outlet brook. Early in the hiking season, side drainages may complicate travel. Most times, the foot trail presents a pleasant meandering tour.

Next, cross the 10-foot-wide clear-flowing outlet brook atop stones; high water may require a wading. At 0.5 mile a mossy cascade accents the outlet as it washes over outcrop. Where the trail grows rockier with wet, muddy pockets, evasive paths may disguise the true trail; keep the outlet brook to your right. Soon the trail and brook become more closely paired, and hemlocks wane from the south bank forest.

By 0.9 mile, ascend the ridge to the lake basin, again finding a good earthen path. Arriving at the lake, cross the beaver dam at the outlet, now crowded with silver logs, to reach a shoreline outcrop for an open view spanning the length of this long, deep lake and taking in its shrub banks and enfolding conifer-deciduous rims.

Find a campsite above the outcrop. To round the shore to the main body of the lake requires some determination and bushwhacking through thick spruce and hobblebush.

Regularly stocked with fish, Jockeybush Lake offers anglers a challenge, if not always success. A fishing tube or small raft earns portage, freeing anglers from the shrubby entanglements of shore. Frogs and toads animate shore, while insect hatches lift from the surface. Return as you came.

NIAGARA FRONTIER

At the northwestern extreme of New York State the Niagara Frontier celebrates the migration west and the feat of the Erie Canal. This land block boasts an inspired locale snuggled between Lake Erie to the west and Lake Ontario to the north. The Alleghenies nudge from the south, while the dramatic Finger Lakes Region stretches east. Two famous rivers punctuated by raging falls grace the region, the Niagara and the Genesee.

Visitors to the area find lowland forest, plain, and swamp, with a comfortable rural backdrop beyond the frenzy of Buffalo and Rochester. The deep gouge of the Genesee River Gorge proves an unforgettable exception.

28 ERIE CANAL HERITAGE TRAIL

General description: The retired towpath of the Erie Canal provides a carefree avenue for hiking, cycling, jogging, and exercise walking, while tracing the past.
General location: Between Lockport and Rochester.
Special attractions: Historic canal, museum, lowland forest, rural setting, greenway parks, historic canal communities.
Length: 63 miles one way from Lockport to Rochester. The trail continues east to Pittsford, but Spencerport at 50 miles or Henpeck Park at 55 miles both mark better endings for hikers.
Elevation: The trail is flat, at about 550 feet in elevation.
Difficulty: Easy.
Maps: Recreational Map and Guide to New York State Canals, a New York State Canal Corporation brochure.
Special requirements: None.
Season and hours: Spring through fall, daylight hours.
For Information: New York State Canal Corporation.
Finding the trailhead: Find the western terminus at Locks 34 and 35 in downtown Lockport at the corner of Cottage and Main streets, opposite the Lockport Municipal Building and Visitor Center, where brochures are available. Multiple north-south roadways cross the canal trail providing convenient access or egress from the tour.

The hike: In the nineteenth century, the Erie Canal opened up the remote western hinterlands to settlement and commerce, linking the Hudson River to the Great Lakes. Today, the historic canal serves recreationist, naturalist, and historian, offering a gentle escape from the settled, commercial world it fostered. The towpath variously shows a paved, fine cinder, or gravel surface. Communities that sprung up along the canal continue to offer services and conveniences to canal travelers.

On a west-to-east journey along the northern towpath, descend along locks 34 and 35, where impressive gates of wood and steel close at an angle, sealed by the force of the water. Chambers fill and empty in fifteen minutes time; boats rise to head west, drop to head east. Detour to the Canal Museum to find historic photos, artifacts, and accounts of this great engineering feat.

Where the trail crosses the grate of a thundering spillway, interpretive signs explain the operation and history of the canal. Dubbed the "Long Level," the canal tour from Lockport to Rochester is lock-free. At 0.25 mile the trail passes through tree-shaded Upson Park and travels a bypass route around the New York State Canal Corporation maintenance yard, one of a handful of breaks in the towpath tour.

Ensnared by wild grape and poison ivy, locust, mulberry (recalling an early venture into the silk industry) box elder, tall sumac, willow, cottonwood, walnut, and fruit trees shape an intermittent tree border. Queen Anne's lace, chicory, daisy, black-eyed Susan, mullein, tiger lily, and dozens of other wildflowers shower the trailside with color. As sun often rains on the corridor, carry plenty of drinking water. The canal typically funnels a cool breeze off the Great Lakes.

Erie Canal and bikeway.

ERIE CANAL HERITAGE TRAIL

Orchards, cornfields, and cropland; farmhouses and silos; and historic homes comprise much of the setting. The levee stands high enough above the flat terrain to provide a fine overview. Where marshes claim the levee base, cattails and loosestrife grow. Gulls, kingfishers, swallows, herons, and vultures share the corridor.

At a few of the greenways, picnic tables and chemical toilets serve towpath travelers. A marina and a few primitive boat docks access the 60-foot-wide canal. Muggy summer days find local boys splashing about in the cool, murky green.

As the towpath passes through the small community of Gasport at about 6 miles, it crosses a site to release water. Here, as elsewhere along the tour, the primary community lies south of the canal. Single-lane bridges regularly span the canal and towpath; all date back to the 1910s.

Towns mark off the tour: Middleport (10 miles), Medina (15 miles), Albion (25 miles), Holley (35 miles), Brockport (40 miles), and Spencerport (50 miles). Attractive brick buildings with old-style business fronts add to their charm.

Past Bates Road, the towpath shows a hardpan dirt surface. At about 17 miles it passes over Culvert Road, the only road that travels under the Erie Canal. Noted in Ripley's Believe It or Not, this 1823-built road shows a stone block construction and dripping archway. To appreciate the unusual feature, one must drive Culvert Road.

A few broad waters along the canal route break the trancelike spell of the continuous 60-foot band. Where the towpath approaches Albion (25 miles), ivy climbs an old brick chimney next to a weathered-board outbuilding and tower. Past Albion, the riprap of the canal bank shows a reddish hue, giving the canal a new signature look.

At Fancher Bridge (about midway between Albion and Holley) the towpath surface changes to rock or coarse-grade gravel, making boots the preferred footwear. Here, too, the trail crosses over a watergate to an overflow pond.

A finer gravel surface leads to NY 260. East past Gallop Road Bridge, the towpath halts, putting hikers onto Canal Road for 0.2 mile. The tour then resumes on the northern towpath, where a canal breach feeds a lake on the south shore.

East past Brockport and Adams Basin the tree border fills out, casting shadows over the trail and closing out views, as the landscape makes a transition from rural to rural-suburban. At Canal and Union in Spencerport, travelers may detour to Towpath Park on the south shore, a greenway with tables and benches—a likely stopping point.

Another potential end comes on the east side of the NY 386 bridge at the Town of Greece's Henpeck Park (55 miles). In the 1800s, Henpeck, the port of South Greece, boasted 8-Mile Grocery, a post office, school, apple dryhouse, two doctors, and a community of twenty-five homes. Briefly, here, the towpath is again paved.

To the east, the towpath quickly changes to an urban route with some critical road crossings. At Long Pond Road, cross over the road bridge, following Erie Canal Heritage Trail markers, to resume the eastbound tour along the south shore—now more an urban bike lane.

The route parallels NY 390 and requires a crossing of NY 31 (a feat of patience and good timing). More city road crossings and a railroad overpass advance the tour. At Lock 32 Canal Park (off NY 65), the trail arrives on the north shore, passing through the tree-shaded linear park, bringing home the tour at 63 miles. Painted blue and gold, Lock 32 and gatehouse command the scene; an observation deck overlooks the lock.

29 ALABAMA SWAMPS TRAILS

Overview

Once the site of ancient Lake Tonawanda, the vast marshes north of Alabama represent a critical wildlife habitat and an exciting natural area. Together Iroquois National Wildlife Refuge and the adjoining New York State Wildlife Management Areas open the gate to some 20,000 acres of prime wetland, maintained in a fairly wild and protected state.

General description: Five easy walks scattered through this protected wetland introduce the habitat and its wildlife.
General location: 6 miles south of Medina.
Special attractions: Bird watching; nesting eagles; marshes, wet meadows, and wooded swamps; spring, summer, and fall wildflowers.
Length: Trails range from 0.5 mile to 5 miles in length.
Elevation: The terrain is virtually flat at an elevation of 600 feet.
Difficulty: Easy.
Maps: Iroquois National Wildlife Refuge Trails and Overlooks brochure; Oak Orchard/Tonawanda Wildlife Management Areas brochure.
Special requirements: Onondaga Nature Trail is off-limits to hiking during shotgun deer season, and hikers may want to avoid Feeder Road during its two months of hunting season. Contact the National Wildlife Refuge (NWR) for dates.
Season and hours: Year-round, dawn to dusk. NWR Headquarters: 8 a.m. to 4 p.m. weekdays; also open weekends during the spring migration.
For information: For Kanyoo, Feeder Road, Onondaga, and Swallow Hollow trails, contact Iroquois National Wildlife Refuge; for the Oak Orchard Environmental Education Center trails contact the New York State Department of Environmental Conservation, Region 8.

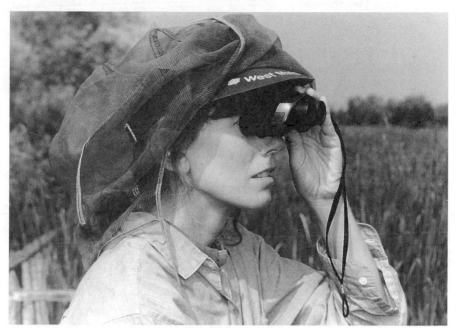
Birdwatching, Oak Orchard Wildlife Management Area.

Finding the trailhead: From the junction of New York 63 and New York 77 in Alabama, go north on NY 63 for 0.8 mile and turn left (wcst) on Casey Road to reach the refuge headquarters in 0.6 mile. Continue west on Casey Road another 0.8 mile and turn north on NY 77 (Lewiston Road) to reach the marked trailhead for Kanyoo Trail on the right in 0.9 mile. Gated Feeder Road lies east off NY 77, 300 feet farther north.

For the other three trailheads, from the junction of Casey Road and NY 63 (east of the headquarters), go north on NY 63 for 0.1 mile and turn right (east) on Roberts Road. In 1.1 miles, turn north on dirt Sour Springs Road to reach Onondaga Nature Trail on the right in 0.8 mile. For Swallow Hollow Trail and the Oak Orchard nature trails stay east on Roberts Road, go 1.5 miles past the intersection with Sour Springs Road, and turn north on Knowlesville Road. Find Swallow Hollow Trail on the left in 1.8 miles; Oak Orchard on the right 0.1 mile farther north.

The hikes: The **Kanyoo Trail** doubles as a winter ski trail and has two interlocking, color-coded loops: blue and yellow. An external-loop tour travels 1.2 miles and includes the boardwalk section of the blue trail overlooking Mohawk Pool.

Begin to the right of the kiosk, passing through a meadow of black-eyed Susan, chicory, and milkweed. Cross over the wide swath of a ski trail, entering the woods of aspen, cherry, and silver and red maple. Go right on the blue trail for a counterclockwise tour. The trail bypasses ski

ALABAMA SWAMPS TRAILS

trails and benches, coming to the boardwalk at 0.5 mile. Shaggy-headed cattails, vegetated waters, snags, and bird boxes comprise the view.

From the boardwalk the trail returns to a moist woodland. At 0.75 mile, go right on the yellow trail to close the loop. An observation deck set back in the woods holds a tree-funneled look at Mohawk Pool. A few tulip trees join the mix as the tour draws to a close; stay right at the junctions.

At 2.5 miles long, gravel **Feeder Road** cuts south to north through a four-leaf clover of marsh pools, offering peripheral looks at the wetlands. To travel closer to the individual pools, hike along the dividing dikes, but remember these side "trails" are closed during nesting season, March 1 to July 15; heed all posted notices.

The sun-exposed road tour passes between fields and a wetland mosaic of open water, cattail marsh, snags, and bulrushes. The far edge of the pools shows a broken tree line, but trees rarely grace the southern extent of the roadway. Where they do occur, cottonwood, sumac, maple, and elm comprise the mix, with wild grape, honeysuckle, and brambles weaving a dense thicket. At times, insects chew the leaves beyond recognition.

The road hugs the feeder canal save where the two bow apart at Sutton's Marsh. A cacophony fills the air. Heron, kingfisher, red-winged blackbird, geese, killdeer, and hawk suggest the raising of binoculars. Wildflowers spangle the roadside; black-eyed Susan and milkweed claim the field.

About midway lies a house and gate. At the fork at 1.85 miles follow the unkempt two-track straight ahead for Feeder Road. The now wooded corridor continues north to Dunlop Road in West Shelby. While the possibility for spying different birds exists, most hikers turn around at the fork. Be especially alert along this far end of the tour during hunting season.

At a separate location, **Onondaga Nature Trail** (3 miles round trip) visits Onondaga Marsh and the woodland to its east.

A gravel dike enters the refuge, dividing shallow Onondaga Marsh with its snags, cattail islands and mazes, aquatic mammal trails, herons, ducks, geese, and muskrats. Vultures roost atop the snags. Milkweed, thistle, mullein, daisy, and other wildflowers color the tour. In the more extensive marsh, red maples win a foothold.

From the end of the marsh (0.3 mile), the trail passes from a fern meadow to a scenic woods of maple, ash, planted pine, aspen, and black cherry; midway, the woods transition to hemlock, birch, and beech. The trail halts at a bench past a huge American beech. Dogwoods and tulip trees sprinkle springtime through the canopy. Return as you came.

To the east, 2-mile **Swallow Hollow Trail** lassos Swallow Hollow Marsh, traveling foot trail, boardwalk, and dike.

Begin at the south corner of the parking area for a clockwise tour; the trail returns at the middle of the lot. Initially, cottonwood, maple, ash, and hornbeam enclose the raised boardwalk, but before long, hikers find the first marsh overlook. Cattail, willow, buttonbush, and nightshade frame and sometimes intrude on the scenic walkway as it alternates between cotton-wood-maple woodland and willow-buttonbush habitat.

At 0.4 mile the boardwalk ends after crossing a duckweed-painted side water. At the T-junction with a gravel dike, go right, traveling between the creek channel and marsh woodland. Willow-buttonbush islands and bulrush bars add interest to the marshy terrain, while turtles sun on the logs. The trail concludes touring hardwood forest, spruce plantation, and boardwalk.

Across the way, at the Oak Orchard Wildlife Management Area Environmental Education Center, six unmarked interlocking trails radiate from the picnic pavilion, to explore North Marsh. Mowed track, foot trail, and boardwalk explore the site's wetland, ponds, fields, and woods.

The mowed path beneath the power pole to the north accesses the Orchard Trail, North Trail, and Old Field Trail, ending at Podunk Road. The three paths entering the woods at the southeast corner of the picnic area access the Shoreline and Catwalk trails and eventually the link to Swallow Hollow.

For the best tour, duck into the woods on the leftmost trail at the southeast corner of the picnic area for the 0.5-mile **Shoreline/Catwalk Tour**. The path passes through dense 10-foot-high shrubs, with aspen, honeysuckle, and herbaceous plants. Keep left to reach the rustic board-walk of weathered wood overlooking the cattail marsh. Willow, maple, wild grape, and a bit of buttonbush frame the tour. Tall cattails seal out the view from the bench at 0.3 mile, but the platform ahead applauds the vast open pond and textured mosaic of North Marsh. At 0.4 mile turn right to close the loop, coming out amid the trees below the pavilion; the path straight ahead leads to Swallow Hollow located across the road.

30   *PEANUT LINE TRAIL*

General description: A part of the Conservation Trail (CT) linking Buffalo to the Finger Lakes Trail, this former rail corridor travels city, suburban, and rural countryside.

General location: Between Tonawanda and Akron.

Special attractions: Portions of paved bicycle/pedestrian way; wildflowers and wildlife sightings.

Length: 17 miles one way.

Elevation: The trail is virtually flat.

Difficulty: Easy, save for overgrown segments.

Maps: Finger Lakes Trail Conference, the Conservation Trail maps (sheets CT 9, CT 10, and CT 11).

Special requirements: None.

Black-eyed Susans.

Season and hours: Spring through fall, 6 a.m. to 10 p.m.

For information: Finger Lakes Trail Conference.

Finding the trailhead: From Interstate 290 in greater Buffalo, take exit 3 for U.S. Highway 62/Niagara Falls Boulevard and go north on U.S. 62. Within a couple of miles, cross the Ellicott Creek bridge and turn left, entering the northern portion of Ellicott Creek Park. Find the first orange blaze on a tree near the mapboard at the entry parking area.

The hike: From Ellicott Creek Park (a developed Erie County park), follow the minimally blazed route east; orange blazes mark changes of direction and intersection crossings only.

From the crosswalk at Niagara Falls Boulevard, a paved bike trail continues the tour, briefly following an exposed utility corridor to parallel above the Ellicott Creek canal. A high shrub border entwined with wild grape abuts the popular hiking, cycling, and jogging route. As the trail nears the Sweet Home Road underpass, it traverses a greenway with picnic tables.

Cardinals, rabbits, mother ducks with their ducklings, carp, and field mice enliven the tour. Where the trail emerges from the I-290 underpass at a pedestrian bridge crossing the canal, depart the bikeway (do not cross the bridge), follow the CT to North Forest Road (2 miles), and turn left. Areas of phragmites and purple loosestrife crowd the roadside marshes. Look for blazes on the street and utility poles. At the intersection with Dodge Road take the mowed greenway east passing between Dodge Road and the utility line.

At 2.3 miles the route crosses a four-lane divided road, John James Audubon Parkway, to follow the raised two-track of the former railroad grade. The tour character changes from commercial to residential, with more trees and shrubs filling out border of the 50- to 100-foot-wide corridor. Cottonwoods, maple, sumac, and planted trees edge the route. More road crossings follow.

East of New York 270, the Peanut Line parallels a thin drainage congested with willow, loosestrife, cattail, and teasel. Gradually the corridor grows more isolated from its surroundings, but the grasses of the rail bed remain trimmed to ankle height. Newer residential developments again open the corridor. At 4.5 miles the grade edges the playing fields of Williamsville North High and Casey Middle schools.

A quarter mile east of Paradise Road (6.2 miles), croaking frogs betray a pond hidden beyond the leafy border. Beware poison ivy beyond the mowed track. Overgrown pockets lead to and from Got Creek bridge, and some remnant ties mark the route. As the trail arrives at Transit Road/NY 78 (6.9 miles), it skirts a lumber yard where a former rail spur leads into the building.

Crossing Transit Road may require patience; beyond lies a rich green aisle. Where the Peanut Line/CT passes through the town of Clarence, "no trespassing" notices mark intersections. According to the Town of Clarence Highway Department, these notices apply only to forms of non-pedestrian

PEANUT LINE TRAIL

travel; hikers are free to pass. At Shimerville Road the route changes to single-lane gravel.

From Goodrich Road (9.9 miles), the rail trail passes through the Clarence Highway Department parking lot and along a power line. The vegetation grows unruly for a spell as the trail changes from suburban to rural. Later a 5-foot-wide earthen lane opens up. In the morning and evening hours, the trail grows more animated with flight, song, and browsing creatures. Cultivated and open fields contribute to the view.

At 10.4 miles, Herr Road marks a more troubling overgrown stretch with brushing, overhanging vegetation; keep a third eye out for poison ivy. Despite periodic clearings, this middle stretch welcomes only determined hikers.

Pushing out of the tangle at Utley Road, find a nice tiger lily patch and a genuine "no trespassing" sign. Detour right on Utley Road, turning left on Clarence Center Road for 0.4 mile. Meadowlark, yellow warbler, wood-chuck, and garter snake, along with a reprieve from bushwhacking, make the road passage bearable. Resume the trail on the right at the end of a guard rail, crossing a duckboard plank through cattails.

The trail becomes passable but far removed from a Sunday stroll. At 15.3 miles the Peanut Line meets a second rail line; follow it left and again bear left in 0.5 mile, touring a tree-buffered coarse-gravel route better suited for boots. Butterfly-weed, chicory, black-eyed Susan, Queen Anne's lace, and the red floral spears of the sumac adorn the route. At Clarence Center Road, a paved bicycle path continues the tour.

Where the bike path emerges at Jackson Street, the CT turns right on Jackson, crosses Buell Street, and continues east on Brooklyn Street to Akron Falls Park (17 miles). For an alternative end, follow the bike trail less than a mile to its end at Cedar Street/NY 93 near Eckerson Avenue in Akron.

31 *TIFFT NATURE PRESERVE*

Overview

Near the Lake Erie shore, this 264-acre urban sanctuary marks a success story in land reclamation. Its low grassland hills (formerly a small landfill), wetland woods, thickets, ponds, and marsh support a thriving bird population, while offering a peaceful retreat from Buffalo's city pace. Five miles of trail and three boardwalks tour the preserve.

General description: Four easy nature walks examine most of the preserve's trails, ponds, and habitats.
General location: In south Buffalo, 3 miles from downtown.
Special attractions: 75-acre freshwater cattail marsh; bird and wildlife watching; flowering annuals, shrubs, and aquatic plants; viewing blinds; visitor center; Sunday guided walks.
Length: Hikes range from a fraction of a mile to 1.3 miles.
Elevation: The preserve lies at an elevation of 600 feet. The Mounds Trail shows a modest elevation change.
Difficulty: Easy.
Maps: Preserve brochure.
Special requirements: Entrance fee.
Season and hours: Year-round, except holidays. Trails: dawn to dusk; center: 9 a.m. to 4 p.m., Tuesday through Sunday.
For information: Tifft Nature Preserve.
Finding the trailhead: From New York 5 in south Buffalo, take the Tifft Street/Fuhrmann Boulevard exit. Westbound traffic, go 0.5 mile south from the exit, turn left under the freeway, and again turn left on a one-way road, merging with traffic exiting from NY 5 East. Go 0.5 mile north on the one-way road to reach the preserve parking lot on the right (east). Locate the trailheads near the visitor center cabin or 0.1 east of the cabin, where the service road crosses a bridge over the southeast arm of Lake Kirsty.

The hikes: The following four tours represent a few logical trail combinations for taking in the preserve highlights.

Find the **Mounds Trail**, a 0.6-mile loop, on the opposite side of the road from the visitor center; three mowed tracks greet hikers. Take the left prong for a rolling clockwise tour of the four grassland mounds. Grasses, bird's-foot trefoil, teasel, dandelion, buttercup, vetch, chicory, and black-eyed Susan weave a wind-bowed carpet, while a few planted pines, fruit trees, and shrubs dot the slope.

Stay right to top each of the four mounds, gathering overviews of the preserve and the Lake Erie setting. Views take in the close-by fields, lakes, ponds, and marshes, the Buffalo city skyline, Lake Erie, and abandoned industrial buildings and grain elevators. Atop the fourth mound, find two mowed tracks; both return to the visitor center.

The 1.3-mile **Mounds Bypass-Snakeroot Loop** rounds the southeast arm of Lake Kirsty, with a Warbler Walk detour.

Begin a counterclockwise tour near a pair of benches on the right, prior to the service road bridge. Bear left on the mowed track, passing below the mounds, skirting the lake rim of cottonwoods and shrubs. Blue and yellow wildflowers speckle the grassland, while dogwood, aspen, sumac, willow, mugwort, and viburnum fill out the lake buffer, screening out views. Songbirds enliven the area, and weathered beaver-cuttings spot the shore.

Stay left crossing the causeway; silvered snags rise up to the right. Just ahead, go left on the wood-chip path of the Snakeroot Trail to continue the loop. Eight to ten-foot high shrubs enclose the trail.

Heritage Boardwalk, Tifft Nature Center.

TIFFT NATURE PRESERVE

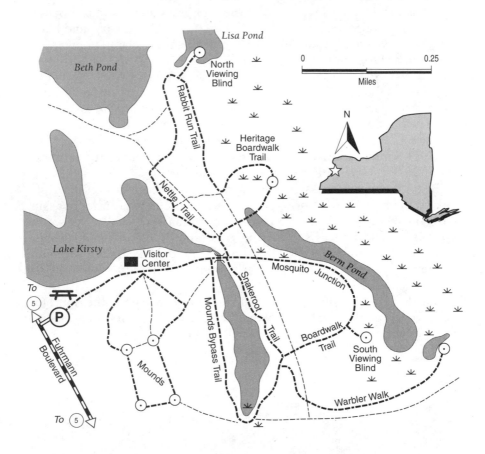

At 0.4 mile, detour right on the wide unmarked Warbler Walk and stay on it, bypassing a bench and crossing over a service road, before coming out at an open marsh view. Snags claim this end of the marsh, dense cattails the far end. Tree swallows roost in the small snags; often a night heron hunches near shore.

As the Warbler Walk continues, looks grow restricted until the trail ends atop a 10-foot-high mound (0.75 mile). From here, enjoy a grand look at the cattail sea, with South Viewing Blind across the way. Highway noise, shipping traffic on Lake Erie, and a silent industrial plant confirm that this is indeed an urban wild.

Return to the Snakeroot Trail and resume the loop, bypassing the Boardwalk Trail to South Viewing Blind. A spur to the left offers an open lake vista, where on our visit a painted turtle had chosen to lay her eggs;

yield the right-of-way to nature. At a second spur to shore, a beaver-fallen cottonwood offers seating. Close the loop at the bridge.

Start the **Berm Pond Hike**, a 0.7-mile loop, by crossing the bridge and going right where the service road forks. At the three-way junction in 0.1 mile, go straight, traveling the elevated boardwalk of Mosquito Junction, skirting Berm Pond.

At some 5 to 6 feet off the ground, the walk parts a dense stand of tall feathery-headed phragmites; midwalk lies an observation deck. Aquatic plants coat the pond's surface, as does a dandruff of cottonwood seeds. Cattail, loosestrife, and bulrush contribute to the marsh tapestry. A foot trail continues the tour, passing amid a scenic cottonwood wetland.

At 0.3 mile find a second boardwalk curving left to South Viewing Blind; the earthen trail ahead holds the loop's return. South Viewing Blind consists of a broad open-air deck masked by a 7-foot wall, overlooking the marsh and Berm Pond. Circular and oval cutouts allow visitors to manipulate their cameras, binoculars, and scopes for ideal viewing.

Return to the junction at 0.3 mile and follow the earthen trail left. Turn right on either the service road or Snakeroot Trail to end the loop at the bridge.

Start the **Heritage Boardwalk-North Viewing Blind Hike**, a 1.2-mile loop, by crossing the bridge and going left at the service road fork. In 250 feet turn right, following a wood-shavings path amid cottonwoods, shrubs, nettles, and mugwort, to Heritage Boardwalk.

The scenic walkway overlooking the aquatic vegetation cuts the end of Berm Pond. Cattail and phragmites shape a wetland border and form island clusters. Red-winged blackbirds, tree swallows, and frogs animate the scene. Benches invite study.

The boardwalk ends amid a sea of cattails, replaced by an earthen trail passing through a willow habitat. At 0.4 mile, meet Rabbit Run, a former railroad bed now favored by eastern cottontails, and turn right on the grassy lane.

Cottonwood, aspen, sumac, and white-berried shrubs frame the route. At the next junction, go right for North Viewing Blind; straight holds the return. Trail and boardwalk reach the blind in 0.1 mile. Here a similar 7-foot wall with viewing cutouts overlooks Lisa Pond, where duckweed, duck potato, and arrow arum coat and claim the shallows, and snags and nesting boxes pierce the pond. A former grain elevator on the Buffalo River looms over the north end of the marsh.

Resume the counterclockwise tour on Rabbit Run, touring an open corridor of cottonwoods and shrubs. Bypass the right turn to Beth Pond and continue straight ahead. Where the trail crosses over a service road at 1 mile, follow the Nettle Trail along the thick shrub border of Lake Kirsty, but beware of the signature nettle. Where the Nettle Trail again meets the service road, turn right to close the loop in a few strides.

Overview

At this 3,100-acre county forest, hikers travel former farmland that was abandoned at the turn of the century and reforested beginning in 1928. Today, the tall plantation pine and spruce along with the native hardwoods provide a shady retreat for tranquil strolling and nature study.

General description: Three easy trails tour the planted and natural wood stands along the Dresser Creek drainage.
General location: 10 miles northeast of Springville.
Special attractions: Plantation pine and spruce, mixed hardwoods, maple sugaring operation.
Length: Old Scarbuck-Extension Trail, 3.7 miles round trip; Silent Woods Trail, 1.5-mile loop, with option of Conservation Trail extension; Sugarbush Trail, 1.6-mile loop.
Elevation: Elevation changes range between 150 and 300 feet.
Difficulty: Easy.
Maps: Sardinia 7.5-minute USGS quad. Erie County Forest trail maps posted at Old Scarbuck gatehouse and snowmobile warming hut.
Special requirements: Bring water; water at site nonpotable.

Dresser Creek hiker bridge, Erie County Forest.

ERIE COUNTY FOREST

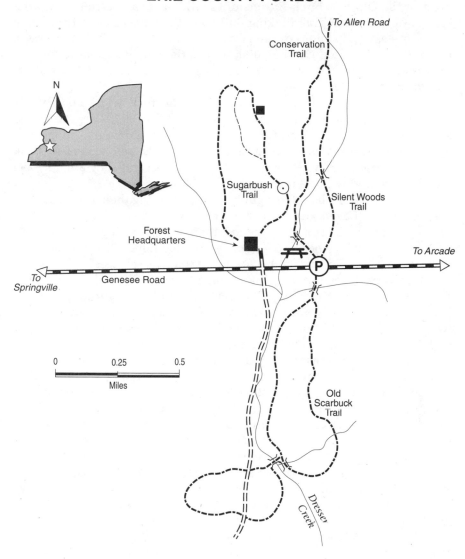

Season and hours: Spring through fall, daylight hours.
For information: Erie County Parks, Recreation and Forestry Department.
Finding the trailhead: From the intersection of Buffalo and Main streets in Springville, go east on Main Street/New York 39 for 1.3 miles and turn north on NY 240. Go 2.9 miles and turn right on Genesee Road in East Concord. The Department of Forestry entrance lies on the left in 3.4 miles. Start Sugarbush Trail west of the buildings; find Old Scarbuck and Silent Woods trails 0.1 mile farther east on Genesee Road.

The hikes: Head south from the gatehouse, for the yellow-blazed figure-eight of the **Old Scarbuck-Extension Trail**. On a shared route with the orange Conservation Trail (linking Buffalo to the Finger Lakes Trail), pass through a spruce plantation interwoven by maple and pine, crossing a footbridge in 250 feet. On the far shore lies the loop junction; follow the yellow and orange blazes straight ahead for a clockwise tour; the yellow-blazed return lies to the right.

Dogwood, fern, and wild raspberry add to the tour, while a boardwalk eases passage through a damp meadow opening. By 0.5 mile spruce alone claim the way; low barren branches give the plantation an out-of-focus appearance. At the woods road turn right; a blue ski trail heads left. Look for the foot trail to resume on the left at 0.75 mile, traveling a maple-ash woods with muddy pockets even in drought years.

As the trail descends into a gully, hemlocks bring their rich signature shade. Stay on the marked route, heading right for a stone-stepping crossing of a small creek. The trail ascends, then levels, touring mixed woods. At 1.2 miles a rickety bench overlooks a wooded slope. Descend and bear right, crossing a tributary footbridge above the Dresser Creek confluence.

Stay with the familiar yellow-orange blazes, continuing left to the Dresser Creek footbridge. For Old Scarbuck Trail alone turn right at this bridge, following the yellow blazes back to the start. For the figure-eight tour, cross the bridge, finding the extension loop. Bear left for a clockwise tour, ascending and paralleling Dresser Creek downstream.

At 2 miles the Conservation Trail and extension loop part company. Follow the yellow blazes across a dirt road and into the woods. Despite a steep downhill slope to Hyler Creek drainage, the trail affords no views. Round away from Hyler drainage through a berry patch and along a hemlock-deciduous flat, crossing a snowmobile route at 2.5 miles. The trail then descends, closing the extension loop at Dresser Creek bridge.

Follow the yellow trail left to close the original loop, traveling along and above Dresser Creek. From a hemlock-shaded woods road, the trail turns right angling up a spruce-clad slope. At 3.4 miles the trail levels, crossing wet areas to close the loop at the initial bridge. Return to the trailhead.

The **Silent Woods Trail** heads north off Genesee Road, reaching the loop junction in a matter of feet. Go straight for a rolling, clockwise tour; to the right lies the return. Amid planted pine, maple, and black cherry, follow shallow Dresser Creek upstream, cross its bridge, and enter a grassy field. Continue north along the wooded border, re-entering the woods on the right at 0.2 mile.

On breezy days the treetops groan and sway. A chest-high tubing, part of the foresters's maple sugar operation, may web the woods. A small boardwalk crosses a moist bottom thick with nettles and fern; the green strikes a bold contrast to the dry needle mat elsewhere. At 0.6 mile, the Conservation Trail heads north (left).

For the Silent Woods loop alone, go right slowly descending to a T-junction with a snowmobile trail (0.9 mile). Turn left finding a steeper descent to the Dresser Creek crossing. Soon the trail turns right off the snowmobile route, ascending through spruce. Cross the snowmobile path once more before descending to close the loop at 1.5 miles.

To lengthen the tour, the **Conservation Trail** heads north at 0.6 mile for 1.5 miles, reaching Allen Road. It tours maple woodlot, mixed forest, gully, and field, following lightly trafficked foot trail and eroded woods roads. Along Dresser Creek drainage the trail traverses private land and bypasses a small cabin; keep to the trail. When ready, return as you came to Silent Woods Trail.

The **Sugarbush Trail** heads north along the west edge of the Forestry Department lawn; follow the blue arrows and diamonds of this dual-purpose cross-country ski/foot trail. Young pine plantation and a maple-black cherry forest next claim the 3-foot-wide trail. Some fern, club moss, beech, and a spotty presence of hemlock add to the tour.

At 0.75 mile the trail tops out and comes to a junction. To the right lies the Sugar Trail; continue straight for the Sugarbush Trail, touring mature maple forest. Where the trail appears to turn left at 1 mile, continue straight ahead, following the markers for a steady downhill, bypassing a rustic cabin and entering a younger forest.

At 1.3 miles a trail arrives on the left. Again plastic tubing from the sugaring operation may overlace the trail. As the trail enters a field, look for turkey and ruffed grouse. Past a bench seat with a southwest view, the forestry buildings come into sight. Continue between field and forest and across the lawn to close the loop back at the buildings.

33 *LETCHWORTH STATE PARK*

Overview

Letchworth State Park encompasses the 17-mile-long Genesee River Gorge, featuring three major waterfalls and some elegant side-creek falls, 400- to 600-foot sheer sandstone-shale cliffs, points of historical note, and second-growth forest. Numbered trails explore the developed park of the west rim; four of these provide a survey of the area.

General description: The four walks of varying length hug the rim and overlook the falls on the Genesee River, tag the river shore, travel a spine between the river and Silver Lake Outlet, and visit an historic grave.

General location: 35 miles south Rochester.

Special attractions: Genesee River Gorge, falls, cliffs, vistas, museum, memorials, historic Glen Iris Inn.

Length: Gorge Trail, 7.75 miles one way; Saint Helena Trail, 1.5 miles round trip; Kisil Point Trail, 2.8 miles round trip; Mary Jemison Trail, 2.5-mile loop.

Elevation: Elevation changes range between 100 and 300 feet.

Difficulty: Easy.

Maps: State park map.

Special requirements: Entrance fee.

Season and hours: Spring through fall, 6 a.m. to dusk.

For information: New York State Parks, Genesee Region.

Finding the trailhead: From the New York 36/New York 408 junction in the village of Mount Morris, go north on NY 36 for 1.1 miles and turn left, reaching the Mount Morris entrance to the state park in 0.4 mile. From Mount Morris entrance, find the trailheads off the main park road. Locate Kisil Point Trail 4 miles south, Saint Helena Trail 10.8 miles south, Mary Jemison Trail/Council Grounds 14.9 miles south, and the Gorge Trail (upper trailhead) 15.8 miles south (0.4 mile north of the southern entrance).

The hikes: The popular **Gorge Trail** (Trail 1) represents the premier hiking tour within the developed park. For a downstream tour, cross the park road

Genesee River Gorge, Letchworth State Park.

from the upper trailhead parking lot, pass under the railroad bridge, and follow the rockwork steps that switchback downhill to the gorge rim.

The first rim vista (0.25 mile) overlooks the 70-foot horseshoe drop of Upper Falls. A plume of mist shoots up and out from the white rushing fury, nurturing the green cloak of the east wall. Only the heavy railroad footings from High Bridge steal from the natural wonder and photographer's image.

As the well-groomed trail continues, it presents new perspectives. Basswood, maple, oak, and spruce overhang the route; poison ivy drapes the edging stone wall and abrupt slope to the river. As the trail skirts a landscaped day-use area, it offers downstream looks at the delicate streamers of side-creek falls and the bulging west cliff.

Next find a side perspective of a waterfall of Niagara proportion— Middle Falls. A viewing deck below Glen Iris Inn (0.75 mile) serves up a grand look at this 107-foot-high, 285- foot-wide waterfall, thundering over an abrupt river ledge. Follow the yellow blazes up and away from the inn.

From this point on, the trail frequently travels the thin woods-and-grass buffer between the rim and the park road. After passing through a mixed evergreen stand planted in 1917, on a roadway island green find an obelisk dedicated to New York's First Dragoons of the Civil War. Reach Inspiration Point (1.4 miles), a roadside vista with an upstream view of Middle and Upper Falls and High Bridge. Interpretive signs now mark the tour; views come piecemeal.

Travel the rim, descending its tiers, coming to the side trail with 127 steps descending to Lower Falls. A broad vista deck, a river bridge, and a 0.1-mile upstream spur present this 50- to 60-foot waterfall, showing a slight crescent and an entourage of lower cascades. From the bridge, take a closer look at the platy shale and sandstone seams of the cliff.

Retrace your steps and resume the downstream hike at 3.25 miles, skirting below Lower Falls day-use. Hemlock and beech offer a rich shade. At the junction at 3.5 miles bear right, bypassing a restaurant, to again travel near the park road. At 4.25 and 4.75 miles, hikers again share roadside vistas with motorists, now overlooking Big Bend. Copper-gilded vultures soar on the thermals, catching the sun on their ebony wings.

At 5.65 miles, tag Great Bend Viewing Area to overlook the dizzying 550-foot cliffs, the scoured bowl curvature, and muddy green Genesee River. Afterward, descend fairly steeply, crossing a footbridge over a charming side water. Still the trail flipflops from rim to road. At 6.6 miles the Gorge Trail explores the beauty at Wolf Creek, with views of the eroded and fluted river cliffs, the broad Genesee River, and twisting Wolf Creek Falls within its own narrow canyon.

Now skirt the picnic areas of Wolf Creek, Tea Table, and Saint Helena, with their rustic stone and slab tables. The Gorge Trail ends at the lower Saint Helena Picnic Area, where it meets the Saint Helena Trail, Trail 13.

The **Saint Helena Trail** serves hiker, angler, and kayaker; it contours downhill through an open canopied forest, reaching a three-way junction

LETCHWORTH STATE PARK

at 0.1 mile. Follow Trail 13 straight ahead or take the two-track to the right to reach the river bar. Depending on river flow, a divided bar may greet hikers and require some wading to reach the main river channel. The trail affords a grand interior perspective on the gorge but a limited river acquaintance. Cottonwood, wild grape, grasses, and willow vegetate the bar. Return as you came.

Kisil Point Trail (Trail 18) offers a look at the Genesee River farther downstream and may be accessed from Highbanks Campground (near Loop 100) or a roadside trailhead. Both trails unite just beyond the campground trailhead, traveling the piney outskirts of camp, bypassing an old picnic shelter, coming to a loop junction at 0.4 mile.

The right fork travels the Genesee River side of Kisil Point Ridge; the left fork overlooks Silver Lake Outlet. Go right for a counterclockwise tour. Pine plantation and a mixed deciduous woods cloak the thin, sharp ridge.

At 0.9 mile, the spurs of the loop reunite; continue forward to the end of the ridge and Kisil Point (1.4 miles). The view encompasses the tinsel stream of Silver Lake Outlet, flowing amid a thick swath of green, and the Genesee River Canyon with its steep gray cliffs, eroded silt skirts, and broad floodplain. Return to the junction at 0.9 mile and complete the loop, coming out at the picnic shelter in 2.5 miles. Retrace the initial 0.3 mile.

The **Mary Jemison Trail** (Trail 2) honors a white-woman captive who came to revere the Seneca Indians with whom she lived. The trail begins at the Council Grounds where a statue of Mary Jemison, an 1800s pioneer cabin, and a tribal Council House pre-dating the American Revolution suggest a detour.

The trail itself heads west and negotiates a series of confusing junctions; follow number 2. The trail tours mixed woods of beech, maple, birch, and basswood, hemlock stands, and pine plantation to visit a couple of linear reservoirs. Evidence of beaver activity surrounds the ponds; amid the woods deer commonly cross paths with hikers. Woods road and foot trail comprise this rolling tour.

34 LETCHWORTH TRAIL

General description: This linear foot trail along the eastern rim of the Genesee River Gorge travels mixed woods and snares occasional river overlooks and grand waterfall views.
General location: Letchworth State Park, 35 miles south of Rochester.
Special attractions: Genesee River Gorge with its three major waterfalls and plummeting sandstone-shale cliffs, seasonal cascades and falls, historic canal and rail corridor, wildlife sightings, lush forest, colorful fall foliage.
Length: 26.5 miles one way, including vista side spurs.
Elevation: The trail travels between 800 and 1,200 feet in elevation, with the rim high point found above the falls.
Difficulty: Moderate.
Maps: Letchworth State Park map; Finger Lakes Trail Conference maps, The Letchworth Trail L1 and L2.
Special requirements: None.
Season and hours: Spring through fall, 6 a.m. to dusk.
For information: New York State Parks, Genesee Region.
Finding the trailhead: For the northern trailhead, from the New York 36/New York 408 junction in Mount Morris, go south on NY 408 (Chapel Street) toward Nunda. In 1.8 miles, turn right for Mount Morris Dam. In another 1.7 miles, turn left to reach the dam-overlook, parking area, and

Middle Falls, Letchworth State Park.

trailhead 0.1 mile ahead. Find the southern terminus in Portageville at the northeast corner of the NY 436 bridge, with off-road parking for a handful of vehicles.

The hike: A north-to-south tour between Mount Morris Dam and Portageville travels the undeveloped eastern rim of the Genesee River Gorge, rolling through mixed forest, pine plantation, and meadow scrub. Ravines punctuate the tour, prescribing the line of travel. While few in number, the river vistas are prized, especially along the trail's south end, where rim overlooks applaud two of the three river falls. Solitude abounds, and wildlife sightings vary, with turkey, raccoon, fox, grouse, deer, beaver, frog, and skunk.

Part of the greater Finger Lakes Trail (FLT), the Letchworth Trail is well-marked with yellow paint blazes, FLT markers, and trail registers. The white spurs to the left lead to access points off River Road and opportunities to shorten the tour. The spurs to the right lead to river overlooks. Numbers indicate the Letchworth State Park trails.

Take a moment to enjoy an overlook of the dam before hiking the FLT south (upstream) from the end of the parking lot. Vultures often roost atop the dam; cliffs and the broad green floodplain contribute to the view. The flat trail passes through a corridor of oak, aspen, maple, pine, and hickory, staying mostly within 10 feet of the rim's edge.

LETCHWORTH TRAIL

At 0.6 mile cross the groomed lawn of a picnic and overlook site maintained by Mount Morris Dam. The view brings together the peninsular ridge of Hogback, a pinched river bend, the developed west rim of Letchworth State Park, and the rural countryside beyond. Gravel and a boardwalk ease wet-area travel. Poison ivy, Virginia creeper, waterleaf, witch-hazel, birch, and basswood fill out the sides of the corridor.

Find the first of the ravines at 1.6 miles; many more follow. The trail becomes more rolling as it travels the rim plateau distanced from the edge. Seasonally, the ravines carry water and show small cascades; a few ravines show the remains of old structures.

At 3.1 miles a 50-foot side trail leads to an open vista atop a loose mud-shale slope; stay well back of the dangerous eroding point. Fog sometimes claims the canyon, masking and unmasking the cliff's ragged spires, ribs, and points. A half mile ahead the bending river canyon again draws hikers aside. Where the trail edges a couple of fields with brushing shrubs, be careful of the old fences with their trailing wire.

At 4.6 miles the FLT bears right as a side trail heads left to the road; a pine stand next claims the way. Where the trail crosses the width of a power-line corridor, an 0.8-mile round-trip detour west along the corridor finds a river view.

On the southbound tour large oaks contrast the tall thin trees comprising much of the mixed forest. Where the FLT meets the northern segment of Trail 16 (a mowed track at 7.5 miles), continue south passing through a tight moist corridor of mixed woods and shrubs to cross a second mowed track of Trail 16. Crows put on a noisy filibuster. Stay the yellow trail, next entering a plantation of spiny-armed pines.

To the right at 9.6 miles, white blazes mark a vista detour to Fiddler's Elbow Viewpoint. Travel a deciduous flat and low ridge to the open vista. Hemlock and beech claim the ridge as it overlooks the gorge. Resume the tour south at 10.4 miles. Orange and red mushrooms and yellow fungi pepper the tour. The understory varies from the barren pine plantations to a crush of flora in the moist woods.

Where the trail exits from a deep, steep-forked ravine at 12.1 miles, look for another white-disc trail heading toward the river for a scenic view. It travels the spine of a thin wooded ridge between the forked ravine to the right and a bowled ravine to the left. At the tip, Old Forks Ravine View offers a fine canyon overlook. The river far below shows a split flow; cottonwood, willow, aspen, and meadow shrubs and flora weave a textured river tapestry.

Resume south on the FLT at 13 miles. Some stately trees mark the tour, including a gnarly old oak with eighteen major arm branchings (16.6 miles). At 17.2 miles a small log shelter rests to the right of the trail. Another road access follows, while the ravines ahead shape steeper climbs and descents. At 18.4 miles cross the overgrown road to the abandoned hamlet of Saint Helena.

Follow the woods road of Trail 9 to the left at 19.6 miles. Shortly, the FLT splits away left, only to cross Trail 9 and tour a dark hemlock stand. Where the FLT crosses Trail 9 one last time, ascend the rim of Dishmill Creek, overlooking the creek's many beaver enhancements. As the trail descends, cross a side drainage and bypass a big oak and big shag-bark hickory.

At 21.3 miles the FLT comes out on a closed section of River Road (Trail 8) and follows it to the right, crossing the culvert of Dishmill Creek. Leave the road at 22.5 miles and round the gate to the right, as the Genesee Valley Greenway Trail (Trail 7) continues the tour.

A tracked earthen path paints a black stripe down the grassy lane of what once was the Pennsylvania Railroad; alongside find the ditch of the 1862-1878 Genesee Valley Canal. Discarded rail ties hint at the past. Birch, basswood, beech, maple, and tulip trees overlace the route, weaving a scenic green tunnel, but ravenous mosquitos speed steps.

A beaver pond and lodge mark the old canal, as do reeds, ferns, young woods, and the occasional cattail patch. At 24.4 miles, exit onto and cross the park road below Parade Grounds Picnic Area and follow the greenway to the river's rim.

At 24.6 miles flat rocks along the rim's edge serve up a spectacular look at the 400-foot cliffs both upstream and directly across the river. Deep in the canyon, the broad Genesee River flows over outcrop. To the right at 25 miles a look across the canyon finds the 200-foot waterfall on Deh-Ga- Ya-Soh Creek. Nearby, a short side trail leads to a view of the 107-foot Middle and 70-foot Upper falls, with a look at High Bridge (a railroad bridge) spanning the canyon.

As the trail rolls through an old landslide area, find views of the upper right side of Middle Falls. Next, descend through a more recent, although stabilized, slide disturbance.

At 25.8 miles a short side trail leads to an imposing look at Upper Falls, the best to be had from either shore. The powerful, surging horseshoe falls seemingly courses right at the spectator. More views follow, with perspectives on the upstream cascades.

After crossing under the railroad bridge, a spur leads to the bridge footing. At 26.1 miles, a 50-foot side falls spills to the river, as the FLT continues along the historic rail and canal corridor. Follow the FLT blazes for a rolling tour, coming out at the NY 436 bridge in Portageville at 26.5 miles.

CHAUTAUQUA-ALLEGHENY REGION

This region occupies the southern corner of western New York shaped by Lake Erie and the Pennsylvania border. The region includes the long flat summits and V-shaped valleys of the Allegheny Mountains, the Upper Genesee River, and Chautauqua Lake and Creek Gorge. The region puts forth a soothing landscape of hardwood-evergreen forests, boulder realms, wildflower meadows, and relaxing waters—the ideal escape for the frazzled and harried.

35 DEER LICK NATURE SANCTUARY

Overview

This hike presents the tranquil beauty of a 400-acre National Natural Landmark that wins over visitors with familiarity versus drama. Quiet hardwood forests, dark hemlock stands, lush meadows, and gentle creeks are the hallmarks of this sanctuary owned by The Nature Conservancy (TNC). Bordered to the north by the South Branch Cattaraugus Creek and New York State's Zoar Valley Multiple Use Area, the sanctuary completes a puzzle of unbroken open space and extends a natural wildlife corridor.

General description: A relaxed day hike strings together the four color-coded trails of this sanctuary.
General location: 4 miles southeast of Gowanda.
Special attractions: Mixed hardwood-hemlock forests, abandoned pasture, meadows, spring wildflowers, fall foliage, quiet.
Length: 5 miles round trip; shorter tours possible.
Elevation: The trail has about a 300-foot elevation change.
Difficulty: Easy.
Maps: Sanctuary map; locator maps posted along the white trail.
Special requirements: No pets, smoking, or picnicking; obey all posted TNC rules.
Season and hours: Spring through fall, daylight hours.
For information: The Nature Conservancy, Central and Western New York Office.
Finding the trailhead: From central Gowanda, go south on New York 62 for 0.5 mile and turn left (east) on Hill Street. In 0.4 mile, turn right on Broadway Road, and in another 0.6 mile turn left on Point Peter Road. Stay on Point Peter Road for 2.3 miles and turn left to enter the sanctuary (0.5 mile past the Point Peter Road-Forty Road fork). Find a small parking area, trail register, and pit toilets near the trail's start.

Forest canopy, Deer Lick Nature Sanctuary.

The hike: The white trail, which traverses the sanctuary from west to east, serves as the main artery, the side-branching colored loops the capillaries. As forest duff can mask the footpaths, keep a keen eye for paint blazes, some of which are faded. For this tour, stay to the white trail entering the sanctuary; pick up the colored trails on the return.

Step over the cable, following a mowed swath east through a transition zone, where wild raspberry, milkweed, and daisy grow amid the field; sumac, apple, and black locust frame the route. To the right lies a small cattail marsh.

Keep an eye out for a good-sized American chestnut to the left. This condor of the plant world has beaten the odds, achieving bloom in 1995; most are cut down by a pervasive blight prior to reaching this size and maturity. Once the food staple of native peoples and early settlers, the chestnut has been virtually lost to modern generations.

Past the first junction a mixed woodland draped by woody vines claims the earthen trail as it traverses a low ridge. At 0.3 mile a gap in the tree cover offers an open look at the ridges rolling away to the northeast. Where the trail mildly descends, eastern hemlock, beech, and big-toothed aspen comprise the canopy. Bird notes fill the air. At 0.75 mile a spring muddies the trail and despite rustic corduroys, proves a nemesis to members of the white-sneaker set.

The white trail crosses Deer Lick Creek, ascends, and curves right at the 1-mile junction with the yellow and Melissa Spring trails. It then travels a

DEER LICK NATURE SANCTUARY

small ridge and wooded plateau marked by huge beech trees, reaching a dead-end at Bear Point (1.25 miles). While the song of the South Branch Cattaraugus Creek carries up the steep slope, the treed rim denies views, save for seasonal glimpses. Do not try to better your view, as the cliffs are dangerous and subject to erosion.

Backtrack to the 1-mile junction to begin picking up the side loops. Go right following the dual yellow-and-white blazes through hemlock-hardwood forest to Melissa Spring in 0.1 mile. To drink from the spring, cup a hand over the lower end of the short vertical pipe and wait for the water to pulse out the top for sipping. Muds again precede the spring.

Continue past Melissa Spring for 0.1 mile to pick up the 1.4-mile yellow loop for a counterclockwise tour. The rolling tour traverses a scenic mature hemlock-hardwood plateau and low ridge before dipping sharply to Deer Lick Creek. Hike upstream a few steps to find the crossing; high water may dictate wading. A waterfall sounds downstream, but the trail provides no views.

The yellow trail next ascends through hardwood forest, passes through a disturbed area of windfalls and snags, and then travels a young maple woodlot ensnared by vines. Ferns dress the floor. Beautiful beech trees claim the rise above the path, as it rejoins the white trail; go right.

In 0.1 mile follow the 1.1-mile orange loop left for a clockwise tour and rolling descent. An old orchard and meadow lie beyond the hemlock-hardwood forest of the trail. The orange loop next follows a small ribbony drainage upstream, touring a moist bottomland of woods and meadow, finding muddy pockets and downfalls to cross.

The trail then ascends steeply near the headwater forks, touring stands of hemlock and hardwood or young maple and mature tulip trees, returning to the white trail. Go left to continue toward the parking lot and to reach the red trail.

In 250 feet find the 0.6-mile red loop heading right. The trail tours a tight stand of small maples and a hemlock rim, overlooking first an abandoned pasture and then a small drainage, before entering the pasture meadow at a gas well. Go right on the overgrown two-track as it swings into the meadow. At the junction in 250 feet, turn left, wading through the tall grasses of yet another doubletrack.

A few abandoned apple trees, popular with area deer, and maple dot the meadow. Black-eyed Susan, milkweed, daisy, clover, and spotted knapweed spangle the tall grasses. The doubletrack gives way to a woods road prior to meeting the white trail; bear right to return to the parking area at 5 miles.

---

36 CHAUTAUQUA CREEK GORGE HIKE

General description: This free-spirited cross-country day hike up Chautauqua Creek Gorge zigzags between wooded banks and requires frequent wadings.
General location: The southwest outskirts of Westfield.
Special attractions: Crystalline waters, cascades, and pools; trout fishing; wildlife sightings; fossils; wildflowers.
Length: 2.5 miles round trip (This and the incremental distances in the text are relative measures, as distances vary depending on number of wadings and crossings).
Elevation: The hike has a 300-foot elevation change.
Difficulty: Moderate.
Maps: None.
Special requirements: This is a low-water tour; boots and wading sneakers suggested. Keep to the creek corridor.
Season and hours: Summer and fall.
For information: Chautauqua County Visitors Bureau or New York State Department of Environmental Conservation (DEC), Region 9.

Finding the trailhead: From the U.S. Highway 20/New York 394 junction in Westfield, go east on NY 394 (South Portage Street) toward Mayville. In 1.3 miles turn right (west) onto South Gale Street. Find a small fishing access at the southeast corner of the Chautauqua Creek bridge; parking for two vehicles.

The hike: A long-time favorite of area locals, this hike offers fun and adventure, exploring the beautiful waters and stunning eroded gorge of Chautauqua Creek. While the anatomy of the gorge extends some 7 miles, private lands patchwork the interior, so hikers must content themselves with a look at the tonsils.

The DEC regularly stocks the creek with trout, and lake trout naturally migrate upstream from Lake Erie. Hikers may spy the DEC fishing regulations posted here and there on the tree trunks.

Descend to Chautauqua Creek from the small fishing access and turn upstream, traveling the east shore, crossing under the bridge. A few willow sprigs dot the rocky bar; sumac, wild grape, maple, aspen, and basswood comprise the wooded shore. For the first 0.1 mile, the loose sandstones of the creek bar torque the ankles. Afterward, broad, flat shale plates alternate with these rocky bars. These "sidewalk" stretches free the eyes to pan the creek and scan the treetops.

Chautauqua Creek.

CHAUTAUQUA CREEK GORGE HIKE

At 0.2 mile comes the first cascade set, flowing over a canted, stepped ledge that stretches the entire width of this broad creek. Over time, the water's movement has polished and rounded the steps. The lower cascade measures 1.5 feet, the upper one is 3 feet. Bleached white logs strew the shore.

Above the cascade the wadings begin, but the water is cool and refreshing, slipping around ankles and caressing calves. Cottonwood, beech, sycamore, and black locust add to the tree border. Pickerel frogs and tadpoles may be spied amid the water-soaked rocks.

A fawn and doe drinking from the stream, a heron flapping to land in a tree, or a chiding kingfisher zipping downstream contribute to a tour. The tracks of raccoon, skunk, and other wildlife often rest between the rocks. Look carefully as some of the loose sandstones hold shell fossils and the shale plates wear the ripples of an ancient sea. Even watching one's feet has rewards.

At 0.6 mile find an abandoned jeep trail fording the creek and the start of the eroding gorge cliffs. The jeep trail continues upstream, running parallel to and crisscrossing the creek, offering hikers an established route versus one of their own devising.

As Chautauqua Creek snakes upstream, sheer shale cliffs shape the outside edge of each bend. At 0.9 mile, a 1.5-foot cascade again stretches the breadth of the creek; white streamers skip over a more broken, layered ledge. Upstream the west canyon wall rises 100 feet, pushing the jeep trail onto the east shore. Shortly after, a 150-foot cliff claims the east shore, putting the jeep trail back on the west shore. Back and forth the ante rises.

At this point follow the jeep trail along the west shore. The trail passes an old building, as it comes to a platform and former dam at 1.2 miles (part of Westfield Water Works). Here, too, a 20- to 25-foot waterfall plummets to a deep green pool; the clear water reveals small fish. Beware of sharp, jagged pipe and concrete found at the site.

Remain on the jeep trail as it continues to hug the creek course, finding a small dam and spillway at 1.25 miles; wire mesh retains the rock of the dam. This site marks both the end of the jeep trail and the ending point for the hike, as private lands lie upstream. Return to the bridge access.

37 ALLEGANY STATE PARK, RED HOUSE LAKE AREA

Overview

This growing "wilderness" state park in southwestern New York (already the biggest in the state) brings together even-height peaks and ridges, V shaped valleys, manmade lakes, second-growth forests, and block-fractured boulder realms. The park's two recreation areas, Red House Lake and Quaker Lake make logical breaks for discussing the park trails. Four trails of varying length represent the Red House Lake Area.

General description: The four trails explore the area ridges and peaks, touring woods and meadows, but offer limited views.
General location: 6 miles south of Salamanca.
Special attractions: Mixed hardwood-evergreen forests, ferns, wildflowers, springs, rocky realms, wildlife sightings.
Length: Red Jacket Trail, 0.7-mile loop; Osgood Trail, 2.7-mile loop; Beehunter Trail, 6.5-mile loop; Eastwood Meadows-North Country-Conservation Trail tour, 7.2 miles one way.

Elevation: The trails show the following elevation changes: Red Jacket, 100 feet; Osgood, 650 feet; Beehunter, 700 feet; Eastwood Meadows-North Country-Conservation Trail, 800 feet.

Difficulty: Red Jacket and Osgood, easy; Beehunter, moderate; Eastwood Meadows-North Country, easy to moderate.

Maps: Allegany State Park Guide Map.

Special requirements: Fee area. Beware of a few bogus trail markings; blue disks mark the official state park trails.

Season and hours: Spring through fall.

For information: New York State Parks, Allegany Region.

Finding the trailhead: From New York 17 west of Salamanca, take exit 19 for the Red House Lake Area, reaching the entrance station in 0.7 mile. The trails radiate from the lake area, off Allegany State Park (ASP) routes 1, 2, and 2A.

The hikes: The **Red Jacket Trail** presents a good area synopsis and begins on the west side of the Administration Building, so pick up your maps and take a look.

Stairs, bridge, and path, all of rustic stone, lead uphill to the marked trail junction beneath a power line. Go right, coming to the loop junction in 250 feet. This split-level loop contours the maple, black cherry, and hemlock cloaked slope above Red House Lake. The green understory

Indian Pipe, Allegany State Park.

ALLEGANY STATE PARK, RED HOUSE LAKE AREA

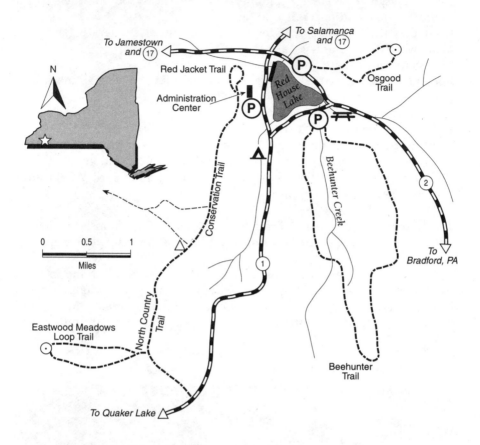

displays half a dozen fern varieties; pines claim the lower slope. At the edges of day, deer browse near the trail.

Views from rustic benches offer open looks at the forest, and leaf-filtered glimpses at Red House Lake, its outlet, the park bikeway, and a round-topped hill. Midway, a recessed stone wall and a rusted steel tower semi-hidden in the trees hint at the ski jump that once occupied this site.

The **Osgood Trail** travels the round-topped hill off the northeast end of Red House Lake. East of the ASP 1/ASP 2 junction, turn north off ASP 2 onto McIntosh Trail to find the trailhead just ahead on the right.

Pass through the fruit tree corridor to the left of the sign, entering the hemlock-pine woods, barren of greenery save for that along the springs. Here and elsewhere in the park, the trail is notably rock-free. The area that is now Allegany State Park alone escaped the advance of the Wisconsin glacier that scoured New York State, broadening valleys and depositing rocks across the terrain at the end of the Ice Age.

The trail ascends, crossing the springs at their origins and bypassing a side trail to the left, before reaching the loop junction at 0.2 mile. Continue uphill; the unmarked trail to the right closes the loop. Chipmunk, songbirds, woodpecker, and deer play cards of surprise. Maple, beech, oak, ash, and black cherry join the evergreens. As the trail contours left above the McIntosh drainage, flat rock slabs punctuate the forest.

At 1.4 miles find the hill's meadow crown and a funneled look west out a break in the tree rim. Go left, passing between the trees to descend the ridge. At 1.8 miles the trail passes through an attractive meadow plateau drained by springs; logs ease soggier crossings.

Where the trail enters an area of moss-and-fern decorated rock slabs, be watchful. A well-worn false trail heads straight downhill, while the loop curves right. Neither path showed a marker near the junction in 1995, but trail crews should have the problem corrected for the 1996 hiking season. Continue contouring and descending to the right to close the loop at 2.5 miles, to reach the trailhead in 2.7 miles.

South of Red House Lake, the **Beehunter Trail** travels the ridges drained by Beehunter Creek. Look for the trailhead on the west side of the field opposite the bathhouse and west of Beehunter Picnic Area (both off ASP 2A).

The trail ascends steadily and steeply for 0.2 mile, attaining the spine of the ridge for a more comfortable tour. Thick grasses spread beneath an open forest of oak, maple, ash, and hemlock. Filtered views east span the Beehunter Creek drainage to a sunbathed ridge. After 0.9 mile a pinched trail rounds the east side of the upper ridge, touring amid brambles, nettles, and ferns. Mossy, slick rocks comprise the trailbed; the blue disks wane. Big black cherry and young beech briefly comprise the forest, as the trail descends.

At 2.2 miles find and cross 15-foot-wide Beehunter Creek with its clear water and rock and gravel bed; it requires wading at times of high water. Disk markers return as the trail again climbs, following a side drainage and crossing the small headwater forks. The rich even-aged forest of 18-inch-diameter hardwoods, the flowing green carpet, and open midstory call to mind a city park atmosphere.

As the trail tops a broad saddle, turn left and ascend the ridge; oak and beech trees return to the mix. At 3.5 miles the trail tops out, now descending via the forested ridge. Red-berried elder gains a stronghold, displaying bright sprays of red berries in August. By 4.5 miles the trail leaves the ridge and levels. Look below the trail at 5.1 miles for a scenic fern-draped split rock with equisized 10-foot by 10-foot rock halves.

Passing through a hemlock grove, the trail comes to a T- junction at a nature-softened woods road; descend left. Stay on the woods road, crossing over a service road to enter a field. Amid the field, find a dirt road with a trailhead sign. Turn right following the dirt road downhill and bear left past the restrooms to reach the bike trail (6.25 miles). Now, go left crossing over Beehunter Creek to close the loop at Beehunter Picnic Area, 6.5 miles.

Hikers may shorten or extend the **Eastwood Meadows-North Country-Conservation Trail Tour**. The described trek passes south to north from the trailhead on ASP 1 (4 miles south of Red House Lake Campground) to the Administration Building.

From ASP 1, a rolling northbound journey alternately tours stands of beech, maple, and hemlock and the shrub-fern meadow clearings from the former ski runs. The white blazes of the North Country Trail join the blue disks of the state park.

At 0.5 mile the North Country Trail turns right; go left to add the Eastwood Meadows Loop. For the meadow tour, where the trail meets a grassy woods road (0.75 mile), turn right to find the ends of the loop on the left in 500 feet. Go left for a clockwise tour. The forest sameness relaxes eye and soul; big-toothed aspen whisper in the canopy. The trail remains flat until 1.4 miles, where it again rolls, generally ascending.

At 1.9 miles find the loop's return to the right, while a limited vista lies 100 feet ahead. The view pans west across a meadow clearing and the Bay State Brook drainage, locating another Allegany ridge.

The loop resumes, descending through a similar forest but with a shrubby understory of nettles and brambles. While not exactly a gauntlet, hikers must evade the prickly overhanging branches. Black cherry remains the giant of the woods. By 2.4 miles, ferns replace the nettles for carefree strolling. Close the loop at 2.9 miles and return to the 0.5-mile junction.

Northbound, the North Country Trail offers an idyllic stroll, showing a modest gradient and troublefree path. A hemlock-hardwood forest enfolds the route, ferns embroider the sides, and snags open up the cathedral. Ahead, a midstory of red-berried elder alternates with the spatially open forest.

By 4.3 miles the trail tags the high point, but the event may easily go unnoticed. With the descent, elder becomes more prevalent. Upon crossing a drainage, look for the next trail junction (4.8 miles). Here the North Country Trail and the west arm of the Conservation Trail (CT) both head left; continue forward, following the blue-blazed route of the east arm of the CT to the Administration Building.

The east arm passes an earthen-floor lean-to that actually does lean. Next to it, a decrepit, mossy road-width bridge spans a drainage; look for the trail's crossing just upstream. The trail starts out level, touring amid mid-aged hardwoods, hemlock groves, and pockets of young beech and shrubs. As the trail descends past large upturned roots (5.6 miles), the west arm of the CT returns on the left; bear right, descending to the Administration Building.

Briefly, mossy rock slabs alter the forest appearance. At 6.5 miles the descent accelerates with uneven steep spurts. As the trail edges meadow clearings, noise from the campground carries up slope. Beneath a power line at 7.1 miles find the trailhead sign for the CT and turn right, descending past an old foundation to reach the Administration Building.

Overview

Conceived to bring a "wilderness playground" to western New York, this 64,000-acre state park succeeds. Hikers find solitude, challenge, and natural beauty amid the terrain of even-height peaks and ridges and V shaped valleys. Four trails represent the offering of the Quaker Lake Area.

General description: These trails travel ridges, tag peaks, explore a boulder realm, and visit a natural spring.
General location: 6 miles south of Salamanca.
Special attractions: Mixed hardwood-evergreen forests, springs, wildflowers, block-fractured boulder caves.
Length: Mount Tuscarora Trail, 5 miles round trip; Three Sisters Trail, 2.5-mile loop; Bear Caves-Mount Seneca Trail, 3 miles round trip; Bear Springs Trail, 0.5 mile round trip.
Elevation: Trails show the following elevation changes: Mount Tuscarora, 750 feet; Three Sisters, 500 feet; Bear Caves-Mount Seneca, 500 feet; Bear Springs less than 100 feet.

Forest, Allegany State Park.

ALLEGANY STATE PARK, QUAKER LAKE AREA

Difficulty: Bear Springs, easy; the others, moderate.

Maps: Allegany State Park Guide Map.

Special requirements: Fee area. Bring flashlight for looking at boulder caves; be prepared for stooping and squeezing. Expect small rooms and passages less than 200 feet long. Consider taking the naturalist's tour to locate the openings.

Season and hours: Spring through fall.

For information: New York State Parks, Allegany Region.

Finding the trailhead: From New York 17 west of Salamanca, take exit 18 for the Quaker Lake Area and go south on NY 280 for 4 miles to reach the entrance station. Find the trails off Allegany State Park (ASP) routes 3 and 1.

The hikes: The **Mount Tuscarora Trail** starts 0.2 mile south of the Quaker Lake entrance station; road shoulder parking only.

The foot trail heads west off ASP 3, traveling a dark hemlock-hardwood forest, ascending parallel to a drainage. At 0.5 mile, the trail curves right and with another burst of climb tops the ridge (0.7 mile). Although the park map shows a view, time has stolen it.

The ascent calms as the trail traces the ridgeline. Indian pipe, baneberry, huckleberry, witch-hazel, striped maple, beech, and small oaks contribute to the tour. The trail claims the first summit (elevation 2,064 feet) at 2.25 miles. It then ascends to travel the next ridge tier to the abandoned fire tower (elevation 2,144 feet) at 2.5 miles. An out-of-place tulip tree or an occasional hickory rises amid the oaks and maples.

Missing its lower flight of stairs and several of its landings, the fire tower now serves only as a landmark and destination. Trees completely enfold the site. Although the trail continues along the ridge to Coon Run Road, turn around and return as you came.

The **Three Sisters Trail** travels to only one sister—West Sister—and begins west of the rental office; find the rental office west of the ASP 1/ASP 3 junction.

Pass into a pine-hardwood forest with a shrubby understory, bypassing a pine-hemlock stand and crossing under a power line. The midstory fern, nettle, and bramble sometimes swipe at hikers. Crossing a footbridge at 0.4 mile, the trail traverses both grassy meadow and open forest—a virtual sauna on sunny, humid days. Pockets of bee-balm, a red member of the mint family, adorn the drainage.

The steadily ascending trail can be rocky, with rustic corduroys aiding passage over soggy reaches. Gradually, the forest fills out. At 1 mile the trail tops and follows the ridge to the left. Red-berried elder interweaves the ridge forest, as the hiker passage grows squeezed. The matted-grass trail ascends and rounds through a beech grove, tagging the top of West Sister (1.4 miles), but it delivers no view.

As the trail drops away from the summit, be aware the grassy footpath can be slippery when wet. At 1.8 miles a large rock slab offers a natural crossing to a spring. After passing under the power line, the foot trail meets Ranger Trail (a road) near cabins 1, 2, and 4. Follow the markers descending Ranger Trail. Prior to reaching ASP 3, take the footpath heading left into the woods to return to the pine-hemlock stand near the start. Turn right to end the hike.

The preferred access to the **Bear Caves-Mount Seneca Trail** is the eastern one; go 1.4 miles east on ASP 3 from the ASP 1/ASP 3 junction. Find parking on the south side of ASP 3, the trailhead on the north.

This trail offers a different look at the park, ascending a broad, worn trail up a steep bouldery slope, reaching an entire community of the massive boxy boulders and outcrops. Crossbedding, balanced rocks, eroded nooks, fissures, and overhangs plus the adorning moss, lichen, and fern contribute to the discovery. At the base of the rocky realm, the primary trail heads right; a secondary trail rounds to the left.

Go right, rounding and ascending, to traverse the wooded top of the rocks. At 0.2 mile the trail overlooks the first cave opening, an inconspicuous natural spacing in the sandstone conglomerate. The small rooms and thin passages (enlarged joints) intrigue the curious. As the trail traverses the top of the rocks, look over the edge to spy a deep narrow fissure. Similar features comprise the caves, only overlaying rocks conceal them.

At 0.3 mile a second cave opening calls the intrepid hiker to literally drop in. By 0.4 mile the trail is again at the base of the rocks, touring the familiar Allegany forest intermixed with bramble, fern, and red-berried elder. The trail descends and then crosses Slide Hollow; high water may dictate wading. Follow the blue-marked trail uphill to the right; a side path descends along the drainage. Bee-balm puts its red signature to the scene.

The trail contours then turns sharply right for a steep assault on Mount Seneca. Clintonia, trillium, and Mayflower decorate the floor. At 1.3 miles push through the congestion of red-berried elder, wild raspberry, and gooseberry to emerge at the summit (1.5 miles). The top holds a look at the wooded ridge of Mount Onondaga to the northeast and the immediate peak to the east. While the trail continues, return as you came.

Bear Springs Trail begins on the west side of ASP 1, 2.2 miles north of the ASP 1/ASP 3 junction.

Enter a woods of maple, black cherry, and hemlock to the left of the sign. The trail slowly descends. The spatially open forest shows a lush fern floor and a profusion of woods flora not seen elsewhere in the park. Oxalis, Mayflower, whorled begonia, trillium, and orchid contribute to the array. Soon after crossing a drainage, the trail reaches the 6-foot-high stonework grotto protecting the spring. Although the trail continues, traveling field and hardwood forest and meeting old woods roads, return as you came.

FINGER LAKES REGION

In central New York, the vast Finger Lakes Region enjoys a signature landscape. The long, thin glacier-gouged lakes look as if Mother Nature raked her fingers down the state's middle. Dramatic east-west river gorges, with spirited falls, tumbling cascades, and imposing cliffs likewise contribute to the region's singular image. Rolling woods and grasslands, low steep-flanked ridges and hills, vital wetlands, and diked ponds complete the terrain and vary the discovery.

The long-distance Finger Lakes Trail unites the splendors of the region. Discover the history of early New York at the site of a Sapony Indian village or while strolling lands awarded the soldiers of the Revolutionary War.

Overview

The Barge Canal and Seneca River isolate this 3,100-acre interior island, where eighteen dikes create an extensive network of ponds, drawing waterfowl to the area. Low, rolling hills (drumlins deposited by glacial action 10,000 years ago), planted floodplain, unkept fields, and hardwood stands complete the island mosaic. The vital habitat supports some two hundred bird species, as well as woodchuck, rabbit, deer, fox, turtle, frog, fish, and newt. Management roads and dikes suggest the tours, while offering easy strolling.

General description: This relaxing loop strings together views of a dozen ponds, as it travels untamed and cultivated fields, wetlands, and woods.
General location: In north central Cayuga County, about 25 miles west of Syracuse.
Special attractions: Bird watching, impoundment ponds, fields, marsh, low-elevation hardwoods, spring and summer wildflowers.
Length: 3-mile loop (3.4 miles, with the Pump Pond spur).
Elevation: The trail shows less than a 100-foot elevation change.
Difficulty: Easy.

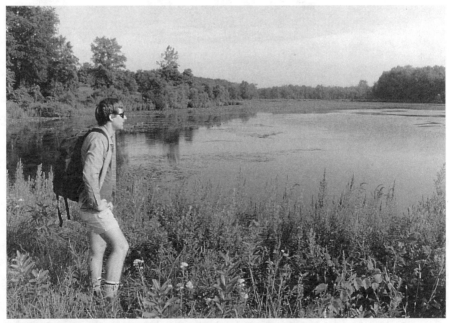

Breeder Pond, Howland Island Wildlife Management Area.

HOWLAND ISLAND WILDLIFE MANAGEMENT AREA

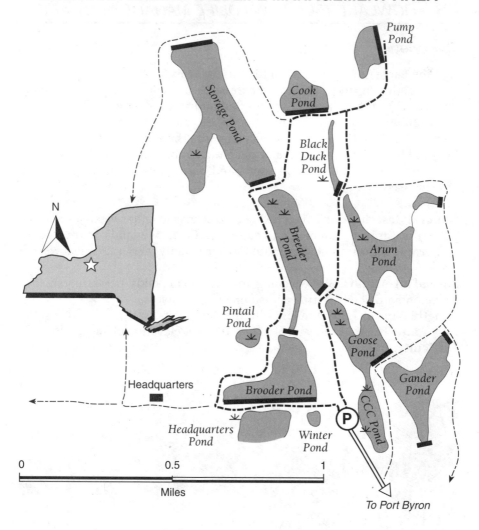

Maps: Howland Island Wildlife Management Area brochure.

Special requirements: Bring insect repellent and mosquito netting for a more enjoyable visit. Hikers may choose to avoid the area during hunting season; contact the Department of Environmental Conservation (DEC) for dates.

Season and hours: Spring through fall, daylight hours. Closures occur April 1 to May 31 for waterfowl nesting.

For information: New York State Department of Environmental Conservation, Region 7.

Finding the trailhead: From Port Byron at the junction of New York 31 and New York 38, go north on NY 38 for 1.8 miles and turn left onto Howland Island Road, at the sign for the wildlife management area (WMA). Stay on Howland Island Road, crossing the steel-deck bridge to reach the island, in another 1.8 miles; the route changes to gravel. Find trail parking at the road barrier in 0.8 mile. (From the Interstate 90, take exit 40 at Weedsport and go west on NY 31 to Port Byron).

The hike: Round the WMA barrier and continue along the gravel road, going left at the junction in 250 feet for a clockwise tour. Locust, maple, hickory, oak, willow, and apple shape a border congested with vines and shrubs. Beware of poison ivy amid the grassy edge. With the turn, the trail passes between Winter Pond, a small, lily-capped square at the foot of a slope, and Brooder Pond, an enormous, mostly vegetated water to the right. Croaking bullfrogs and a "brooder's" plop cause eyes to dart.

The quonset hut of the headquarters appears on the hill to the west, as Headquarters Pond replaces Winter Pond on the left. Trees and shrubs rim half this large, lily-ringed open water; a planted field extends up the western slope. Reflections of trees and passing clouds call to photographers.

Near the end of Headquarters Pond, cattail, loosestrife, tag alder, and milkweed overtake the shore. Swallows perch on the line overhead, while red-winged blackbirds animate the marsh. At 0.4 mile lies a three-way junction, follow the grassy doubletrack heading right, edging Brooder Pond. Queen Anne's lace, daisy, chicory, loosestrife, clover, milkweed, and a host of other wildflowers bring splendor to the tall-grass field. Monarch butterflies alight on the milkweed.

Past a spruce stand, Pintail Pond catches the eye with its roundish shrub islands, nesting boxes, and lily pad mosaic, rimmed by tall wetland and meadow. Yellow warblers, kingfisher, and ducks add to a growing list of sightings. On a channel to the left, look for turtles slipping off logs.

As the left side of the trail changes from meadow to cornfield, Breeder Pond replaces Brooder Pond on the right. The presence of hikers sometimes offends the feeding geese, causing them to march out of the field in comical haughtiness.

At 1.3 miles the trail tours a corridor with cottonwood and basswood, coming out on a dike between Breeder and Storage ponds. A heron lifting off the water, raining drops from its wings, or an osprey sometimes atop the large snag on the east shore of Breeder Pond may engage the eye. Under a cottonwood at the end of the dike, find a junction; go left for the loop. Black walnut trees and a mild meadow slope now frame the tour.

At arrowhead-shaped Cook Pond (1.75 mile) turn right, bypassing a small extension of Black Duck Pond where a birdhouse holds center stage. At the upcoming T-junction a detour left finds Pump Pond in 0.2-mile; the loop continues right, traveling a straightaway often enclosed by elm, locust, and walnut. Black Duck Pond may be glimpsed beyond the shrub tangle. A better view of this long, thin duckweed pond comes at the junction at 2.15 miles; go right for the loop.

The trail passes between Black Duck and Arum ponds to round above the latter. Trees keep Arum Pond a puzzle, pieced together by stolen glances. Ahead, an open meadow shore spans to Arum and Goose ponds.

Overgrown jeep tracks arrive on the right and left, as hikers near the dike between Breeder and Goose ponds.

The vegetated ponds hold a lesson in succession. Purple loosestrife, an exotic, overwhelms the CCC Pond at 2.9 miles; while pretty in its July bloom, loosestrife displaces native vegetations. With a mild ascent, the trail bypasses an overgrown track on the right, to close the loop at Winter Pond. Return to the trailhead.

40 BEAVER LAKE NATURE CENTER

Overview

At this 550-acre Onondaga County Park, 9 miles of superbly groomed nature trails and boardwalks explore lake, marsh, meadow, and woods habitats for outstanding wildlife sightings and nature study. The trails welcome all abilities, and repeat tours bring new appreciation; ask the park's "one-hundred milers" who regularly tour the eight trails. The three hikes described below sample five of the trails. The site's interpretive panels, benches, observation platforms, a blind, and high-powered binoculars enhance a visit.

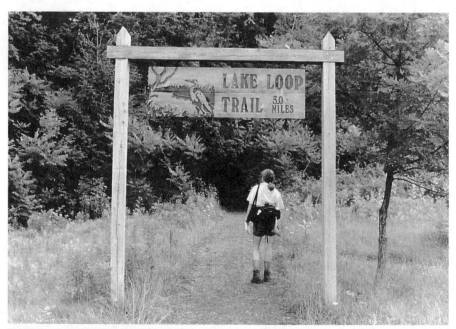

Trailhead sign, Beaver Lake Nature Center

BEAVER LAKE NATURE CENTER

General description: The selected trails are all easy, ranging from a fragment of a mile to 3 miles in length, with Lakeview Trail having the most convenient lake access.

General location: 15 miles northwest of Syracuse.

Special attractions: Thirty thousand spring-migrating Canada geese, ten thousand fall migrants; songbirds, osprey, heron, deer, fox, beaver, frog, turtle, and toad; pitcher plants; spring wildflowers; massive beech trees and hemlock hollows.

Length: Lake Loop, 3-mile loop; interlocked Hemlock Hollow and Bog trails, 1 mile round trip; Lakeview Trail, 0.3-mile loop.

Elevation: Trails are virtually flat.

Difficulty: All easy.

Maps: Beaver Lake Nature Center flier.

Special requirements: Token vehicle fee. Carry repellent.

Season and hours: Year-round, dawn to dusk; building opens 8 a.m. In winter, the trails are popular for cross-country skiing and snowshoeing; snowshoes are provided free of charge.

For information: Beaver Lake Nature Center.

Finding the trailhead: From New York State Thruway Interstate 90, take exit 39, go north on Interstate 690/New York 690 for 5.8 miles, and take the second Baldwinsville exit as indicated for the nature center. Go west on New York 370 for 2 miles. There, turn right on East Mud Lake Road, following the signs; the nature center is on the left in 0.7 mile. The Lake Loop starts to the right of the visitor center, the other named trails start to the center's left; scenic carved signs identify each trail.

The hikes: A woods walk characterizes the early distance of the **Lake Loop**, which seldom hints at centrally located 206-acre Beaver Lake. The wide wood-chip path travels amid spruce-pine woodland, towering tulip and beech trees, and a congestion of young, spindly maples. Virginia creeper, poison ivy, and fern contribute to the understory. Where Lake Loop crosses the other park trails, signs indicate the junctions.

At 0.5 mile the loop follows a boardwalk over the lake outlet, where white water lilies decorate the flow in summer, and turtles sun on the logs. Highbush blueberry, alder, nettles, dodder, fern, and cattails rear up in the wetland tangle. At 0.7 mile an elevated bench overlooks Beaver Lake.

Duckweed coats a small inlet drainage where cardinal flowers decorate a log. At 1 mile a wide foot trail replaces the boardwalk, and at 1.25 miles side trails branch right to three lean-tos and left to a canoe landing site; periodically, the county offers guided canoe trips. In the wet ash-maple woodland, poison ivy abounds.

At 1.7 miles the loop again travels a boardwalk passing a small catfish water, with rimming cattail, loosestrife, and arrowhead. The trail then passes through pine plantation and meadow, skirting below the Vann Road lake overlook. At 2.25 miles the trail crosses a service road.

Where Lake Loop meets the **Teal Marsh Trail** (2.5 miles), follow the Teal Marsh Trail left to complete the circuit. A quick spur left leads to a water-lily cove. Hemlock hollows and transition woods alternately claim the route, as it passes a small wetland pond and picnic shelter, reaching the walkway to the visitor center (3 miles).

En route to the visitor center, bypass the Hemlock Hollow, Bog, and Lakeview trailheads. With **Hemlock Hollow Trail** being the lone access to the **Bog Trail**, these two hikes naturally combine. The Hemlock Hollow Trail swings a 0.4-mile loop through a dark hemlock woods with oak, birch, beech, and interspersing witch-hazel. Midway the ladle-shaped Bog Trail branches west, traveling boardwalk and trail along a former island, now a marshy Beaver Lake peninsula.

By keeping right at the two initial Bog Trail junctions (the loop), hikers explore the length of the peninsula. Spurs lead to a bog-pond overlook, a one-story lake observation platform, and a couple of lakeshore accesses. At the lake platform, high-powered binoculars pull cross-lake herons into close scrutiny. On the return take the boardwalk loop capping the tour with a marsh study. Sweet gale, arrowhead, cranberry, loosestrife, and pitcher plant number among the discoveries.

The wheelchair-accessible **Lakeview Loop** draws a figure-eight through similar deep woods, with plaques explaining the intricate habitat interactions. A beautiful big oak marks the second loop junction. Off the second loop, spurs lead to two lake vistas. At the larger viewing stop, travelers find benches and telescopes, including one telescope low enough for comfortable use from a wheelchair.

An osprey snatching a fish from the lake, the growing wake of a beaver, or some thirty thousand migrant geese awaiting the spring thaw in Canada in turn captivate visitors.

Late March to early May marks the peak time for viewing Canada geese; in fall a smaller contention stops over on the lake.

41 HIGH TOR WILDLIFE MANAGEMENT AREA

Overview

Three separate land parcels comprise High Tor Wildlife Management Area (WMA); this trail explores the southernmost and largest of the three. Hikes in this 3,400-acre parcel follow service road, jeep track, and foot trail, exploring wetland, gully, woods, and field. An occasional interpretive sign introduces the natural history.

General description: With side spurs to a wildlife pond and an overlook of Conklin Gully, this barbell-shaped tour showcases the WMA's varied habitats and hill-and-gully terrain.
General location: 6 miles south of Canandaigua Lake, 3 miles east of Naples.
Special attractions: Striking 400-foot-deep chasm, isolated waterfall, wildlife ponds, wildlife sightings, wildflowers.
Length: 7.5 miles round trip.
Elevation: The trail shows about a 400-foot elevation change.
Difficulty: Easy.
Maps: Wildlife management area brochure.
Special requirements: Sun-drenched tour; bring water.
Season and hours: Spring through fall; daylight hours.

For information: New York State Department of Environmental Conservation (DEC), Region 8.

Finding the trailhead: From the junction of New York 53 and New York 21 in Naples, go south on NY 53 for 0.8 mile and turn left (east) toward Italy Valley on Ontario County 21. In 1.9 miles turn left on Bassett Road. Find trailhead parking 0.3 mile ahead on the left.

The hike: Hike the tree-lined service road north, rounding the gate and passing between two wildlife ponds. Cattails and marsh grasses shape the rim; a scummy mat coats the pond to the left. Clover, daisy, chicory, buttercup, and morning glory sprinkle the grassy shoulder. Swallowtail, monarch, and admiral butterflies flutter about ankles and flowers.

At 0.1 mile go left on the primary service road for a steady moderate ascent; the secondary road to the right marks the close for the lower and larger loop of this lopsided barbell tour. Maple, oak, and hickory now comprise the tree border distanced from the trail by a 10- to 30-foot-wide shoulder. Yellow warbler, muskrat, hawk, ruffed grouse, and white-tailed deer bounding through the tall grasses enrich a tour.

At 1.2 miles a spur to the left leads to Campsite One. The DEC makes camps available only to educational groups with written permission; phone Region 8 at 607-522-3323 for camp information. A 0.1-mile detour to the camp finds a picture-pretty circular pond rimmed by cattails and noisy with bullfrogs.

At the four-way junction at 1.4 miles, the service road continues north to the upper loop and Conklin Gully; the overgrown doubletrack to the right begins the lower loop; and a detour left (west) on the orange Bristol Hills Branch of the Finger Lakes Trail (FLT) leads to another, larger wildlife pond (1.6 miles). A deciduous border rims two-thirds of this pond. Snake, frog, and birdlife number among the sightings.

Return to the junction at 1.4 miles and continue north toward Conklin Gully, following the eastbound Bristol Hills Branch of the FLT. Past a cattail wetland, look for a roadside post with double orange blazings just as the road curves right (2.1 miles). Take a couple of steps north past the post, turn left, and follow the FLT (now a foot trail) into the woods.

The trail descends sharply through full cool woods, crossing over a blue-blazed doubletrack. Pass beneath the broken arm of a granddaddy oak, boasting a 6-foot diameter and twelve major branchings; paying homage to this tree alone justifies the tour. At 2.75 miles reach a grassy woods road. Turn right staying with the FLT to close the upper loop. To add a side trip to Conklin Gully, turn left following the blue blazes.

The side tour quickly curves right for a serious descent on a broad, exposed road corridor offering looks north. Cross a small, steep ravine at 3 miles and ascend to round the nose of a ridge for a grand overlook of the "gully" — a rather unassuming characterization for such an awesome chasm (3.25 miles). Keep well back from the edge as it has a dangerous unstable overhang.

Majestic oak, High Tor Wildlife Management Area.

At Conklin Gully, sun-beaten 400-foot-tall gray-brown cliffs open to the sky with a crystalline waterfall slipping through a green wooded seam halfway down the north wall. Elsewhere, pine and aspen dot the shale mudstones. Free from protective barriers, this site extends perhaps the most heart-thumping gorge vista in the entire state.

Retrace your steps uphill to the 2.75-mile junction (3.75 miles), and resume the upper loop, ascending the grassy doubletrack straight ahead. Orange FLT and blue blazes now point the way. At Campsite Two (4 miles), a rim view pans north overlooking the nearby wooded ridges and farms and Canandaigua Lake. Pass through the parking area to the service road and head left.

The upper loop closes back at the 2.1-mile junction (where the FLT entered the woods as a foot trail). Continue straight (south) on the service road past the cattail pond, returning to the 1.4/1.8-mile junction at 4.7 miles. Now, turn left (east) on the overgrown doubletrack for the lower loop; the parallel tracks remain clear for easy walking. Again, the set-back woods provide but spotty shade.

At 4.8 miles an interpretive sign explains the snapped treetops and missing branches; they are the legacy of a 1991 ice storm. The trail next rounds a wildlife pond at least ten times the size of the previous ones. Snags, open water, marsh islands, and noisy dragonflies comprise its persona. Detour onto the levee for an unobstructed view.

An ascent through a long narrow meadow of elbow-high grasses inter-woven with white, pink, and yellow wildflowers leads to a T-junction at 5.8 miles. Here the loop turns right; the path downhill to the left leads to more wildlife ponds, beginning in 0.5 mile. Stay the loop, ascending a daisy-clad road.

The trail tops out at 6.25 mile and descends via a similar long meadow corridor. By 7 miles, spruce plantations alternate with the meadow openings. Where the lower loop closes (7.4 miles), turn left to return to the trailhead.

42 INTERLOKEN NATIONAL RECREATION TRAIL

General description: This linear multi-use route strings north to south through New York State's lone national forest, exploring natural and planted forests, meadow, transitioning shrublands, and pond habitats.

General location: 10 miles northeast of Watkins Glen, between Seneca and Cayuga lakes.

Special attractions: Habitat diversity, bird watching, fishing, wildlife sightings, cultural history, wildflowers.

Length: 12 miles one way.

Elevation: The trail travels from a low elevation of 1,300 feet in the south to a high of 1,850 feet on Hector Backbone.

Difficulty: Moderate.

Maps: Finger Lakes National Forest brochure; U.S. Department of Agriculture (USDA) Finger Lakes National Forest map.

Special requirements: Be prepared for muddy patches.

Season and hours: Spring through fall.

For information: Finger Lakes National Forest, Hector Ranger District.

Finding the trailhead: From the New York 227/New York 96 junction in Trumansburg, go north on NY 96 for 1.5 miles and turn left onto Seneca County 143 for 4.8 miles. Turn right on County 146 for 1 mile and then go left on Parmenter/Butcher Hill Road for 0.6 mile; the northern trailhead is on the left.

For the southern trailhead, at the Schuyler County 5/New York 79 intersection in Burdett, go 0.9 mile east on NY 79 and turn left on Logan Road/County 4 for 1.1 miles; there turn right on Wycoff. In 0.5 mile, go right on Burnt Hill Road for 0.4 mile; the trailhead is on the left.

The hike: Once inhabited by Iroquois Indians and later partitioned into military parcels and given to veterans of the Revolutionary War, the gentle ridges and open flats of this national forest eventually returned to government hands through a farmer's relief act during the Great Depression. Stabilized through reforestation, the land once again thrives, serving interests of naturalist and recreationist.

Interloken Trail, Finger Lakes National Forest.

INTERLOKEN NATIONAL RECREATION TRAIL

To Seneca Falls

Parmenter Road

To (414)

To Trumansburg

146

To (414)

Townsend Road

To Trumansburg

143

N

To (414)

Seneca Road

To Trumansburg

Teeter Pond

To (414)

Searsburg Road

1

To Trumansburg

Hector Backbone

Potomac Road

0   1   2

Miles

Foster Pond

Picnic Area Road

Blueberry Patch Rec. Area

Mathews Road

To Trumansburg

227

4

Burnt Hill Road

To Ithaca

79

Wycoff Road

79

To (79)

To Watkins Glen

On a north-south tour, the orange-marked trail enters a mature mixed woods with a lush understory. An aspen-shrub complex, a woodlot of young maple and seedling pine, and an open meadow variously claim the route. At 1.25 miles cross Townsend Road, and at 1.5 miles, cross a 10-foot-wide drainage that may require wading during high water. Veer left for a mild ascent leading to a gate; pass through, leaving all gates as you found them.

Stay with the orange blazes, wading knee-high grasses, descending to and crossing Seneca Road; bypass the No-Tan-Takto Horse Trail. Next, the national recreation trail (NRT) passes through an aspen-shrub complex, reaching Teeter Pond (2.5 miles). This expansive marsh and open water attracts warm-water anglers and wildlife. Snags, shrub islands, and reflections of the cloud-filled sky add to its welcome. Pass to the right of the pond.

Leaving the pond at 2.8 miles, tour a full mixed forest, coming to a gate at the corner of a large pasture. Follow the diagonal staked course of the NRT, touring knee- to waist-high grasses sprinkled with clover, daisy, and buttercup, to cross Searsburg Road at 3.2 miles.

A mowed swath enters the woods for a gentle climb, but muddy passages can weigh down boots. Green leaves stretch from the lower story to the canopy, with a bright azalea patch at 3.8 miles. Sightings of red eft, deer, and warbler spice the journey.

At a signed junction with the Backbone Trail, continue straight for the NRT, touring a pine plantation with accents of fairy slipper. Back amid an oak-maple woodland, bypass private property on the right. As the trail curves left and slowly rises, re-routes evade some of the more impassable muddy reaches. A thinned forest of big trees and boardwalks precede the shrubby outskirts of Foster Pond.

Reaching the outskirts, follow the tracked path straight ahead. Here the Backbone Trail (northbound) heads left; in 200 feet, its southbound counterpart journeys right. Now bear left for the Interloken Trail, rounding the south shore of Foster Pond amid grass and shrubs.

Turn right at the marked junction at 5.75 miles. This is the first of three junctions where side trails branch east (left) to Potomac Road. Ski markers and ribbons help mark the route as it still travels aisles of thick grass and shrubs; orange blazes resume in the woods as boardwalks ease passage.

At Picnic Area Road (6.9 miles), hike west (right) along the road for 0.2 mile, bypassing Blueberry Patch Recreation Area to pick up the NRT as it resumes south, entering pines. At 7.4 miles a side trail heads left and at 7.5 miles, the Ravine Trail heads right; continue straight ahead.

Pass from a younger woods of maple and big-toothed aspen to a more mature, mixed complex, coming to a gate and another pasture stretch. The footpath now angles uphill to the left, with a microwave tower visible to the east, ridges and farmland sweeping west. While tall grasses overhang the path, it is more passable than it first appears.

From Mathews Road return to woods, soon passing amid snags and 8-foot-tall shrubs. At 9.1 miles cross the overgrown corridor of a forlorn Burnt

Hill Trail. Planted and natural woods alternately claim the rolling meander. Upon meeting the Gorge Trail, follow it right for 0.1 mile, and then go straight where the Gorge Trail turns right. Mature oaks and flavorful early-summer strawberries slow strides, but beware of poison ivy when reaching for berries.

Pine, spruce, and larch plantations now interrupt the deciduous stands. At 10.2 miles travel the levee of a small wildlife pond at a corner junction of Burnt Hill Road; the scummy crescent percolates with frogs. As poison ivy abounds, keep to the thin hiker track. Continue straight past South Slope Trail.

At 11 miles meet the Finger Lakes Trail (FLT) and bear left. A 0.2-mile detour right leads to the FLT Trailhead on Burnt Hill Road. At the trailhead an interesting historical display features an 1864 handwritten letter from an area farmer to his wife that recounts the taking of Atlanta.

A lean-to presides in a grassy clearing to the left of the NRT at 11.1 miles; continue straight following the FLT/Interloken Trail marked with white and orange blazes. With a rolling descent, travel a woodland-shrub bog, bypassing a frog pond, crossing through a gap in a stonewall, and traveling along the boardwalk to reach the southern terminus (12 miles).

43 TAUGHANNOCK FALLS STATE PARK

Overview

While the Finger Lakes Region boasts several prized east-west gorge features with similarly named trails, each has a unique signature. For this park, Taughannock Falls autographs the park with a flourish. Cradled in a cliff amphitheater and spilling 215 feet from a hanging canyon, the waterfall conjures images of Yosemite National Park and ranks as the tallest falls east of the Mississippi River.

General description: A pair of trails explore the belly of the gorge and its canyon rim for exciting views.
General location: West side of Cayuga Lake.
Special attractions: Rich geologic, natural, and cultural history; waterfalls; Taughannock Creek; 400-foot cliffs.
Length: Gorge Trail, 1.5 miles round trip; Rim Loop, 3.5-mile loop.
Elevation: The Gorge Trail shows a 100-foot elevation change, the Rim Loop about a 550-foot elevation change.
Difficulty: Easy.
Maps: State park brochure.
Special requirements: No swimming in Taughannock Creek.
Season and hours: Spring through fall, daylight hours. The Gorge Trail remains open year-round.

Taughannock Falls, Taughannock Falls State Park.

TAUGHANNOCK FALLS STATE PARK

For information: New York State Parks, Finger Lakes Region.

Finding the trailhead: From the junction of New York 13/34 and New York 89/96/79 (the corner of State and Meadow streets) in Ithaca, go north on NY 89, staying on it for 9.1 miles. Turn left (west) to enter the trailhead parking lot; trails leave the southwest corner of the parking area.

The hikes: The Gorge Trail and Falls Overlook on the north rim tender the best canyon-Taughannock Falls vantages, but hiking the Rim Loop grants perspectives otherwise denied. The trails start from a site once occupied by Taughannock Indian camps and a cabin that sheltered a soldier in the Revolutionary War.

For the **Gorge Trail** (an interpretive trail), hike west along the paved walk. Next to the trail information hut the South Rim Trail veers left; continue west into the gorge.

At 0.1 mile an impressive 15-foot ledge spans the 75- to 100-foot width of Taughannock Creek. At the north corner the falls spills at an angle, with chutes carving deep channels in the sedimentary ledge. The uniformly flat bedrock of the creek amazes, planed long ago by torrents of melting ice and rock. Hemlock, basswood, maple, and oak overhang the improved surface trail. In another 0.1 mile a second ledge spans the width of the creek; this one measuring 2 feet high.

Steep wooded slopes yield to skyward-stretching cliffs. Where a woods buffer isolates the trail from the creek, side paths branch to shore. Swallows, hawks, and cardinals dwell in the canyon, as do great-horned owls, whose appetites spelled an end to a peregrine release program in the 1970s.

By 0.5 mile the sandstone-shale cliffs become more prominent, steep, eroding, and jointed, with boxy overhangs and tenuously held trees. Sycamores join the ranks. Across the bridge the waterfall amphitheater humbles onlookers. With multiple streamers and wisping spray the 215-foot vertical falls plunges to an awaiting pool 30 feet deep. The spray nurtures greenery cloaking the canted base of the 400-foot cliffs. Who could ask for a more lovely or authoritative stop sign? Return as you came.

For a clockwise tour of the **Rim Loop** start on the South Rim Trail near the trail information hut. Ascend stairs and trail to top the rim at 0.25 mile, turning right (upstream) for a mild ascent alongside a mesh fence. A mixed deciduous-hemlock forest shades the trail; deer encounters may enhance a tour. By 0.5 mile open views replace teasing glimpses of the gorge, with up-canyon views spotlighting the upper reaches of Taughannock Falls.

At 0.8 mile the rim terrain puts the hiker trail onto Gorge Road to round a steep side drainage. Afterward the buffer between trail and road remains thin. At a U-shaped scouring of the rim, a dizzying look down applauds the canyon bottom. The trail next travels a broad wooded plateau and rounds a deep gash in the gorge rim, passing amid cedar, birch, willow, berried shrub, tiger lily, daisy, and harebell.

At 1.75 miles cross the hiker bridge over Taughannock Creek, prior to a road bridge and the park boundary. Upstream a 100-foot falls spills at a hairpin turn of the now-pinched gorge; downstream a strong tree-capped rim, jutting points, vertical cliffs, and an ancient plunge pool washed by the slow-moving stream comprise the scene.

Resume the loop, following the North Rim Trail through a small field, bearing right to follow the mowed shoulder of the park road for 0.4 mile. Back on the rim, the trail travels a narrow hemlock-hardwood corridor, once more alongside a wire-mesh fence. At 2.5 miles find Falls Overlook for a bird's-eye view of the rock amphitheater and starring falls. This vantage presents the upstream water flowing up to and over the abrupt ledge of the hanging valley and the full length of the 215-foot drop. Taughannock House, a luxury hotel from the 1860s to the turn of the century, formerly claimed this view.

The trail now descends, skirting a picnic area and later the campground. Views span downstream, taking in the broad creek bottom, wooded canyon, Cayuga Lake, and its east ridge. With the descent, the tour grows sunnier. At 3.25 miles stone stairs lead to NY 89, reaching the north side of Taughannock Creek bridge. Turn right, cross the bridge, and return to the parking area.

General description: Part of the greater Finger Lakes Trail (FLT), this trail rolls from rim to drainage, touring hemlock glen and hardwood forest between Spruce Pond and Cuyler.

General location: 25 miles southeast of Syracuse.

Special attractions: Hang-gliding site and vista, waterfalls, deep hollows, a lean-to, wildlife sightings, fall foliage.

Length: 12 miles one way.

Elevation: The trail shows a 750-foot elevation change, with the high point at Jones Hill Summit (1,964 feet).

Difficulty: Strenuous.

Maps: Morgan Hill State Forest brochure; Finger Lakes Trail Conference map, The Onondaga Trail, Section 01.

Special requirements: This trail travels both public and private lands, so keep to the trail and obey posted notices.

Season and hours: Spring through fall.

For information: New York State Department of Environmental Conservation (DEC), Region 7.

Finding the trailhead: From Interstate 81, take exit 14 for Tully and go east on New York 80 for 4.5 miles, passing through Tully and merging with New York 91 North. At 4.5 miles, turn south on gravel Herlihy Road, go 1.9

Curved snag.

ONONDAGA TRAIL

miles, and continue straight at the junction to reach the Spruce Pond Fishing Access in another 0.1 mile; parking for ten vehicles.

For the southern terminus, in Cuyler, follow Lincklaen Road west for 0.7 mile; where it crosses New York 13, the road name changes to Tripoli. At the intersection with West Keeney and Eaton Hill roads, turn left on West Keeney Road. Look for the step-ladder stile crossing the fence on the right. Limited road shoulder parking exists for shuttle vehicles.

The hike: This orange-blazed route travels foot trail and woods roads, touring Labrador Hollow State Nature Preserve, Morgan Hill State Forest, and private land. When following woods roads, keep a sharp eye out for where the foot-trail segments resume. A long lapse between markers may indicate a need to backtrack and find the trail.

For a north-south tour, cross the earthen levee of square Spruce Pond and strike up the beech-and-maple wooded slope. Where the climb levels off, ferns and brambles find habitat. A dark spruce plantation, aspen-ash woods, and an aisle of fragrant azalea in turn claim the way.

Atop Jones Hill, enter Labrador Hollow—a unique area (no camping, no fires)—rounding above the steep western slope. Faint side paths branch to the rim for obscure, seasonal views; keep to the orange trail to traverse the meadow gap of the hang-glider takeoff (1.5 miles). Open views pan the steep-sided north-south valley of oval Labrador Pond. Would-be hang gliders must secure a special permit from the DEC.

Follow the doubletrack south, descending the rim. On this poorly marked segment, keep an eye out for the foot trail heading left into the deciduous forest at 1.7 miles. The tour again flipflops between road and trail; keep left, continuing to descend.

The route contours and changes direction for a sharp descent to the gulf rim of Tinker Falls Creek (2.5 miles). The severity of the slope restricts views of the 50-foot falls, where droplet streams weep from an overhang. A few steps to the right, though, affords a look into the cliff bowl and gorge; the trail continues left. Do not approach the dangerous, sloughing edge or attempt any cross-country travel to gain a better falls perspective.

Cross Tinker Falls Creek just upstream from the overhang, for a steep angular ascent to a woods road; follow it left a few steps to pick up the foot trail on the right. The tour again alternates between foot trail and woods road as it ascends, curving away from the Tinker Falls drainage. Cross the nose of a ridge and descend through plantations of spruce and tamarack to cross Shackham Road at 4 miles.

Amid a conifer-hardwood forest, follow Shackham Brook upstream, crossing its footbridge. Just ahead white side trails travel either side of Enchanted Hollow; cross over the hollow to follow the second one, a woods road, upstream for unobstructed views and easier walking. A 0.2-mile round-trip detour finds a stepped cascade spilling over bedrock ledges.

Return downstream and resume the Onondaga Trail as it contours the hemlock-spruce slope, still following Shackham Brook upstream. Bypass a blue trail to the left. Before long the trail hooks left, now paralleling upstream along aptly named Hemlock Brook. Past an 8-foot waterfall and camp flat, reach a lean-to overlooking the steep-sided drainage (5 miles). Descend to and cross Hemlock Brook atop flat stones. The foot trail now angles sharply up the wooded slope.

Where the tour again follows a woods road, be alert for where the foot trail descends to the left; do not be confused by the orange snowmobile markers on the road straight ahead. The trail now dips through a steep side drainage and ascends to cross Morgan Hill Road at 6 miles.

Angle across the road, picking up the trail as it ascends. Stay to the orange-blazed route, as white trails branch left to the Morgan Hill bivouac area. Spruce wanes from the mix. Continue to watch for the Onondaga trail markers, as truck trail and snowmobile routes interweave the area. The tour passes amid plantation and mixed woods, with some big-diameter trees. At 7.3 miles traverse the breadth of an open utility corridor.

After crossing a lightly used truck trail (8 miles), the trail rolls and contours, crossing two more woods roads. Maple, beech, black cherry, and tamarack cloak the slope. The interval between blazes grows longer, but still frequent enough to reassure. Woodpecker, grouse, and deer may surprise.

At 8.8 miles the trail enters private property for the remainder of the tour. Uneven foot trail and overgrown jeep track lead the way. Watch for blazes as the trail descends through woods and bramble-fern patches, frequently changing direction. At 10 miles cross the first of two hollows. Here the brook pours over slate and shows a steep gorge downstream.

Ascend for a rolling tour along the hemlock-clad rim of the downstream gorge; watch your footing. The brook flows 80 to 100 feet below. Despite a few markers being down, the trail remains followable. Ahead the trail and drainage both bend left to reach Cardinal Hollow. Descend and cross this larger brook where wading may be required.

Turn upstream, cross a rocky side drainage, and ascend the slope to parallel Cardinal Hollow upstream. On woods road, ascend away from the hollow, then veer left descending via woods path to Spicer Falls, 11.7 miles. Best views of this two-stage, 60-foot waterfall come when autumn denudes the trees. Follow the drainage rim downstream to cross a stepladder stile over a fence. Descend and pass through a cow pasture, ending the tour at West Keeney Road (12 miles).

45 *WATKINS GLEN STATE PARK*

Overview

This park presents one of the premier gorge and waterfall tours in the Finger Lakes Region and in the country. Charged with excitement, the tour brings together majestic 200-foot cliffs, nineteen waterfalls punctuating a 545-foot drop of Glen Creek, turbulent chutes, deep plunge pools, and scenic bridges, tunnels, and twisting staircases.

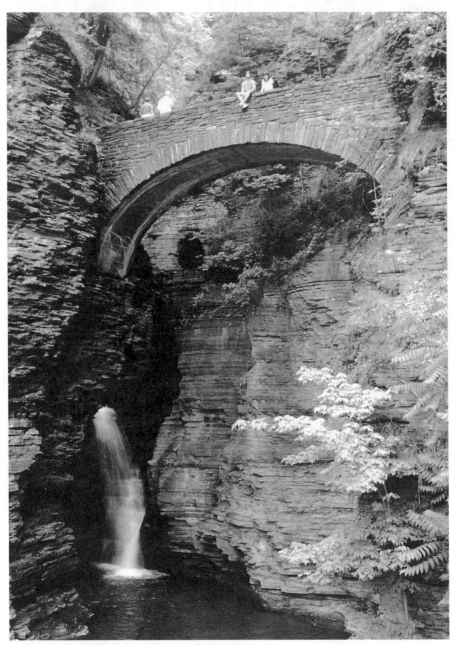

Sentry Bridge, Watkins Glen State Park.

General description: The north shore loop examines the gorge from within and above, while the south rim hike travels the wooded rim to an upstream manmade lake.

General location: In the village of Watkins Glen.

Special attractions: Waterfalls, cascades, chutes, and still-water calms; brooding cliffs; diverse woods.

Length: Gorge Trail-Indian Trail Loop, 2.8-mile loop; South Rim Hike, 3.5 miles round trip.

Elevation: The loop shows a 600-foot elevation change, South Rim about a 700-foot elevation change.

Difficulty: Easy to moderate.

Maps: State park brochure.

Special requirements: Fee parking; lot may fill at peak times. Beware, springs and waterfalls dampen the steps and walks.

Season and hours: Mid-May through November 10; daylight hours.

For information: New York State Parks, Finger Lakes Region.

Finding the trailhead: In Watkins Glen, find the park entrance west off Franklin Avenue/New York 14, south of 4th Street.

The hikes: If a trail choice must be made, make it the **Gorge Trail.** A shuttle bus runs between the lower concession and upper entrance for those who have time for just a one-way tour and for those who choose to descend rather than ascend the trail's 832 steps; purchase tickets at the gift shop.

The bustle at the park entry echoes the site's roots as a private resort in the late 1800s. Off-hour, off-season, and rainy day visits allow for a quieter, unhurried communion with the gorge grandeur. An upstream tour starts at the west end of the parking lot; bring plenty of film.

Early looks feature the stone arch of Sentry Bridge and bulging canyon walls shaping a keyhole view of a falls recessed in the shadows. The trail now ascends the first of three tunnels bored into the rock, coming out at Sentry Bridge for an up-canyon view of the pinched gorge, long-distance views at Watkins Glen, and close looks at the jointed layered rock. The tour crisscrosses Glen Creek four times.

At 0.1 mile the Finger Lakes Trail (South Rim Hike) heads left; remain in the gorge, skirting the Timespell laser show setup. As the trail ascends the stairs to Cavern Cascade, look down to see a heart-shaped plunge pool. Now pass behind the droplet curtain for a unique perspective; ahead lies the Spiral Tunnel staircase, which opens to a view of the suspension bridge. Keep to the gorge passing under the bridge.

As the canyon walls cup and divide, each bend holds an aura of mystery. A leafy bower claims the Narrows, while a dry, concave bowing of the gorge characterizes the "Cathedral." A tiered upstream cascade feeds the 60-foot plunge of Central Cascade, the highest in the park. At 0.7 mile Rainbow Falls showers over the south rim. Beyond lies a bridge and Spiral Gorge, a darker, more brooding passage.

WATKINS GLEN STATE PARK

To Chequaga Falls

14

Village of Watkins Glen

To Geneva

Gift Shop

Sentry Bridge

Cavern Cascade

Point Lookout

Central Cascade

329

Indian Trail

Gorge Trail

Rainbow Falls

Mile Bridge

South Rim Trail

0.5

0.25

Miles

0

Jacob's Ladder

To Watkins Glen

409

Glen Creek

To 329

Punch Bowl Lake

329

To Townsend

N

The trail returns to the glaring light at Mile Point Bridge. Continue west along the north wall, bypassing both the bridge and a trail to the right. Amid the calm above the lower-canyon storm, ascend the stairs of Jacob's Ladder to Indian Trail (the loop's return) and upper entrance (1.5 miles).

Look for the **Indian Trail** to head right just beyond a midway bench on Jacob's Ladder. A low rock wall or mesh fence edges the broad trail as it tours the north rim and slope. Evergreens, dogwood, oak, maple, beech, sassafras, and black cherry contribute to a forest roster concealing Glen Creek.

At 1.8 miles the spur from Mile Point Bridge arrives on the right; at 2 miles the trail overlooks Rainbow Falls. Staying along the rim, find a Central Cascade overlook for a totally new perspective. The trail then skirts a cemetery and descends sharply, bypassing a lean-to, to reach the suspension bridge. Lovers Lane arrives on the right; continue straight ahead (east) to Point Lookout and the park entrance.

A detour onto the bridge provides a grand look 85 feet down to the creek and out the canyon, while Point Lookout offers a fine cross-gorge view. Descend the stairs meeting the Gorge Trail at Spiral Tunnel and retrace the first 0.25 mile.

The **South Rim Hike** shares the first 0.1 mile with the Gorge Trail. After crossing Sentry Bridge, veer left on the Finger Lakes Trail (FLT), ascending some one hundred steps to the south rim. Turn right on the service road, following the white blazes of the FLT. At 0.25 mile find a tiny lily pond, topped by just a few blooms. Ahead, stone pedestal and disk slab tables mark a forlorn recreation site.

Bear right, ascending the chestnut oak and hemlock rim, bypassing spurs to the south entrance and much later the campground. At 0.75 mile a lean-to presides next to the trail; upstream from the lean-to, a stairway descends to the gorge. For much of this tour, appreciation of the gorge is audio rather than visual.

Follow the wide trail ahead at 1.2 miles, passing under a scenic railroad bridge where a robust deciduous vegetation interweaves the rusting trestle. Pine, cherry, hickory, and ash briefly frame the tour. As the trail veers toward the rim, a ragged vertical outcrop attracts attention.

The trail next rounds the nose of a hemlock-shaded point for filtered looks at Glen Creek. Stay the white blazes, descending in spurts to Punch Bowl Lake (1.75 miles). Overlook the dam and its vertical falls and then dip to where beaver gnawings dot the lakeshore. Bullfrog, cedar waxwing, and red-winged blackbird animate the site. Marsh grasses claim the upper lake, while cattail peninsulas extend to the open water. Much of the pond shows aquatic plants. At the site, picnic tables remain usable but a restroom facility has collapsed.

Return as you came or follow the FLT upstream.

Overview

Buttermilk Falls caps a dramatic 500-foot freefall of Buttermilk Creek that occurs over a distance of 0.75 mile. Cascades, rapids, bedrock slides, emerald pools, platy cliffs, and a 40-foot spire rock comprise the prized setting.

General description: Easy interlocking trails explore the Buttermilk Creek gorge, its upstream glen, and Treman Lake, while a first-rate interpretive loop examines a unique marsh.

General location: Southern outskirts of Ithaca.

Special attractions: Buttermilk Falls and Creek, upland forest, marsh, scenic rockwork dam, wildlife sightings.

Length: Gorge-Rim Loop, 1.7-mile loop; Bear Trail-Treman Lake Loop, 3.5 miles round trip; Larch Meadows Trail, 1-mile loop.

Elevation: Gorge-Rim Loop shows a 500-foot elevation change; Bear Trail-Treman Lake Loop, a 150-foot elevation change; Larch Meadows, virtually flat.

Difficulty: Easy.

Maps: State park brochure; Larch Meadows Trail brochure.

Falls on Buttermilk Creek, Buttermilk Falls State Park.

Special requirements: Fee area. Wear repellent in meadows.
Season and hours: Spring through fall (gorge trails close November 10); daylight hours.
For information: New York State Parks, Finger Lakes Region.
Finding the trailhead: From the junction of New York 79 and New York 13/34 (the corner of Seneca and Meadow streets) in southwest Ithaca, go south on NY 13/34 for 1.8 miles and turn left to enter the main area of Buttermilk Falls State Park. For the upper area, continue 0.1 mile farther south on NY 13/34 and turn left (east) on Sandbank Road. Go 2.2 miles and turn left on West King Road. In 1.2 miles turn right on the park road to reach the upper day-use area in 0.8 mile.

The hikes: In the main area, find the popular **Gorge-Rim Loop** near the swimming hole at the base of Buttermilk Falls. Cross the dam and ascend along the south wall. Broad Buttermilk Falls sheets over a magnificent canted cliff sloping to the manmade pool. Crossbeds accent the light-colored rock, and small ledges fold the waters into cascades.

A steep stairway ascends alongside the falls, isolating aspects of the watery spectacle. Beech, hemlock, and a burst of understory greenery contribute to a tour. Prior to reaching the upper level of the falls, the stairs turn away. At 0.2 mile a three-tier, three-dimensional falls graces the creek. One level spills through a grotto, where the gorge walls pinch together; some ten falls accent this tour.

Cascades, historic plunge pools, eroded cliff scallops, and hemlock coves delight. The trail affords perspectives from below, alongside, and atop the cascades. A lean-to lies uphill to the right just prior to a crescent footbridge at 0.5 mile that crosses Buttermilk Creek to the north wall and Rim Trail. Stay along the south wall for the full 1.7-mile loop.

A ribbony side falls washes over the cliff, as a split-level hourglass falls punctuates the creek. Next find Pinnacle Rock, a 40-foot chiseled gray spire isolated from the cliff; delicate ferns decorate the erosion-resistant ledges. Maple, ash, and basswood shade the trail as it nears West King Road (0.8 mile).

Here Bear Trail continues upstream on the south shore. For the Gorge-Rim Loop alone, cross the road bridge and turn left on the Rim Trail, a wide dirt lane isolated from the edge by a wire-mesh fence. Past an overlook of Pinnacle Rock, the trail gently descends. At 1.1 miles the side trail arrives from the creek; views are few and short-lived.

As the descent steepens, the trail shows a paved surface, and the corridor grows more open. Beyond Buttermilk Falls Overlook (a filtered view), the trail descends and contours the slope above the campground road to exit at the refreshment stand.

For a longer creek tour, delay taking the rim return at 0.8 mile; instead follow the **Bear Trail** upstream to **Treman Lake Loop**. Bear Trail travels the broad wooded glen upstream, passing some 40-feet away from the stream. Hemlock, basswood, maple, oak, and beech shade a plush, green

BUTTERMILK FALLS STATE PARK

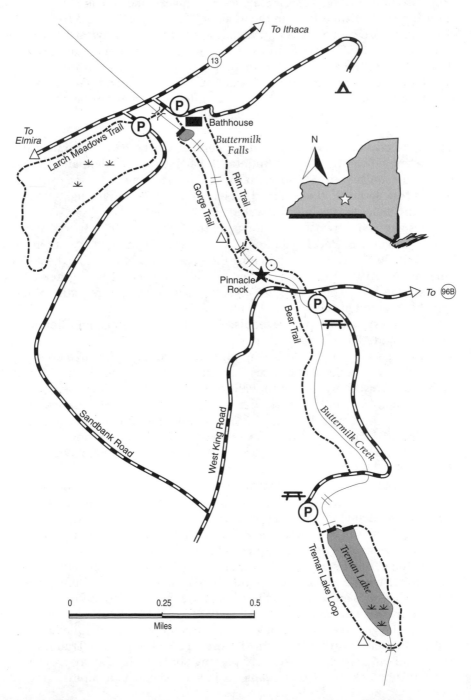

0   0.25   0.5

Miles

understory. Side trails descend to the bank, while skunk cabbage claims the moist slopes. In 0.75 mile (1.55 miles), the trail comes out at a picnic area. Continue upstream along the creek, or follow the road to the site's comfort station, where the Treman Lake Loop starts.

A counterclockwise tour stays along the south shore bypassing the dam and spillway feeding the picnic area falls. The tour continues amid the mixed deciduous-hemlock forest; cross-lake views find an attractive cliff scallop and cove. The trail ascends drawing 100 feet above the water. Geese occupy a small island.

Cross a side-drainage footbridge and round the upper marshy head of Treman Lake, bypassing an orange-blazed trail near a second lean-to. Next, cross the scenic stone bridge over Buttermilk Creek to travel the north shore, closing the loop; stay low along the rock wall leaving the bridge.

Stairsteps ascend a knoll for an overlook of the lake's cattail waters before the trail returns to shore. Sunfish guarding their gravel-cleared nests or a snapping turtle may delay hiker's strides. Beware of poison ivy along shore.

Another set of stairs leads to a second vista featuring the attractive stonework and natural cliff outcrop that form the dam's curvature. Continue rounding the lake, staying left to cross the stone dam and outcrop to close the loop. The trail returns to the comfort station at 2.6 miles (3.4 miles), to West King Road at 3.5 miles (4.3 miles), and to the lower park via the Rim Trail (5.2 miles).

Start the **Larch Meadows Trail** next to the ballfield restroom, 0.1 mile south of the main entrance off Sandbank Road. A fine brochure (available at the entrance station or trailhead) explains this unique habitat, part of ancient Cayuga Lake.

Until 1779 this site held a Sapony Indian village comprised of log cabins. That year, during the Revolutionary War, word of the advance of the Sullivan Campaign forced the tribe to flee their village. When the troops later overtook the site, they torched all the cabins, ending an era.

For the hike, follow the southern edge of the ballfield, bearing left prior to the end of the field on a wide mowed swath. The trail tours habitats of mixed woods; skunk cabbage wetland; stands of willow and spreading black walnut; and waist-high ferns, grasses, and wildflowers. Passing a 4-foot-diameter sycamore, the trail meets and briefly follows a service road to the right. The trail then resumes to the right, returning to the ballfield to close the loop.

CENTRAL-LEATHERSTOCKING REGION

Squeezed amid the Adirondacks, the Catskills, and the Finger Lakes Region, this region occupies the belt buckle of the state and celebrates the countryside made famous by James Fenimore Cooper. The region boasts shining lakes, forested ridges, swamps, fields, caverns, and caves. A section of the original Erie Canal channels hikers through the past. A tranquil pastoral setting claims the outlying territory.

47 OLD ERIE CANAL HERITAGE TRAIL

General description: This multi-use national recreation trail travels the towpath of the Erie Canal between DeWitt and Rome, passing museums, parks, and historic structures.

General location: East of Syracuse.

Special attractions: Historic canal, towpath, aqueducts, culverts, and cannery ruins; trailside museums; Green Lakes State Park; wildflowers; and wildlife sightings.

Length: 36 miles one way, with a 2.2-mile interruption between Durhamville and State Bridge (New York 46 and New York 31); the tour thrice requires road travel to bridge towpath units.

Elevation: The flat trail travels at an elevation of 425 feet.

Difficulty: Easy.

Maps: State park flier.

Special requirements: Pick up a flier for Old Erie Canal for both its map and mileage log. Wash after any contact with the canal waters. Find restrooms and drinking water at Cedar Bay and Poolsbrook picnic areas and at Green Lakes State Park. Tour fees collected at museums and at Erie Canal Village.

Season and hours: Year-round, dawn to dusk.

For information: New York State Parks, Central Region.

Finding the trailhead: From Interstate 481 in East Syracuse, take exit 3E for New York 5/New York 92 and go east toward Fayetteville. In 0.8 mile, where NY 5 and NY 92 split, go north (left) on Lyndon Road for 0.8 mile, bearing left on Kinne Road. Go 0.4 mile and turn right on Butternut Drive to find Ryder Park and the western trail terminus on the right in 0.1 mile. Find the eastern terminus west of Rome, off NY 46.

The hike: This linear New York State Park salutes a 36-mile vestige of the historic 363-mile Erie Canal, which linked the Atlantic Ocean and Great Lakes, opening the West to transportation and commerce—a great boon to nineteenth-century New York State and one of the great engineering feats

Stonework arches, Old Erie Heritage Canal State Park.

of the day. The trail follows the old towpath plodded by the barge-towing mules from 1825 to 1918.

The trail variously shows cinders or a natural surface. Footbridges at Cedar Bay and Poolsbrook picnic areas, at Green Lakes State Park, and opposite the Fayetteville side canal allow passage between the north and south shore for the western end of the tour. Road bridges serve the eastern end.

Virginia creeper, poison ivy, and wild grape entangle the diverse tree border of maple, locust, box elder, elm, ash, sumac, black willow, dogwood, honeysuckle, and Japanese barberry. Queen Anne's lace, chickory, purple loosestrife, dandelion, and spotted knapweed color the towpath sides.

For the most part, the corridor remains undeveloped, with a few encroaching residences where the trail nears towns. Parallel roadways sometimes add noise, but mostly the hike brings relaxation, following the straightaways and gentle bends of the canal. Woodchuck, painted and snapping turtle, kingfisher, yellow warbler, rough-winged swallow (that nest in the unmortared stonework), blue-gill, and carp share the canalway.

On a west-to-east tour from Ryder Park Nature Area in DeWitt to the out-skirts of Rome, find mileage markers and crossroad labels regularly marking the distance; these travel aids wane by later miles. A 6-foot-wide cinder trail crosses over Butternut Creek for overlooks of the cut stones and concrete of a lateral aqueduct. Frog and turtle hide amid the algae, while carp part the murky water. A cattail marsh lies beyond the trees to the left, as the route rounds the bald hill of a former landfill to reach the northern towpath.

Cross under the rustic steel footbridge that leads to Cedar Bay Picnic Area on the south shore, bypassing the Canal Center. Despite the building having been closed now for several years, the grounds still hold an old tow hoist and watering basin from the canal days and a memorial honoring Moses DeWitt (1766 to 1794).

The tour now slips into character with areas of intermittent and full shade and uninterrupted overlooks of the canal. Where the Erie Canal widens into a pond beyond Burdick Street, a side canal paired with its own tow-path trail arrives from Fayetteville; a footbridge ties this spur to the national recreation trail. Notice the big cut stones of the side canal.

From Manlius Center at 3 miles, a sparsity of trees makes for a hot passage, while an old barn alongside the trail hints at the rural canal set-ting. From the footbridge to Green Lakes State Park (4.6 miles), a 0.2-mile service road ascends to a New York 290 crossing. With the park facilities located well south of the highway, plan on a mile detour for drinking wa-ter and restrooms, but the park invites with two deep lakes.

At Kirkville Road, a couple of picnic tables and a small lawn invite a stop and offer fine looks at the canal rockwork. The water shows but minimal movement, hinting at the original need for the towpath to move the barges from point to point. Cross-canal views find an unruly growth of trees and shrubs isolating the corridor. Generally, the canal channels with it a refreshing breeze.

OLD ERIE CANAL HERITAGE TRAIL

Past Poolsbrook Road (7.3 miles), the corridor again becomes more sun exposed; at the road crossings, the towpath typically opens up. As the canal widens to a pond, cross-canal views find scenic Poolsbrook Picnic Area with its park benches and tables shaded by scenic willow and apple trees. Where the canal again narrows, a footbridge crosses to the picnic area.

A small trailhead parking lot serves towpath travelers at White Bridge Road (8.6 miles). The corridor itself remains little changed, as the dense leafy border of the far shore continues. Past Bolivar Road, a scenic gape-board barn and a silo overlook the towpath.

At Lakeport Road (10.9 miles) search the southwest corner of the canal to find an old cannery ruins; cross the road bridge to reach the Chittenango Landing Canal Boat Museum (open daily 10 a.m. to 4 p.m. July and August; irregular hours other months). The site includes both indoor and outdoor exhibits, with three original dry dock bays being rebuilt with the original stone, replica sawmill and blacksmith buildings, and a mule-drawn steamboat and fine pictorial history.

The towpath narrows approaching and leaving Canaseraga Road at 12.5 miles. Hayfields and cornfields add to the serenity of the tour. East of Fuller's Bridge, cross from the northern towpath to the south shore at West Shore Railroad (14.9 miles). Where the trail meets Bebee Bridge Road, turn north (left), cross the bridge, and continue east along the northern towpath.

At 16.4 miles the canal parallels State Street into Canastota, as the towpath now becomes a residential greenway. At Buck Street, the towpath disappears; follow Canal Street east 0.3 mile, picking up the towpath past New York 13. On the north side of Canal Street, look for the Canastota Canal Museum, which houses canal artifacts and photos in a building on the National Register of Historic Places, circa 1874.

Where the towpath halts at North Court Road (19.5 miles), bear left, angling across the road to again pick up the northern towpath at the edge of a cornfield. Canal Road maintains a parallel course, the area remains rural, and more waterflow constructions mark the tour. By Cobb Street, leafy trees overlace the route for a scenic stroll.

At 22.3 miles the trail detours from the towpath for 0.3 mile, crossing Interstate 90 on an overpass. Afterward, the towpath resumes only briefly before reaching the 2.2-mile travel gap at Durhamville (22.4 miles). End the tour here or pick up the trail on the north side of NY 31 at State Bridge. Another 11.4 miles of the tour remain, passing through the rural countryside first on the southern towpath, crossing to the northern towpath at Lock 21 (31 miles), but the closeness of NY 46 intrudes.

October through April, hikers may take the tour all the way east to the privately owned Erie Canal Village off NY 46, a re-created canal-era community. May through September, when the village closes its section of towpath for its mule-drawn canal boat tours, end the hike at Fort Bull Road (35 miles).

General description: This Beaver Creek State Forest circuit travels the wooded and meadow outskirts of Brookfield Swamp.

General location: In southeast Madison County, 1 mile north of Brookfield.

Special attractions: Hemlock-hardwood forest and conifer plantation, spring and summer wildflowers, wildlife sightings.

Length: 9.5-mile loop.

Elevation: The trail shows about a 200-foot elevation change.

Difficulty: Easy to moderate.

Maps: Brookfield Trail System brochure.

Special requirements: None.

Season and hours: Spring through fall.

Beaver Creek and Brookfield Swamp, Beaver Creek State Forest.

For information: New York State Department of Environmental Conservation, Region 7.

Finding the trailhead: From the junction of Fairground Road and Main Street (Skaneateles Turnpike) in Brookfield, go north on Fairground Road for 1 mile to find trailhead parking on the left. Arriving from U.S. Highway 20, turn south on Bliven Road between Bridgewater and Sangerfield, coming to a Y-junction in 1.4 miles. Bear left on Fairground Road and continue 3 miles to find the trailhead on the right. Parking for five vehicles.

The hike: Part of an extensive 130-mile trail system serving foot, horse, and snowmobile travelers, this well-marked circuit stays primarily on trail and closed woods roads linked by two short truck-trail segments open to vehicles, maximum speed 25 miles per hour. The rolling trail rarely comes in contact with Brookfield Swamp, centerpiece of the tour.

Hike the gravel track west from the parking lot for a clockwise tour. Scarlet tanager, woodchuck, and rabbit may number among the early wildlife sightings. Birch, alder, and shrubby deciduous frame the open trail. Keep to the gravel path, crossing the horsebridge over Beaver Creek; high railings protect horse and rider.

Pause on the bridge for the best view of Brookfield Swamp. Far-stretching views north and a more restricted view south present the attractive marsh. Dark-flowing Beaver Creek meanders through the broad swamp bottom, framed in turn by bog grass, wetland shrubs, and trees. Lilies and other aquatics decorate the shallow edge, and dragonflies buzz the surface.

A mowed swath continues the tour, with a scenic row of maple and black cherry trees toward the swamp, a tidy pine plantation to the left. Rock walls sometimes border the route, while wild strawberries offer tasty bites in June.

At the 0.8-mile junction turn right to traverse a low hemlock-clad ridge, for a cool, shady passage. Oxalis and Mayflower decorate the floor. Descending the ridge, cross a small drainage dotted with false hellebore. An aspen stand and spruce plantation now vary the walk. Amid the long grassy meadows dotted by pine and aspen, keep an eye out for turkeys. Occasional engine sounds precede the crossing of Beaver Creek Road (2.2 miles) and the start of a truck-trail segment. Travel the semi-shaded dirt road uphill, bypassing a connector to the greater Brookfield Trail System on the left at 2.4 miles. At 2.7 miles turn left, entering the woods, bypassing a small rock-lined pond built for fire protection in the 1930s. Descend and cross a side brook below the rock ruins of an old dam, and follow the levee to the right (downstream) along an old ditch.

Crossing back over Beaver Creek Road, follow the Glenn Bacon Trail, a mowed swath touring an open meadow corridor, with full-skirted spruce, woody shrubs, hawkweed, daisy, buttercup, and various floral stalks. Before long the trail ascends sharply and steadily through mixed forest, then levels to traverse another long meadow, coming to a tribute

BROOKFIELD SWAMP LOOP

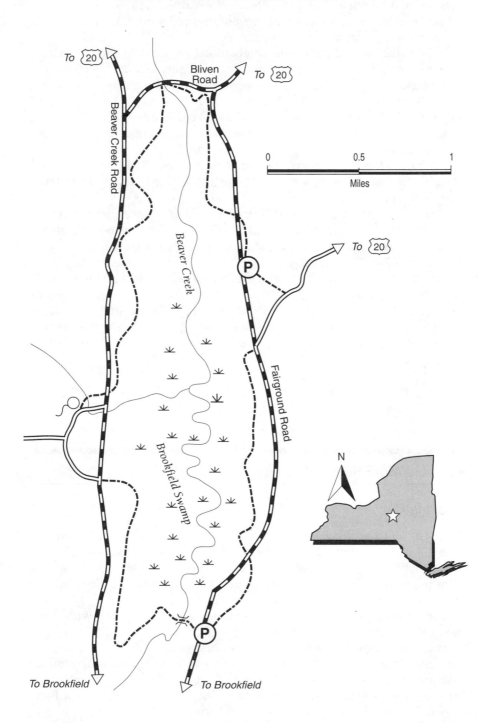

to Glenn Bacon, a horseman who advanced recreational opportunities in the area. A bench and picnic table overlook Brookfield Swamp and the wooded east ridge—a textured tapestry of mottled wetland, shrubs, leafy trees, and sharp plantation outlines.

Stay on the mowed track, alternately touring open field and spruce corridor. As the tour can be hot and humid, carry plenty of water. A bandanna for the head and insect repellent bring some tranquility during bug season. The trail rolls as it approaches Bliven Road for a road-bridge crossing of Beaver Creek (5.2 miles). A few rural homes come into view.

On the opposite shore, the trail passes between meadow and plantation. Amid the mixed woods at 5.9 miles, a regal 4- to 5-foot-diameter white pine presides trailside. Soon the trail crosses Fairground Road, touring amid meadow and tamarack, bypassing the primary trailhead for equestrian users at 6.4 miles.

Remain on the east side of Fairground Road, ascending a grassy doubletrack amid a cedar-hardwood forest. The trail tops out meeting a truck trail at 6.9 miles; turn right, staying on the truck trail descending to Fairground Road (7.5 miles).

Angle left across the road and descend via foot trail, passing through meadow and crossing drainages. Past the tamarack seed orchard, a spruce corridor claims the tour. At 9 miles, again cross Fairground Road for a brief swing along the wooded east slope, coming out opposite the parking area; cross the road and close the loop.

49 GLIMMERGLASS STATE PARK

Overview

In the heart of James Fenimore Cooper country, the wooded flank of Mount Wellington and the field, shrub, and woodland habitats of this state park provide an understated setting for Hyde Bay on Otsego Lake—the "glimmerglass" jewel of the area. Amidst this soothing backdrop, hikers enjoy short outings and subtle discoveries.

General description: Casual hikes explore lake cove, pond, woodland, and field habitats.

General location: 8 miles north of Cooperstown.

Special attractions: Historic estate, bird watching, spring and summer wildflowers, fall foliage.

Length: Otsego Lake-Mount Wellington Hike, 3.5-mile loop; Beaver Pond to Woodland-Field Loop, 2.2 miles round trip.

Hyde Hall, Glimmerglass State Park.

Elevation: The Otsego Lake-Mount Wellington Hike shows a 500-foot elevation change; the other is flat.
Difficulty: Easy.
Maps: State park brochure.
Special requirements: Fee area.
Season and hours: Spring through fall.
For information: New York State Parks, Central Region.
Finding the trailhead: From U.S. Highway 20 in East Springfield, turn south on Otsego County 31, following the signs for Glimmerglass State Park. In 3.9 miles turn right (west) to enter the park. From Cooperstown go 8 miles north on County 31 to reach the turn for the park entrance.

The hikes: For the **Otsego Lake-Mount Wellington Hike**, from the parking area west of Hyde Hall Mansion, at the end of the public road, walk the closed service road west. A tight array of thin trees and big white pines choke out early Hyde Bay-Otsego Lake views.

At 0.2 mile look for a roadside post and orange banding on the trees, the start of the Mount Wellington Trail, but delay taking it. Stay on the service road to complete the lake loop first. In 100 feet, a gap offers an open view of the lake with the attractive serial ridges beyond. The lake's sparkle inspired James Fenimore Cooper to dub it "Glimmerglass" in his popular tales about a frontier hero, "the Leatherstocking."

Where the service road forks, go left for a clockwise tour, rounding above the lake shore. Morning sightings of deer add to a tour; lake views remain filtered. The loop's return travels slightly higher up the slope, passing amid hemlock, birch, waterleaf, ferns, and a few reeds.

Return to the roadside post (0.9 mile) and follow the orange route up the flank of Mount Wellington. The trail ascends the broad back of a side ridge for a comfortable tour. Mixed-age evergreens and hardwoods weave a high, full, and restless canopy. Where the ridge flattens, ferns grace the slope. Again, deer may be spied.

After a brief dip the ridge again flattens before rounding the upper edge of the wooded slope, reaching a lake overview (1.7 miles). In summer, trees filter much of the view. The trail now arcs back along the broad summit; moister areas hold distinct pockets of at least four varieties of fern. Bold displays of five-finger fern particularly delight.

At 2.2 miles arrows point where the trail departs the plateau to contour downhill; still the big-diameter trees engage. In 0.5 mile the trail enters the sharpest descent of the tour. At 3 miles turn left along a utility corridor. Beware of the animal burrows masked by the tall grasses, and watch for the next blaze that points downhill to the right.

Descend through a dense patch of big-leafed plants, reach the service road, and turn right, following the road between the twin gate cottages and beneath the domed arch of Tin Top. Cross the grounds of Hyde Hall Mansion, formerly owned by Lieutenant George Clarke (a New York State governor from 1736 to 1744) and return to the parking area. The mansion, a dignified stone-block manor, is open for guided tours summer weekends or by appointment.

For **Beaver Pond to Woodland-Field Loop**, begin at the parking lot for the Beaver Pond Trail, reached opposite the entry to the park's main beach. The hike starts on the gated service road east of the lean-to, next to a privy. But first, admire the shallow pond from the parking area, as a thick shrub border completely isolates it from the trail.

A mowed swath with stonedust added allows for wheelchair access, as the trail curves right, rounding between some picnic sites. The trail next travels the shrub-lined corridor between meadow and pond. Hawkweed, iris, buttercup, and clover sprinkle color. In winter the trail doubles as a cross-country ski trail.

At the Y-junction (0.4 mile) go left for the Woodland-Field Loop, now traversing a tall-grass field; the tour no longer is wheelchair-accessible. Pass through the Shadow Brook covered bridge (another remaining estate structure), and take the first left for a clockwise tour of the outer woodland-field circuit. Swallows nest in the bridge rafters; views of Shadow Brook quickly vanish.

The trail passes through an open transition zone between field and woods; along the outer park, view the rural neighborhood. At 1 mile briefly enter a woodland pocket of big oaks, well worth slowing to get to

GLIMMERGLASS STATE PARK

know. At the upcoming junction keep left; at the 1.2-mile junction, turn right. A left at 1.2 miles leads to the headquarters.

The trail, now a doubletrack, passes amid a gallery of magnificent old maples. Where the doubletrack bears right, continue straight on the mowed track, soon traveling amid a young succession forest. Return to the covered bridge at 1.6 miles and retrace Beaver Pond Trail to the trailhead.

Overview

A quiet wooded setting, gentle terrain, and 35-acre Bowman Lake are the hallmarks of this state park. Bordered by 11,000 acres of state forest land, the park contributes to a broad open space for wildlife and a tranquil arena for hikers. The long-distance Finger Lakes Trail (FLT) passes through the park, and a fine nature trail encircles the lake.

General description: A pair of well-marked, rolling walks journey through natural hardwood stands and conifer plantations to visit a fire tower and explore the lake basin.

General location: 8 miles northwest of Oxford.

Special attractions: Lake setting, diverse hardwood forests, scenic rock walls, fire-tower access, bird watching.

Length: FLT to Berry Hill Fire Tower, 5.6 miles round trip; Nature Trail, 1.3-mile loop.

Elevation: The FLT to Berry Hill Fire Tower shows a 360-foot elevation change, the Nature Trail a 100-foot change.

Difficulty: Easy.

Maps: State park brochure; Finger Lakes Trail Conference map, Sheet M24.

Special requirements: Fee area. Expect some soggy stretches.

Season and hours: Spring through fall, daylight hours. Nature Center: Friday evenings and weekends, during summer.

For information: New York State Parks, Central Region.

Finding the trailhead: From the junction of New York 12 and New York 220 at the village green in Oxford, go 6 miles west on NY 220 and turn right (north) on Steere Road. In 1.4 miles, find the park entrance on the left.

The hikes: To hike the **FLT to Berry Hill Fire Tower**, follow the signs through the park for "beach parking" and start at the northwest corner of the northernmost parking area. Look for the white blazes of the FLT heading north (right).

Pass through woods, quickly meeting the park road. There turn left on a wide grassy swath to reach an FLT destination sign; bear right per the sign for Berry Hill Fire Tower. The trail travels a rich woods of hemlock, maple, yellow birch, and black cherry, following the small inlet brook upstream. Abundant lady fern, Mayflower, oxalis, and club mosses create a vibrant contrast to the leaf mat elsewhere. Patterned fungi riddle logs and snags. Mouse and woodpecker share the woods.

Small meadows of fern, false hellebore, grasses, moss, and forget-me-not enshroud the springs, while muddy pockets record the tracks of last night's wildlife. Amid an area of pines, bypass a tree-painted mileage notice, remnant rock walls, and a trail register.

Berry Hill Fire Tower.

BOWMAN LAKE STATE PARK

Berry Hill
Fire Tower

P

To East Pharsalia

0   0.25   0.5

Miles

N

Tower Road

Finger Lakes Trail

To East Pharsalia

Preston Road

*To
Norwich*

Steere Road

P

Bowman Lake

Nature
Center

P

Park   Road

*To
Norwich*

To Oxford

Ahead, a forest lane lined by big maple and black cherry gives way to
a rolling tour through natural and planted woods. Cross over Preston Road
and through a rock-wall egress for a scenic straightaway through fern-lined
plantation. Gradually, the forest includes more hardwoods, with maple
and ash dominating the wetter areas.

At 1.8 miles cross gravel Tower Road, touring a red pine plantation;
some of the plots show tidy rows. At 2.25 miles, the FLT returns to Tower

Road, following it to the right. Skirt a field and turn left on the side road at 2.6 miles to reach the fire tower and rustic cabin atop grassy Berry Hill.

The public may ascend the six-story tower, but the upper loft remains closed. Still the perch affords a fine overview of its south-central New York neighborhood, a landscape of low ridges, rolling fields, and wooded hills. Wild strawberries atop the hill suggest the site's name. Return as you came.

The red-marked **Nature Trail** starts at the nature center; look for a trail sign on the building's northwest corner. The trail heads north through the mixed forest of the developed park for a counterclockwise tour, thrice crossing park roads. Expect rocks, roots, and soggy stretches; rangers recommend hikers inquire about trail conditions before starting.

In 0.2 mile skirt the western edge of the northern parking lot for the beach. Where the trail overlooks Bowman Lake, springtime hikers spy Canada geese and their trailing young. At the northwest corner of the parking area the red trail curves west into the woods, as red squirrels chide from the treetops.

Hemlock and tall deciduous trees weave a rich shade, while small drainages thread the woods. Bypass some picnic sites and cross a foot-bridge over the rocky inlet; birch, ash, and beech favor this wetter site. At 0.5 mile reach a cattail shore where remnant footboards hint at a former interpretive site. Views still present the marshy shore, semi-submerged bullfrogs, and maple-willow edge, as well as length-of-the-lake views at the earthen levee.

Ascend steeply from the lake and pass a remnant stone wall, touring amid congested spruce and moist meadow habitats. Woods roads briefly continue the tour, before the marked trail climbs and contours the wooded west slope. Upon descent, turn right on a woods road, rounding the lake. At 1.1 miles a footpath travels even closer to shore.

Bullfrogs, sunfish fiercely protecting their cleared-gravel nests, and tadpoles animate the water, while a few irises grow along the levee shore. From the levee, signs point uphill to the right. Skirt the picnic area and return to the nature center (1.3 miles).

CAPITAL-SARATOGA REGION

At this east-central New York region, with the capital complex at its core, hikers can retrace the march of the British in 1777; explore Helderberg Escarpment; visit field, forest, and wetland habitats; and venture to the Taconic Crest. Five major rivers thread through the region, and vistas sweep the Mohawk and Hudson valleys, the Adirondacks, Massachusetts, and Vermont. The region offers quiet nature strolls and vigorous hikes, with a range of tours in between.

Cannon, Saratoga National Historic Park.

51 WILKINSON NATIONAL RECREATION TRAIL

General description: An interpretive loop through fields and woods retraces the British march and visits sites where fortifications stood and battles raged during the Revolutionary War.

General location: Saratoga National Historic Park, 30 miles north of Albany.

Special attractions: Historical sites, interpretive boards, mixed woods, untamed fields, wildflowers, wildlife.

Length: 4.8 miles round trip, including Freeman Loop.

Elevation: The trail shows a 150-foot elevation change.

Difficulty: Easy to moderate.

Maps: Wilkinson Trail flier.

Special requirements: The park collects a nominal per-person fee from hikers; a per-vehicle fee for the auto tour. Upon payment, receive a trail pass good for seven days; keep it with you while hiking. Request a trail flier, which contains the map and corresponding descriptions to the lettered interpretive stations. The park service encourages hikers to wear bright colors October through November. Carry plenty of water.

Season and hours: Early April through November. Grounds open sunrise to sunset; visitor center: 9 a.m. to 5 p.m.

For information: Saratoga National Historic Park.

Finding the trailhead: From Troy, go 17.5 miles north on U.S. Highway 4 and turn left (west) to reach the Saratoga National Historic Park access road. Go 2.3 miles to the visitor center.

From New York State Thruway Interstate 87 south of Saratoga Springs, take exit 12 and follow the well-marked route to the park. It travels New York 67 east, U.S. Highway 9 north, New York 9P east, New York 423 east, and New York 32 north to enter the park in 12 miles; be alert for the frequent turns.

The hike: The two Battles of Saratoga fought in the fall of 1777 marked the turning point in the American Revolutionary War. Colonist victories over the British in this key area along the Hudson River convinced the French that the Americans could prevail. When France then declared war on Great Britain, the tide turned toward American independence. This national recreation trail (NRT) revisits those crucial battle scenes.

Exit the back door of the visitor center and turn right, bypassing cannons and memorials, crossing the lawn to reach the trail kiosk in 500 feet. Hike past the kiosk coming to a junction and interpretive post A; bear left for the trail. White stakes with a "WT" for the Wilkinson Trail clarify junctions; such stakes also identify the interpretive sites.

The wide mowed track passes through a shrubby transition habitat; woods of planted pine, maple, oak, aspen, and fruit trees; and rolling untamed fields of thigh-high grasses and wildflowers. Islands of trees typically spot the fields. The National Park Service (NPS) manages the property to communicate the look of the land during the campaign of 1777. Only a few rooftops break the spell.

Downy woodpeckers telegraph their locations in the woods, while songbirds spread cheer in the field. The NRT occasionally crosses a horse trail and slips across the auto-tour route four times.

At 0.6 mile a spur to the left leads to Stop 7 on the auto tour. Follow it to Breymann's Redoubt, converging on a paved walk to find interpretive boards, a pair of cannons, and posts outlining the site of the German breastwork, a crude log barrier that measured 200 yards long and 7 feet high that secured the British right flank.

Despite this defense, colonists overwhelmed the site, driving off the Crown Forces on October 7, 1777. Bear right on a paved lane descending from the redoubt to find the Boot Monument, a tribute to Benedict Arnold who received a leg wound while distinguishing himself in the fray.

Return to the Wilkinson Trail and turn left, reaching the loop junction and post C (0.9 mile); go left for a clockwise tour. Aster, Queen Anne's lace, golden rod, and spotted knapweed interweave the autumn fields. Crossing the tour road for the first time (1.1 miles), pass through a pine corridor, soon

WILKINSON NATIONAL RECREATION TRAIL

reaching the Liaison Trail at post D. Continue straight ahead for the full tour; turn right on the Liaison Trail to shorten the loop by 2 miles.

The woods framing the Wilkinson Trail grow more mixed with maple, oak, aspen, black cherry, elm, hornbeam, and hophornbeam. The second road crossing soon follows. The trail now travels a wooded plateau between the Mill Creek and Great Ravine drainages. When the British marched along this route in 1777, old-growth trees 6 feet in diameter cloaked the highland. Today, white-tailed deer commonly cross the path.

A couple of plank crossings precede the footbridge at post F (2 miles). Upon crossing the bridge, bear right; this open field would have been cultivated in the eighteenth century. Cross the tour road, still amid field. Butterflies, crickets, and grasshoppers divert the eye. The blooms of spring and the seed pods of fall bring a special beauty to the field.

Where the trail enters a deciduous stand at 2.25 miles, an autumn collage of leaves adds to the richness of the tour. Descend steeply, cross a ravine, and ascend the opposite slope to tour a low ridge clad in pine. Past post J, traverse a long open field. At the base of a rise, cross over a horse trail, ascending to meet a paved walk at 3.2 miles. Go left to add a clockwise tour of the 0.6-mile Freeman Loop; the Wilkinson Trail bisects this loop.

This circuit and its spurs visit the John Freeman Farm and Balcarres Redoubt, noting the battles of September 19 and October 7, 1777. Visitors look upon posts outlining a British fortification that withstood the fiery American onslaught; a monument to a fallen American Captain; Bloody Knoll, named for the many casualties of October 7, 1777; and an obelisk and exquisitely crafted cannons. Interpretive panels, some with recorded messages, relate the history, while lilacs recall the farm. The Liaison Trail also rejoins the tour at this site.

At 3.8 miles return to the junction with the Wilkinson Trail and turn right, crossing over and departing Freeman Loop. Pass through field and pine stand to cross the tour road (4 miles). Past post N (the last of the interpretive sites), cross over a horse trail, reaching a T-junction with a mowed path. Go right, following the sign to the visitor center; to left lies Barber Wheatfield, another battle site. Close the loop at post C in another 0.1 mile, and bear left retracing the first 0.6 mile to the visitor center (4.8 miles).

52 TACONIC CREST TRAIL

Overview

Two day hikes from Petersburg Pass encapsulate the attributes and demerits of the 35-mile-long Taconic Crest Trail, stringing from southwest Vermont through New York to end at Pittsfield State Forest in Massachusetts. Both of these hikes travel hardwood forests and serve up multi-state views. One visits a geologic oddity; one tops a mountain.

General description: These round trip hikes introduce the Taconic Crest and its neighborhood.
General location: On the New York-Massachusetts border south of Vermont, off New York 2.
Special attractions: Multi-state vistas, a snow hole, a former ski area, colorful fall foliage.
Length: Snow Hole Hike, 5.1 miles round trip; Berlin Mountain Hike, 4.6 miles round trip.
Elevation: From a trailhead elevation of 2,100 feet, the trail to the Snow Hole climbs 200 feet. The trail to Berlin Mountain climbs 700 feet, reaching a summit elevation of 2,798 feet.
Difficulty: Both moderate.
Maps: New York State Department of Environmental Conservation, Petersburg Pass Scenic Area flier (generally available at the start of each trail).
Special requirements: No camping in Williams College Hopkins Memorial Forest or on private land. Use care crossing NY 2.
Season and hours: Spring through fall, daylight hours.
For information: New York State Department of Environmental Conservation, Region 4.

Finding the trailhead: From the New York 22/New York 2 junction, go 5.3 miles east on NY 2 to reach the large, open parking lot for Petersburg Pass Scenic Area on the right.

The hikes: If time allows for only one hike make it the **Snow Hole Hike**. Free from vehicle use, this hike presents a more serene look at the area by traveling a woods road better suited for foot travel.

From the Petersburg Pass parking lot, cross to the north side of NY 2, taking one of the steeply ascending foot trails behind the "Town of Petersburg" sign. In 250 feet these spurs meet the Taconic Crest Trail as it arrives on the right. Over-the-shoulder views find Petersburg Pass and Mount Raimer. At 0.1 mile a spur leads to a western perspective overlooking a steep open slope to the valley below and Adirondacks beyond.

The rolling trail travels 2,250-acre Hopkins Memorial Forest, contouring the Taconic's west flank and traversing the crest. It changes from tall, full-canopy forests of birch, beech, maple, black cherry, and oak to areas of low-stature trees with shrubby understories.

At 0.4 mile bypass a spring. At 0.55 mile the RRR Brook Trail arrives on the right. In places, the woods feature highly scenic candelabra-trunked trees, dipping low their shades of autumn. Elsewhere, silver snags (victims of the pear thrip infestation of the late 1980s) draw eyes skyward. Wooden stakes record 0.5-mile increments.

Berlin Mountain, Taconic Crest.

TACONIC CREST TRAIL

0   0.5   1
Miles

Snow Hole

White Rock

Vermont
New York   Massachusetts

Birch Brook Trail

To Williamstown, MA

Taconic Crest Trail

To Petersburg

RRR Brook Trail

To Williamstown, MA

N

Petersburg Pass

P

Mount Raimer

2

To Williamstown, MA

Berlin Pass Trail

To Berlin

Berlin Pass

Berlin Mountain
2,798 ft.

At times a chill air washes up the slope, invigorating leaves and travelers. At 1.1 miles fountains of 3- to 4-foot tall interrupted ferns claim the left side of the trail, while the easy-to-miss Birch Brook Trail appears on the right.

Amid a steady ascent, at 1.5 miles the crest trail briefly crosses into southwest Vermont before returning to New York at White Rock, a signed landmark. The area received this U.S. Geological Survey designation for chunks of milky white quartz scattered throughout the woods. Along the way, open berry fields present vistas of Petersburg Pass and the rolling New York terrain.

From White Rock, drift east, descending into a forest of beech. At the marked junction at 2.5 miles, leave the crest trail, detouring right for a 250-foot descent to the Snow Hole, a cavity in the ground, with jagged, moss-covered chasm walls that meet each other in an ill-fitting bite. Explorers who enter the chasm discover chill air and often snow and ice lingering into summer. This chill supports a boreal understory of hobblebush, club moss, and oxalis.

Area rocks wear the names and dates from visitors from 100 years ago, but the genuine etchings must be sorted from the prankster and contemporary markings. A path overlooks the cavity and its cave-like end. Return as you came.

The **Berlin Mountain Hike** leaves the southwest corner of the parking area, rounding a rock barricade, following white-paint and diamond blazes. A western view overlooks the valley, panning to the Adirondacks.

The trail weaves through a maze of abandoned dirt roads from a former ski area, ascending Mount Raimer. Markers come at regular intervals, with small arrows further assisting hikers through the initial confusion. Birch, beech, and sugar and striped maples overlace the route. After a steep climb at 0.3 mile, the ascent eases. Bear right at the fork at 0.65 miles to reach the crest.

At times the woods open up with fern, bramble, and snags and an open-spacing of maple and birch. Vehicle use sadly mars the route; side trails skirt the worst of the deep-worn scars, mud bowls, and standing water. At 0.85 mile stay along the main gravel road as it curves right, descending through private property.

Ahead, Berlin Mountain boldly greets hikers, with its steep flanks and deep drainage crease. Eastern views find Massachusetts's Mount Greylock, topped by a 100-foot-high war memorial and radio tower.

At Berlin Pass (1.15 miles) blue-blazed trails descend east and west along the old Albany-Boston post road; continue straight, keeping to the main gravel road. Very few markers point the way through private land.

A wooded rolling-ridge ascent delivers the stark summit flat at 2.3 miles. A few concrete remnants hint at the abandoned fire tower. Ringed by small fir, shrubs, and golden rod, the summit serves up a 270-degree view with Albany and the Adirondacks; the Berkshires, Mount Greylock, Williamstown, and North Adams in Massachusetts; and the southern mountains of Vermont and New Hampshire. Return as you came.

53 JOHN BOYD THACHER STATE PARK

Overview

Boasts of this 2,300-acre park include 6 miles of the famous Helderberg Escarpment, one of the richest fossil-bearing formations in the world, dramatic cliffs, Mohawk-Hudson Valley panoramas, Indian trails and tales of Tory spies, waterfalls, and mixed woods. Short trails throw open the pages of the park.

General description: Three easy hikes travel above and below the vertical limestone cliffs and through second-growth woods.
General location: 12 miles west of Albany; 17 miles southwest of Schenectady.
Special attractions: Fossil-bearing limestone cliffs; vistas; historic Indian trade route and a Revolutionary-times paint mine; goshawk, rabbit, deer, and fox.
Length: Indian Ladder Trail, 1 mile round trip; Escarpment Trail, 2.5 miles one way; Nature Trail, 1-mile loop.
Elevation: Indian Ladder Trail shows a 200-foot elevation change; the Escarpment Trail and Nature Trail each show about 100 feet in elevation change.
Difficulty: All easy.
Maps: State park brochure.
Special requirements: Vehicle entrance fee collected Memorial Day through Labor Day. Gates close promptly at dusk for Indian Ladder Trail.
Season and hours: May through mid-November (weather permitting), 8 a.m. to dusk.
For information: New York State Parks, Saratoga-Capital Region.
Finding the trailhead: From the junction of New York 158 and U.S. Highway 20 south of Rotterdam, follow NY 158 south to where it ends at New York 146 in 1.7 miles. Now, take NY 146 west for 2.3 miles, and continue west on New York 156. At its junction with New York 157 in 3.2 miles, go south on NY 157 for 1.7 miles. There turn left (east) on Albany County 256. Go 2.6 miles, turning back onto NY 157, following it left for Thacher State Park. The park straddles NY 157; marked park accesses begin in 0.5 mile. Signs help sort out the later junctions.

The hikes: The park's premier hiking trail, **Indian Ladder Trail**, wraps below the light-colored platy cliffs of Helderberg Escarpment between Indian Ladder and LaGrange Bush picnic areas. At Indian Ladder Picnic Area find the marked trailhead, taking the first right past the entry station.

This trail rounds the escarpment where the Mohawk Schoharie constructed a shortcut to the valley by placing a sturdy notched trunk against the cliff for descending and scaling. Today, stonework steps descend through a rock chasm leading to a viewing platform and the start

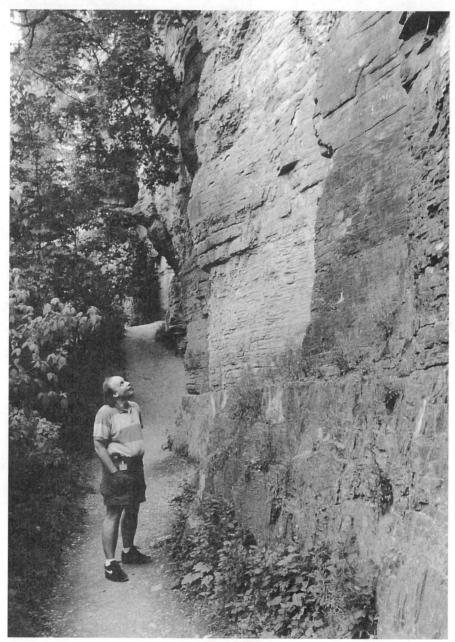

Indian Ladder Trail, John Boyd Thacher State Park.

of an exciting, neck-craning tour at the base of the 100- to 200-foot-high cliffs.

Outward vistas pan the Mohawk-Hudson Valley, but the cliffs truly command with their bulges, overhangs, flutes, fissures, clefts, and hollows. Millions of years ago an uplift of limestone, sandstone, and shale followed by ages of erosion and weathering brought about the site's vertical fracturing, breakaway blocks, and ultimately these startling cliffs. Numbered signs identify cliff features. While some defacing exists, mostly the park succeeds in protecting this geologic treasure.

Cliff scallops and protrusions lend character, as the trail journeys north to east following a broad U-curvature. Outlets to underground streams, Minelot and Outlet falls, and the wooded slope plunging to the valley floor further engage travelers. Nearing LaGrange Bush Picnic Area, beware of a low rock ledge. Return as you came or via the Escarpment Trail.

The thin footpath of the **Escarpment Trail** hugs the fenced escarpment rim, skirting the developed park; it travels from a turnout north of Hale's Cave Picnic Area to Cliff Edge Overlook.

Along the trail, open overlooks and stolen glimpses across the rim's dense shrub cap bring about a new respect for the plummeting cliffs. Views sweep the Mohawk-Hudson Valley and the escarpment arc. On clear days, look for the distant ragged outline of the Adirondack High Peaks and Green Mountains.

A tangle of cherry, birch, cedar, sumac, and wild rose often isolates the trail, providing habitat for rabbit and songbird; beware of poison ivy. At the ends of the tour, one finds the best escarpment profiles; more boots travel the path between Indian Ladder and Cliff Edge Overlook. Ravens, hawks, and vultures soar below the rim. The aqua markers of the Long Path, a New York state through-trail, stamp part of the tour.

The **Nature Trail** or Forest Trail starts on a service road for authorized vehicles only, midway between Lower Paint Mine Picnic Area and the first parking lot for Paint Mine Picnic Area. Find the trailhead next to a roadside table.

The trail crosses a footbridge with upstream views of a pretty stepped creek. A textured woods of maple, hickory, oak, hemlock, and white pine enfolds the tour. This trail too briefly advances the Long Path. After a climb from the creek, the Long Path heads left, the Nature Trail heads right.

Paper birch and aspen add to the mix, and at 0.3 mile the trail tops out. Posts from the former interpretive trail mark the way; stay right at each intersection, following foot trail and woods road. Lady slipper, violet, clintonia, and Mayflower sprinkle the woods, while red eft and frog favor the leafy bottomed puddles. Upon crossing a drainage, the trail meets the authorized-vehicle road; descend right, closing the loop.

JOHN BOYD THACHER STATE PARK

54 FIVE RIVERS ENVIRONMENTAL EDUCATION CENTER

Overview

At this nationally recognized environmental education center, visitors, students, parents, and children examine habitat interrelationships, touring field, forest, meadow, and pond. Six self-guided nature trails explore the grounds. The center takes its name from the five major rivers flowing into the greater area: the Hudson, Mohawk, Sacandaga, Schoharie, and Hoosick.

General description: The easy loops provide opportunities for wildlife sighting and nature study.
General location: Capital District, just west of Delmar.
Special attractions: Bird watching; spring and summer wildflowers; possible sightings of beaver, deer, turtle, frog, bluebird, and Canada goose; small interpretive center.
Length: Trails range from a fragment of a mile to 2.5 miles.
Elevation: Most are flat. Beaver Tree and Vlomankill trails each show an elevation change of less than 100 feet.
Difficulty: All easy.

Goose Pond, Five Rivers Environmental Education Center.

FIVE RIVERS ENVIRONMENTAL EDUCATION CENTER

Maps: Five Rivers Environmental Education Center brochure. Interpretive pamphlets are available at trailheads.

Special requirements: Take necessary precautions for ticks, and carry insect repellent.

Season and hours: Year-round (weather permitting), sunrise to sunset; building: 9 a.m. to 4:30 p.m. Monday through Saturday and 1 p.m. to 5 p.m. Sunday (closed major holidays).

For information: Five Rivers Environmental Education Center.

Finding the trailhead: From the junction of Albany County 52 (Elm Avenue) and New York 443 (Delaware Avenue) in west Delmar, go 1.4 miles west on NY 443 and turn right (north) on Orchard Street at a sign for the center. Go 0.4 mile and turn left on Game Farm Road, reaching the center entrance and parking lot on the right in 0.3 mile.

The hikes: All trails radiate from the interpretive building. The wheelchair-accessible 0.2-mile **Woodlot Trail** heads east at the southeast corner of the parking lot. The loop travels boardwalk and wide, fine-gravel trail through a woodlot of young, skyward-shooting maple, ash, and beech. Flowering shrubs, wild grape, geranium, fern, and Virginia creeper contribute to a dense mid- and understory. Butterflies and hummingbirds frequent the woodlot.

The popular 0.5-mile **Beaver Tree Trail** begins on the south side of Game Farm Road opposite the entrance. The tree-shaded route rings a rectangular manmade pond. Along it, deck overlooks, a spillway, and bridge offer up-close looks at the pond habitat. Duckweed and water plants patchwork the pond's surface, while cattails and purple loosestrife vegetate part of the rim. Ducks and geese rear their young, turtles sun on the logs, and beaver gnawings hint at the trail's name.

To reach Wild Turkey, North Loop, and Old Field trails, hike north from the parking lot toward the maintenance buildings. Find the Wild Turkey Trailhead to the right of the buildings, the other two trails to the left.

The 2.5-mile **Wild Turkey Trail** swings north through open meadow and field. Yellow, pink, and white wildflowers spangle the grassy areas. At 0.75 mile the trail makes a barbell tour through forest and field near the north boundary; arrows guide hikers through the confusing junctions. Second-generation hemlocks and a few big oaks punctuate the tour. The different stages of meadow growth (left wild to the whim of succession or cropped short) support various wildlife communities.

For the 2-mile **North Loop Trail**, bear left following the mowed track away from the trail's information board. Early views pan west to Helderberg Mountains. Rabbit, mourning dove, bluebird, and deer number among the early morning sightings. Where the trail passes between Wood Duck and Goose ponds, turtles, frogs, muskrats, and herons cause fingers to point. Willows and cattails rim the ponds. At junctions, arrows point out the North Loop Trail.

Along the middle third of the loop, the trail tours a dark, deep woods of hemlock, maple, beech, and oak. Some trees approach 18 inches in diameter. Waterplant, trillium, and jack-in-the-pulpit bring a blush of early spring. At 1.75 miles the trail bypasses a log lean-to set back in the woods. Bypassing a picnic shelter, the North Loop Trail follows farm road and grassy track through field, returning to the ponds.

Next door, the 0.5-mile **Old Field Trail** makes a figure-eight tour rounding past Sunfish and Goose ponds and through fields and second-growth woods. Abandoned fruit trees provide additional habitat. Again, the fields show different stages of succession, and a picnic shelter lies off the trail. Old Field Trail ends next to the North Loop Trail information board.

The 0.75-mile **Vlomankill Trail** has the most remote trailhead. Hike north from the parking lot; turn west going past the maintenance buildings, North Loop and Old Field trails, and Goose Lane (a maintenance road); and again turn north to find the marked trailhead. The trail descends fairly steeply, passing through hickory, maple, birch, and pine woods arriving at Vloman Kill (a stream) and the loop. Cross the footbridge for a clockwise tour, journeying upstream.

The trail travels a hemlock-deciduous wooded flat threaded by the slow, murky waters of Vloman Kill. Erosion mars the banks. Greeting hikers at the second bridge crossing is a more picturesque water that spills over canted layered rock, around grassy tufts, and through shallow horseshoe curves. A natural log dam accounts for the difference in flow between the two bridges. On snags, look for the telltale pinhole drillings of a sapsucker. Virginia creeper and poison ivy scale and weave beneath the trees.

CATSKILLS REGION

Sharing the southern tip of New York with the Hudson Valley, this region brings together the chiseled beauty and lore of the Catskill Mountains, the cliff-and-crag realm of the Shawangunks, and outlying wooded ridges parted by thin valleys. This is a countryside of kill and clove drainages, the land of Rip Van Winkle and Sleepy Hollow. Naturalist John Burroughs tracked this land drawing from its inspiration.

Hikes explore forest, field, pond, sapphire lakes, and escarpment rim. Vistas sweep the Catskills, the Mohonks, and the Hudson Valley. The region also boasts one of the finest bird watching areas in the state.

55 BEAR SPRING MOUNTAIN WILDLIFE MANAGEMENT AREA

Overview

At this little-used 7,141-acre wildlife management area in the western Catskills, hiker/horse trails travel long, thin ridges parted by long, thin valleys, touring meadow grassland, second-generation hardwood forests, and ponds. Fork Mountain and Launt Pond trails typify the hiking; Fork Mountain Trail also advances the long-distance Finger Lakes Trail.

General description: Fork Mountain Trail offers a moderately difficult ridge tour, Launt Pond Trail an easy pond circuit.
General location: 5 miles southeast of Walton.
Special attractions: Fishing; bird watching; spring and summer wildflowers; fall foliage; possible sightings of wild turkey, deer, rabbit, gray fox, coyote, skunk, and beaver.
Length: Fork Mountain Trail, 8.4 miles round trip or a 4.2-mile shuttle hike; Launt Pond Trail, 1.2-mile loop.
Elevation: Fork Mountain Trail rolls from 2,350 feet at its northern trailhead to a high of 2,500 feet, ending at 1,250 feet. Launt Pond Trail shows minimal elevation change.
Difficulty: Fork Mountain Trail, moderate; Launt Pond Trail, easy.

Beaver Dam on Launt Pond, Bear Spring Mountain Wildlife Management Area.

Maps: Wildlife management area brochure.

Special requirements: Camping is allowed only at the area's two developed campgrounds; permit required. Vehicle entrance fee or walk-in fee collected at Launt Pond.

Season and hours: May through November.

For information: New York State Department of Environmental Conservation, Region 4.

Finding the trailhead: At the New York 10/New York 206 junction in Walton, go east on NY 206 for 3.5 miles and turn right on Beers Brook Road. At the road fork in 0.4 mile, bear left on West Trout Brook Road and follow it south for 0.7 mile reaching the northern access to Fork Mountain Trail (Trail 5) on the left. To reach the southern trailhead to spot a shuttle vehicle, continue south on West Trout Brook Road for another 3.4 miles. There, bear left on East Trout Brook Road to find trail parking opposite Spruce Grove Horse Camp in 0.1 mile.

For Launt Pond Trail, from the junction of NY 206 and Beers Brook Road, continue east on NY 206 for 0.2 mile and turn south on East Trout Brook Road, reaching Launt Pond Campground and Day Use in 1 mile.

The hikes: For a north-south tour of **Fork Mountain Trail** (Trail 5), from West Trout Brook Road, round the gate and follow the grassy road heading south for a steady, moderate ascent. Blue horsehead-disk and number "5" trail markers indicate the route. Forget-me-not, violet, buttercup, geranium, strawberry, clover, and fern embroider the grassy avenue bordered by hardwood and spruce.

Before long, a broad meadow swath replaces the grassy track. Despite annual mowings that artificially maintain the ridge trail's meadow character and keep it groomed, take the necessary precautions for ticks, and periodically check trouser legs for the unwanted hitchhikers. In fall, sock-piercing seeds also annoy hikers.

By 0.5 mile the sun-drenched trail claims the first rise, rolling along the ridgetop. Restricted western views span the West Branch Trout Brook drainage. Maple, beech, oak, and black cherry comprise the eastern rim of the meadow; 6- to 8-foot-tall shrubs later claim the western edge, stealing all views. After 1.2 miles enjoy a tour segment with a Sunday-stroll ease, save for a few swampy, poorly drained areas. Butterflies, grasshoppers, frogs, and vultures animate the tour; deer make a hasty debut.

At 2.7 miles Trail 4 descends left to Middle Pond; continue straight for Fork Mountain Trail, entering a long ridge descent, wading a misty sea of wispy knee- to thigh-high grasses. By 3.4 miles hemlocks and an attractive fern fringe enfold the narrowed grassy track. Next, the trail steepens for a knee-jarring descent amid lower grasses.

Where the trail curves west and levels, find a junction (3.9 miles), where Trail 5 branches both left and straight. To reach the trailhead across from Spruce Grove Horse Camp, turn left, traversing the upper edge of a meadow, passing below a conifer-hidden pond. From the meadow's end,

BEAR SPRING MOUNTAIN
WILDLIFE MANAGEMENT AREA

To (206) and Walton

To (206) and Walton

Launt Pond

N

Fork Mountain

Middle Pond

West Trout Brook Road

East Trout Brook Road

0   0.5   1
Miles

Spruce Grove
Horse Camp

To (30)

briefly follow a hoof-rutted earthen path and turn right to enter the southern trailhead parking lot (4.2 miles). If a shuttle was not prearranged, return as you came or make a loop.

For a counterclockwise tour of the **Launt Pond Trail**, head north along the east shore from the designated beach area. Groomed lawn, planted shade trees, and picnic tables claim the first 0.1 mile; the west shore boasts a natural wooded ridge. Swallows dart after the insect hatch; newts, frogs, fish, and whirligig beetles stir the surface of the narrow oval.

From the picnic area, part the overhanging shrubs to enter the woods, following a skinny path indicated by yellow nature-trail disks. Beaver gnawings, dams, and lodges, both old and new, may be spied along the loop as it travels a few yards inland from shore. Clintonia, starflower, Mayflower, and violet bring springtime color.

At 0.4 mile continue north away from the lake, turning left at 0.5 mile for a stone-stepping crossing of a braided inlet drainage. In the dark, congested inlet woods, miry segments plague travel.

Look for a beaver dam on the inlet drainage, as the trail returns to Launt Pond. Now, travel the wooded west slope 50 feet from shore. Hemlock and pine shade the trail as it rounds toward the small earthen dam or levee. Cross the spillway and go past the cartop-boat launch and fishing platform to close the loop at 1.2 miles.

56 LITTLE POND LOOP

General description: This day hike stitches together Little Pond and Touchmenot Mountain, touring mixed forest, conifer plantation, and meadow habitats.

General location: In the remote western Catskills, 14 miles northwest of New York 17 at Livingston Manor.

Special attractions: Little Pond, modest views, fishing, spring and summer wildflowers, fall foliage.

Length: 5.3-mile loop, including spur to Cabot Mountain.

Elevation: The loop travels between Little Pond at 2,000 feet and Touchmenot Mountain at 2,700 feet. Find the high point on the side spur to Cabot Mountain, elevation 2,970 feet.

Difficulty: Moderate.

Maps: New York-New Jersey Trail Conference map, Western Catskill Trails.

Special requirements: Fee area. A few climbs require the use of hands.

Season and hours: Spring through fall.

For information: New York Department of Environmental Conservation, Region 4.

Frog catcher.

Finding the trailhead: From New York 30 on the south shore of Pepacton Reservoir, 13.5 miles equidistant from Margaretville and Downsville, turn southeast on Beech Hill Road, go 6.3 miles, and turn left on Beaver Kill Road (Ulster County 54). In 2 miles turn left on Barkaboom Road for 0.2 mile. Now turn left to find Little Pond entrance station in 0.8 mile. The loop starts near the bathhouse/shower facility above the pond.

The hike: This hike explores the gentle western relief of the Catskill Mountains, swinging between Little Pond and Touchmenot Mountain, with a spur to Cabot Mountain. Little Pond, a long lake with a small dam at its developed end, rests between low wooded ridges and sports stocks of pan-sized fish. The pond portion of the hike proves most enjoyable post and prior to the summer vacation season.

For a clockwise tour, follow the yellow-blazed trail between the bathhouse and the upper edge of the picnic area, rounding the east shore of Little Pond. Hemlocks push to the edge of the pond; oaks, birch, beech, and maple fill out the woods. Trillium, oxalis, clintonia, Mayflower, starflower, azalea, and mountain laurel pay tribute to spring. At the small drainages look for the trail to arc deeper into the woods and for the growth of false hellebore and jack-in-the-pulpit. Isolated walk-in sites dot the wooded shore.

After crossing a rocky inlet brook at 0.5 mile, turn right and traverse the wooded bench overlooking the brook's steep ravine. Viburnum and fern dominate the understory. Before long, a beaver dam alters the brook, and snags pierce the pond and the lodge itself. Duckweed and a film of pollen coat the water, as methane gas bubbles to the surface. A cacophony of croaking, knocking, drumming, and shrill notes fills the air.

Climb steadily amid stands of small-diameter trees, meadows of knee- to hip-high vegetation, and mature pine and spruce plantations. From the meadows, glimpse the area ridges. Near the upper end of an overgrown meadow, turn right, following the yellow markers through an area of young maple with a handful of ancient maples.

At 1.25 miles an egress in a beautiful rock wall leads to a more extensive grassy meadow with wild strawberries, a semi-hidden pond, an old rock foundation, and views of Touchmenot Mountain. Traverse the center of the meadow and cross a shale clearing, before returning to a mixed-age woods. At the red-trail junction at 1.7 miles, go left to top Cabot Mountain; go right to continue the loop.

A detour left contours a similarly wooded slope of maple, birch, and beech, coming to the foot of Cabot Mountain and a fairly steep ascent. The moist slope supports nettles, ferns, waterleaf, violets, trillium, and jack-in-the-pulpit. Although steep, the thin footpath retains its earth. Amid the ledges and overhangs, expect to use your hands, and beware a hail of loose rock from any hikers above you.

Traveling the wooded flat at the edge of the slope, look for the open ledge of Beaver Kill Vista at 2.4 miles. While leafy trees filter much of the

LITTLE POND LOOP

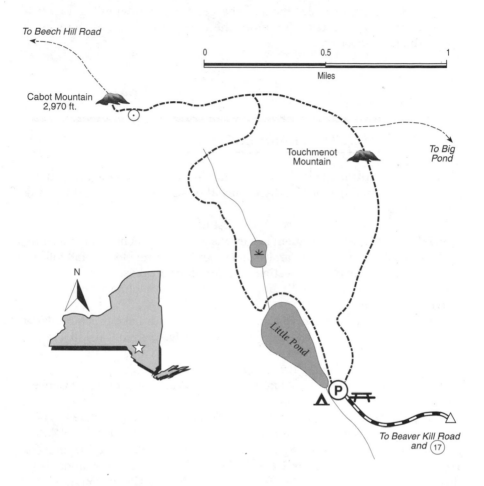

To Beech Hill Road

Cabot Mountain
2,970 ft.

0   0.5   1
Miles

Touchmenot
Mountain

To Big
Pond

N

Little Pond

P

To Beaver Kill Road
and (17)

view, Touchmenot Mountain, the Catskill ridges beyond Beaver Kill, and the glare of Little Pond still reward. Columbine dresses the rock, drawing hummingbirds to the hiker's feet. Past the vista point lies a wooded summit flat with a lush fern floor.

Return to the 1.7-mile junction at 3.3 miles, staying on the red trail for a mildly rolling, shady walk to Touchmenot Mountain. Cross a rocky drainage and climb, finding wooded flats between the steep ledge ascents. At the marked junction at 3.8 miles, go right on the blue trail to close the loop at Little Pond. The red trail turns left for Barkaboom Road and Big Pond in 1 mile.

Continue the ascent of Touchmenot Mountain on the blue trail. Ledge overlooks allow for a forest appreciation but no outward views. Roll along the summit plateau before sharply descending at 4.3 miles. Mosses decorate the platy outcrops, ledges, and isolated rocks. Again use hands to ease descents. Once off the rocks, the trail charges straight downhill amid a rich mixed forest. For the final 0.5 mile, the descent eases; exit the woods above the bathhouse.

57 NORTH-SOUTH LAKE LOOP

General description: This Catskill Mountains loop travels the escarpment and wooded outskirts of North-South Lake, snaring views and passing cultural sites.
General location: 10 miles west of Catskill.
Special attractions: Escarpment ledges, vistas, a monument and nineteenth-century hotel sites, waterfalls, azalea and mountain laurel blooms, fall foliage.
Length: 10-mile loop, with destinations for shorter hikes.
Elevation: The trail shows about a 600-foot elevation change.
Difficulty: Moderate.
Maps: Catskill Forest Preserve Camping, North-South Lake brochure; New York-New Jersey Trail Conference map, North Lake Area Catskill Trails.
Special requirements: Fee area.
Season and hours: Spring through fall.
For information: New York State Department of Environmental Conservation, Region 4.
Finding the trailhead: From New York State Thruway Interstate 87, take exit 20 at Saugerties and go north on New York 32 to the NY 32/NY 32A junction (6 miles from the I-87 exit). Bear left on NY 32A, staying on it for 1.8 miles; there turn west on New York 23A. In 4.8 miles in Haines Falls, turn right on Greene County 18 for North-South Lake Campground, reaching the entrance station in 2.2 miles. Find the trailhead at the upper end of North Lake beach parking, in another 1.6 miles; look for the blue blazes and sign for Artists Rock.

The hike: Although the loop travels the blue Escarpment and yellow Rock Shelter trails ringing the North-South Lake area, it never approaches the lake.

From the upper reaches of the beach parking lot, follow the blue trail left (north), rounding and ascending to Artists Rock; soon a yellow spur arrives on the left. Black oaks, maple, pine, azalea, and mountain laurel decorate the brink, as the broad sandstone ledges form natural avenues. The jut of Artists Rock extends a 180-degree Hudson Valley panorama; vultures sail below the point.

Ascend through forest, top the next ledge tier for a peek at North-South Lake (formerly two lakes), and then round below an immense conglomerate

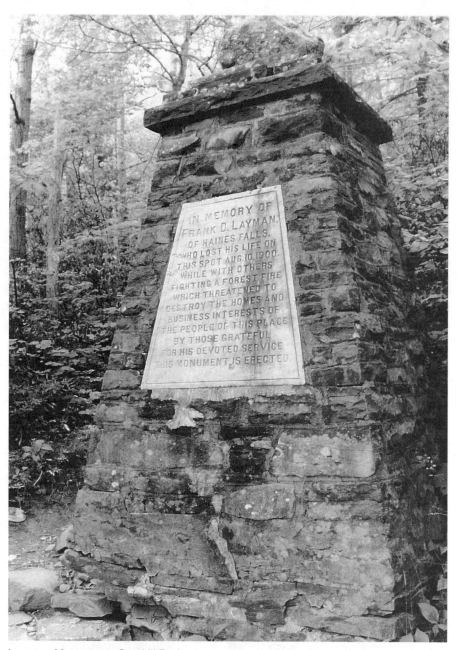

IN MEMORY OF
FRANK D. LAYMAN,
OF HAINES FALLS,
WHO LOST HIS LIFE ON
THIS SPOT AUG. 10. 1900,
WHILE WITH OTHERS
FIGHTING A FOREST FIRE
WHICH THREATENED TO
DESTROY THE HOMES AND
BUSINESS INTERESTS OF
THE PEOPLE OF THIS PLACE
BY THOSE GRATEFUL
FOR HIS DEVOTED SERVICE
THIS MONUMENT IS ERECTED.

Layman Monument, Catskill Park.

outcrop with cobbles eroding from the cliff. At 1 mile a 0.4-mile round-trip detour right leads to Sunset Rock for one of the finest vistas in the Catskills; the loop continues straight ahead.

On the detour, visit the escarpment edge of Lookout Point for northeast views, before reaching a series of plane-topped outcrops comprising Sunset Point. Fissures measuring a foot wide and 20 feet deep isolate the rock islands. Views sweep across North-South Lake and its wooded basin to the swaybacked ridge of High Peak and Roundtop Mountain.

Resume the counterclockwise loop toward Newmans Ledge, ascending along a thin edge with a disturbing drop. Vistas span Rip Van Winkle Hollow to Rips Rock—afterall, this is Knickerbocker and literature's Washington Irving country.

The trail then contours and ascends, tagging a junction below Badman Cave, shaped by an overhang and reached by a rock scramble. Leave the blue trail, now following the yellow Rock Shelter Trail straight ahead for a steady descent amid hemlock, spruce, and oak.

The descent grows rocky traveling alongside the brook draining to Marys Glen. Find the 3-mile junction near a 10-foot waterfall weeping from a rock overhang; bear right staying the yellow trail. The red trail descends to Ashley (or Marys Glen) Falls, a beaver meadow, and the campground. Spring peepers bring vitality to the glen in the evening hours.

Where the yellow trail draws even with the top of the 10-foot waterfall, veer left continuing the loop, descending to Haines Falls Road (4.4 miles). Rocks and roots riddle the trail, while a few maple old-timers grace the woods.

At Haines Falls Road, angle left to reach and briefly walk Schutt Road. At 4.5 miles look for the blue Escarpment Trail (the loop), as it turns left off Schutt Road; this trail has sections of joint hiker-horse usage. Descend along the wide lane, touring hemlock-birch forest, passing segments of colonial rock walls, and crossing an old railroad grade.

With a footbridge crossing of Spruce Creek comes the next junction (5.4 miles); turn right on the woods road, and soon after, bear left on an earthen lane paralleling Spruce Creek downstream. A forget-me-not clad bench separates the trail from the stream. Scenic rockwork marks Spruce Creek as the blue trail turns and ascends away.

Mountain laurel and azalea now fill the midstory with late-spring color and fragrance. With a descent along a rocky drainage, come upon a rock obelisk with a boulder crown. This monument honors firefighter Frank Layman who lost his life in the fire of 1900. Round the obelisk to the left and in a few steps, take a sharp left back uphill to the escarpment (6.4 miles). Vistas feature Kaaterskill drainage and the wooded ridge of High Peak and Roundtop Mountain.

Pass through a rock channel, and ascend and contour along the wooded escarpment. At 6.9 miles continue straight ahead for Inspiration Point, bypassing a second Sunset Rock. Past Inspiration Point, find a picturesque look through the "V" of Kaaterskill Canyon at Hudson Valley. At 7.6 miles

NORTH-SOUTH LAKE LOOP

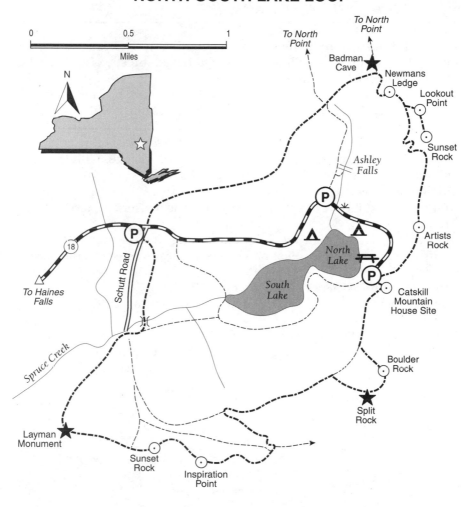

turn right on a woods road reaching a junction; here turn left to stay to the blue trail.

A rocky woods-road ascent between full borders of azalea, laurel, and oak, leads to the next junction where the blue trail heads right on a narrowed forest lane. Follow the signs to Boulder Rock, again turning right at 8.75 miles.

Past Split Rock, where massive blocks have pulled apart from the escarpment face, find Boulder Rock, a naturally transported boulder that came to rest on the escarpment ledge. Bear left meeting the red trail. Here turn right to reach a clearing and sign at 9.6 miles, that together recall Catskill Mountain House, a hotel that hosted presidents and dignitaries in the nineteenth century. Round left away from the sign, bearing right in 0.1 mile to come out at the open parking area above the beach at 10 miles.

General description: Suitable for a day outing or backpack, this hike mainly travels former woods roads through mixed forests, visiting a lake and an abandoned lookout tower.

General location: In the Catskills, about 6 miles west of Saugerties.

Special attractions: Vistas, lake, lean-tos, historic ruins, wildflowers, fall foliage, wildlife sightings.

Length: 13.5 miles round trip, including spur to Echo Lake.

Elevation: The trail shows a 1,250-foot elevation change, with the high point at Overlook Mountain, elevation 3,140 feet.

Difficulty: Moderate.

Maps: New York-New Jersey Trail Conference map, Northeastern Catskill Trails.

Special requirements: Note that both parking and the start of the trail occur on private land; respect all posted notices to preserve the access privilege.

Season and hours: Spring through fall.

For information: New York Department of Environmental Conservation, Regions 3 and 4.

Finding the trailhead: From the junction of New York 23A and Greene County 16 in Tannersville, turn south on County 16 (Depot Street) for 5.5

Overlook House ruins, Catskill Park.

OVERLOOK MOUNTAIN HIKE

To Tannersville

Prediger Road

P

16

To West Saugerties

To Jimmy Dolan Notch

0   0.5   1
Miles

To Indian Head Mountain

Plattekill Mountain

N

Echo Lake

Overlook House Ruins

Overlook Mountain 3,140 ft.

To Mead

miles; the road name changes several times. Turn right on Prediger Road for 0.5 mile, finding trail parking along the right shoulder only. Do not clog the road or block the private residence by parking on the left or too close to the trailhead. Also leave enough space between parked vehicles for returning hikers to pull out safely.

The hike: The southern approach to Overlook Mountain offers perhaps the most popular peak climb in the entire Catskills. This hike takes an alternative approach arriving from the north. While longer, it offers a comfortable grade, a pleasant backdrop, points of interest, and fewer travelers; a detour en route finds charming Echo Lake. Despite the closure of the old lookout tower, side paths along the summit ridge help piece together the panoramic puzzle.

Follow the red markers away from the old cabin, passing through a stile and crossing a footbridge to enter a hemlock-deciduous woodland. Travel an often rocky woods road with a modest incline, coming to the 0.5-mile junction. Continue straight on the red trail for Overlook Mountain; soon the old road tapers to trail width.

Big maples and birch comprise the canopy above a boulder-studded forest floor. Porcupine, deer, red eft, mouse, and toad draw one's attention away from the rolling trail. At 1.25 miles, cross a thin creek, and at 1.9 miles turn right on a woods road, coming to a signed junction. Now follow the blue markers straight ahead for the summit; the red trail turns right toward Indian Head Mountain and destinations west.

At 2.25 miles find Devils Kitchen lean-to, with privy and reliable creek source; on a weekday in June, the lone occupant was a porcupine. Pass through the lean-to's camp and cross the creek footbridge for a steady ascent. Nettles, trillium, clintonia, starflower, and Mayflower sprinkle spring bloom.

Rounding the slope of Plattekill Mountain, bypass a low stone bench and travel the semi-shaded brink of an old quarry, or perhaps a mill site, with stone foundations. Here a footpath parts the vegetation of the old road, azalea brings its fragrant pink signature, and oaks join the mix. A wooded flat precedes the Echo Lake Trail junction at 4.25 miles.

Detour right, following the yellow trail along a former carriage road descending sharply to the lake and lean-to at 5 miles. The lean-to looks out at a grassy shore of Echo Lake. A 0.5-mile path rings the lake, and above it looms the ridge of Overlook Mountain. In spring, thousands of polliwogs blacken the shallows, while small toads seemingly cause the roadbed to percolate. The lake destination ideally serves novice backpackers.

Resume the trek to Overlook Mountain at 5.75 miles, again following blue markers, ascending along an escarpment edge for the next 0.25 mile. Mountain laurel, azalea, and pockets of beech trees adorn the way. A fuller forest follows. At 6.25 miles, bypass an unusual balanced rock on the right as rock ledges and overhangs now characterize the forest. Filtered views find Indian Head and Twin mountains. Beyond find piped water for wetting the brow.

As the trail draws into the open near a signal tower, look for a junction (6.9 miles). Red markers point the way left to the summit. About 0.1 mile straight ahead, two huge concrete shells and other ruins hauntingly echo the bygone elegance of Overlook House, a classic nineteenth-century mountain hotel that stood at this site. Built in 1878, the hotel fell to fire in the 1920s. The shell showing "1928" above its doorway represents an abandoned effort to rebuild. The road continues past the ruins downhill 2 miles to Mead.

From the signal tower, the final 0.5 mile to the fire tower ascends via woods road. Side paths to the right top a ridge ledge for views to the south-southeast from Ashokan Reservoir to the Hudson River, peering down and out Lewis Hollow. The creased rocks shaping the left shoulder of the road also draw hikers over for a closer look.

The nine-story steel-framed lookout still stands, absent its lower flight of stairs. A picnic table welcomes one to stay for lunch, but camping is prohibited near the lookout. Spur trails pierce the ring of trees, reaching vistas. Looks south find Ashokan Reservoir, the Slide Mountain area, Cooper Lake, and Mount Tobias. Follow the wire corridor away from the tower to find outcrops with a western vantage; here views span Saw Kill drainage to Plateau, Sugarloaf, and Twin mountains, with Hunter Mountain rising beyond Stony Clove Notch. The return is as you came.

59 SLIDE MOUNTAIN LOOP

General description: Traveling hemlock-deciduous and fir-birch forests, this popular trail tags the highest point in the Catskills and passes Burroughs Plaque and Curtis Monument.

General location: 16 miles southwest of Woodstock.

Special attractions: Vistas, rare high-elevation fir forest, rock features, commemorative markers, fall foliage.

Length: 7 miles round trip.

Elevation: The trail shows about an 1,800-foot elevation change, with a summit high point at 4,180 feet.

Difficulty: Moderate to strenuous.

Maps: Catskill Forest Preserve Camping, Woodland Valley brochure; New York-New Jersey Trail Conference map, Southern Catskill Trails.

Special requirements: Due to the sensitive nature of this popular forest preserve peak, hikers need to play a protective and respectful role. Do not make this an annual trek as it cannot sustain such heavy foot traffic, and keep your hiking party small. Avoid travel during and immediately following a rainstorm. If the trails are wet, keep to the red Wittenberg-Cornell-Slide Trail, a carriage road that can better handle the foot traffic; do not

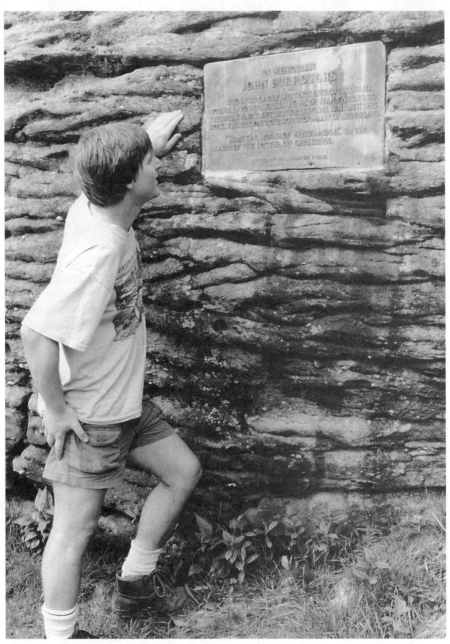

Burroughs plaque, Catskill Park.

travel the delicate Curtis-Ormsbee Trail. Plan a day hike versus an overnight stay. If you do choose to camp, remember, to protect this area's sensitive fir complex there is no camping above the 3,500-foot elevation.
Season and hours: Spring through fall.
For information: New York State Department of Environmental Conservation, Region 3.
Finding the trailhead: From the junction of New York 214 and New York 28 in Phoenicia, go west on NY 28 for 7.9 miles, reaching Big Indian. There turn south on Ulster County 47, go 9 miles, and turn left to enter the off-road parking area for Slide Mountain Trailhead.

The hike: This hike strings together the yellow Phoenicia-East Branch Trail, the red Wittenberg-Cornell-Slide Trail, and the blue Curtis-Ormsbee Trail, for a rolling tour at the western extent of the Burroughs Range.

Rock-hop across the brook-sized West Branch Neversink River, following yellow markers for a rocky ascent; an open forest of maple, birch, and beech clads the slope. Where the trail reaches a woods road at 0.4 mile, follow it right, now contouring the boulder-studded wooded slope. Past a pipe providing water, find the loop junction (0.7 mile). Turn left on the red trail for a clockwise tour, once again following a rocky woods road; be careful not to turn an ankle.

Leafy branches overlace the ascending trail for fragile shade, while seasonal run-offs race over the route. The trail narrows and steepens, soon pulling above the 3,500-foot elevation. Fir, birch, and snags comprise the skyline. Where the trail next contours the slope, it shows a trail width, with close-ranking firs shaping the aisle. Winds assail the ridge, and weather-watchers delight in the rapid cloud changes. At 2 miles the blue trail to the right continues the loop; remain on the red trail to reach Slide Mountain.

The trail to Slide Mountain climbs steadily along the north edge of the ridge, remaining amid the tightly clustered firs. Mayflower, clintonia, and moss touch green to the forest floor. At 2.5 miles a ledge to the left offers a view north-northeast from Overlook to Sugarloaf Mountain with Woodland Valley below.

Just ahead, the trail tops the open ledge of Slide Mountain (2.75 miles). Red markers point downhill to the right, where the trail rounds the foot of the cliff to view a plaque honoring John Burroughs, an early-day environmentalist and writer who introduced Slide Mountain to the world through his essays. The dramatic range arcing from Slide to Wittenberg Mountain carries his name.

On Burroughs's noted trek to this peak, he traveled cross-country from Woodland Valley coming out just north of the summit. He arrived, ascending the slide of 1820; forest has since reclaimed the scar. During his sojourns, he slept beneath the overhang next to which the plaque now rests.

From Slide Mountain, views pan across the spire-topped firs to an all-star line-up of Catskill peaks, including Wittenberg, Plateau, Twin, Indian

SLIDE MOUNTAIN LOOP

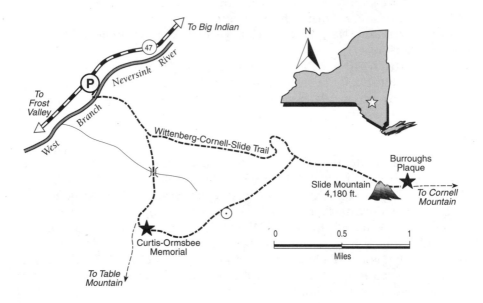

Head, and Overlook mountains. Cornell and Friday mountains form bookends to Ashokan Reservoir.

Return to the loop junction at 3.5 miles and follow the blue-marked foot trail into a fir forest laced with birch and hobblebush. Before long, steep downhill spurts replace the mild descent. The forest grows more open and shrubby, with a meadowy floor. Stones aid the crossing of marshy sites, where the soft ground records the tracks of deer and the occasional print of a misplaced boot.

At 4.25 miles a short spur left leads to a ledge with a Table Mountain vista. With a couple more plunges, the trail offers views spanning the East Branch Neversink River. Some hand assists may be needed for the sharp descents that follow.

Soon, the trail overlooks a rock island pulled away from the slope, before descending to skirt the massive rock. A road-sized gap parts the 12- to 15-foot-tall cliff faces. In places the crossbeds have eroded clear through. The trail now flattens for a comfortable shady woods stroll to the 4.9-mile junction, site of the 2.5-foot-tall marble tribute to trail builders William Curtis and Allen Ormsbee, who designed the scenic blue trail just traveled.

Turn right on the woods road, following the yellow blazes back to the trailhead. While less rocky than the other woods roads comprising the loop, springs can muddy travel. After bypassing a small woods road on the left, cross a three-log bridge over a babbling headwater of the West Branch Neversink. Ahead, rocks prove invaluable for hopscotch travel along the soggy road. Close the loop, and at 6.65 miles, turn left for a rocky descent to the trailhead 7 miles.

60 MOHONK LAKE RESORT – MOHONK PRESERVE

Overview

In the northern Shawangunks, these adjoining private properties offer hikers a diversity of trails, varying in length, challenge, and offering. Mohonk Mountain House, a national historic landmark and commercial resort, has served outdoor recreationists since 1869. While access to the castlelike house (hotel) is restricted to guests, its regal exterior complements the Mohonk Lake setting.

Linked by an extensive network of trails, the woods and rock features of Mohonk Preserve extend the realm of discovery. Mohonk Preserve is the largest visitor/membership supported nature preserve in New York State, with the mission of protecting the ridge for perpetuity.

General description: Three trails, each originating from a separate access point, introduce the Mohonk Area splendor—one of inspiring cliffs, grand views, and fragile habitats.

General location: 6 miles west of New Paltz.

Special attractions: Vistas, dramatic quartz conglomerate cliffs, spring wildflowers and flowering shrubs, fall foliage.

Length: Sky Top Hike, 1 mile round trip; Bonticou Crag Hike, 3.5 miles round trip; The Trapps Loop, 5.25 miles round trip.

Elevation: Elevation changes range between 250 and 300 feet.

Difficulty: Sky Top and The Trapps Loop, both easy. Bonticou Crag Hike, moderate.

Maps: Mohonk Mountain House and Mohonk Preserve trail maps.

Special requirements: These independent, privately owned properties each charge a per person entry fee, with the resort charging a per person parking fee as well. A reciprocity has been struck, where payment for a day's hiking at one site buys same-day hiking privileges at the other. Users accept full responsibility for any risk and agree to follow the posted rules. Weekday and off-season visits to the resort cost less. Hikers should phone the resort prior to visiting to confirm that its trails will be open.

Season and hours: Spring through fall, 7 a.m. to dusk. Mohonk

Mohonk Lake and resort.

Preserve Visitor Center: 8 a.m. to 5 p.m. weekdays, with reduced week-end hours.

For information: Mohonk Mountain House; Mohonk Preserve.

Finding the trailhead: From New York State Thruway Interstate 87, take exit 18 and go west on New York 299 passing through New Paltz and crossing over the Wallkill River bridge. Take the first right, turning onto Springtown Road and bear left at the fork in 0.5 mile. This is Mountain Rest Road; follow it 2.7 miles to reach the preserve visitor center on the right, parking on the left. Continue another 0.7 mile to reach the resort gatehouse on the left.

For The Trapps Loop from I-87, go 7.2 miles west on NY 299, reaching the junction with U.S. Highway 44/New York 55. Go west on US 44/NY 55 for 1.7 miles and turn right for parking.

The hikes: For the shortest route to **Sky Top**, start at the putting green near the front of Mountain House and ascend past the conference building.

The trail transports visitors to a bygone era, crossing ledges, visiting rustic Victorian gazebos, and overlooking Mountain House and Mohonk Lake. Castlelike Mountain House, an architectural collage of frame and stone structures with turrets, balconies, and gables, adds to the enchantment of the deep green lake and white cliff shore. An evergreen-deciduous forest with mountain laurel and berry bushes claims the slope.

MOHONK LAKE RESORT – MOHONK PRESERVE

By Hayes Lookout (0.4 mile), photographers attain a spectacular over-view of Mohonk Lake, Mountain House, the Hudson Valley, and Catskill ridges and peaks; the view excels when splashed with autumn red and yellow. The spur to Thurston Rock offers views at the far end of the lake and The Trapps.

Cross Sky Top Road and ascend the steps to arrive at the Albert K. Smiley Memorial Tower (0.5 mile), a regional landmark named for the founder of Mountain House. Huge stone blocks, a spiral staircase, and long thin tower windows contribute the tower's medieval charm; a 360-degree vista rewards the climb. Return as you came or plot a loop return along the many interlocking trails and carriage roads.

The **Bonticou Crag** hike begins a mile away at the Mohonk Preserve Visitor Center. Follow the red trail east away from the staff parking lot. A detour downhill at the start offers a look at the destination, an immense, jutting skyline cliff.

A woods road replaces the mowed track as it leaves the field to travel a pine-deciduous woods. Birch fill out the midstory, and poison ivy lines the road. In spring, the bloom of dogwoods adds to a tour. Keep left, bypassing the Pond Trail, which descends to round a circular pond.

At 0.5 mile descend to the right, following the blue-blazed Northeast Trail, a canted foot trail. A sharp pitch and marked rise characterize the tour as it crosses a ravine. Soon, round a jumble of chunky boulders at the base of Bonticou Crag. At the 0.9-mile junction avoid the yellow trail to the right that makes a rugged, rock-climbing assault on the summit. Instead, stay with the Northeast Trail for a gentler back-door ticket to Bonticou Crag.

At 1.3 miles go right, still following the blue Northeast Trail, passing between boulders and along the cliff to climb the wooded north slope. Top the ridge, again meeting the yellow trail; this time follow it right. Traverse the summit ridge, as it shows a burst of mountain laurel, low-stature trees, azalea bushes, a variety of wildflowers, and humped outcrops; watch closely for the yellow blazes.

Upon attaining the escarpment ledge, views include the crag overhang, wooded Guyot Hill, the Wallkill and Hudson river valleys, and the Catskill Mountains. Before exploring the white quartz-conglomerate rim, make a mental note of where the trail first reached the escarpment to speed your return; retrace your steps.

For **The Trapps Loop**, hike southeast from the end of the parking turnaround to reach the loop junction at Trapps Bridge. This 0.25-mile connector follows part of the old turnpike; deciduous trees and mountain laurel frame the way. Pass the red Shongum Path on the left, prior to the bridge.

Ascend to bridge level, but do not cross it. Instead, turn left to find The Trapps Loop junction; a signboard and self-pay station mark the site. Follow Overcliff left for a clockwise loop. The shale-surfaced carriage road contours the wooded slope for a gentle ascent, bypassing an impressive scatter of massive rock, a canted rock slab, and a small overhang. Rare gaps offer views across Coxing Kill.

Keep to the carriage road, rounding and descending to the other side of The Trapps ridge, once again touring an area of breakaway boulders beneath a cliff. Bypass the blue Sleepy Hollow Trail, and bear right as an unmarked carriage road arrives on the left.

Rhododendron Bridge (2.6 miles) marks a major junction. For the loop, take Undercliff carriage road to the right; the Laurel Ledge carriage road heads left. Across the bridge, find Old Minnewaska carriage road and Oakwood Drive.

Undercliff again contours the woodland slope. Oaks, maple, birch, and hemlock comprise the woods, with azalea and a few dogwoods displacing the mountain laurel. Wild geranium and jack-in-the-pulpit color the trail's sides. At 3.25 miles again bypass Sleepy Hollow Trail to find early leaf-masked views of The Trapps cliffs and hear climbers overhead.

Old-growth trees rise from the steep slope dropping away from the carriage road. Ahead, find less impeded looks at the 200-foot white quartzite cliffs. Millipedes dot the overhangs, and boulder slabs continue to riddle the base. Forest gaps offer looks to the east-southeast and at a hairpin turn on US 44.

At 4.6 miles the cliffs plunge to the carriage road in dramatic fashion. A memorial and climbers kiosk introduce the early-day climbers who popularized the area and explain the conditions for climbing. Next round a shale slope to close the loop (5 miles); return to the trailhead (5.25 miles).

61 *LAKE MINNEWASKA STATE PARK PRESERVE*

Overview

A former resort and recent battleground between developers and environ-mentalists, this state park preserve presents a tranquil natural realm. The site boasts beautiful white-cliff escarpments, picturesque blue waters, and soothing forests—images to delight poet and photographer. Comfortable carriageways and foot trails travel the preserve for tours of varying length and discovery.

General description: The selected carriageway circuit travels from Lake Minnewaska, around Lake Awosting, and across a Shawangunk escarpment rim for a rich and varied tour.

General location: 10 miles west of New Paltz.

Special attractions: Striking ledges and vistas, attractive mountain lakes, a waterfall, mixed woods, wildflowers, and flowering shrubs.

Length: 11.8 miles round trip, including Rainbow Falls detour.

Elevation: The trail shows about a 600-foot elevation change.

Difficulty: Moderate.

Maps: State park flier; New York-New Jersey Trail Conference maps, Shawangunk Trails-South and Lake Minnewaska Area.

Special requirements: Fee area.

Season and hours: Spring through fall, 9 a.m. to 7 p.m.

For information: New York State Parks, Palisades Region.

Finding the trailhead: From New York State Thruway Interstate 87, take exit 18 for New Paltz and go west on New York 299 for 7.2 miles. At the junction with U.S. Highway 44/New York 55, go west on US 44/NY 55 for 4.4 miles and turn left for the park. The trail starts from the picnic area at the end of the park road.

The hike: From the picnic area, descend via the red trail to the Minnewaska lakeshore. At the northwest corner of the lake (opposite the swimming area), take the green Upper Awosting Carriageway west; a fine-grade slate provides a smooth walking surface. Hemlock, maple, oak, beautiful white birch, and mountain laurel comprise the woods.

The carefree stroll allows eyes and thoughts to roam; the occasional gap offers views north. Deer, grouse, and goshawk may slow strides. The trail shows a mild uphill grade more apparent to the eye than the body. The lure of the forest and song of the birds push aside any road noise. Cyclists may share the way.

At 0.7 mile bypass an old orchard where the snarled trees still flower in spring and rusted pieces of farm equipment blend into the meadow. Along the way, side brooks sheet over outcrops draining to Peters Kill below, and color-coded foot trails branch away. Beneath a powerline, a flat gray outcrop suggests a stop.

Upper Awosting Carriageway. Lake Minnewaska State Park.

LAKE MINNEWASKA STATE PARK PRESERVE

Before long, scenic rock ledges with fern-and-grass topped shelves border the way. At 2.6 miles the aqua-blazed Long Path emerges from a break in Litchfield Ledge. A detour right on Long Path leads to Rainbow Falls.

To view the falls, descend through a deep woods of mature hemlock and beech, crossing a side drainage and Huntington Ravine. Rainbow Falls marks a side stream, plunging to the latter. Its rivulets pour from an overhang, gracing a color-streaked cliff; a growing streamer of algae catches the water. Return to Upper Awosting Carriageway (3.2 miles) and resume the hike west to Lake Awosting.

Gradually, the terrain flattens. At the carriageway junction at 3.75 miles, turn right now following a black-blazed earthen carriageway for a counterclockwise tour of Lake Awosting. The dam presents an open lake view, animated by ducks, geese, and shorebirds. Pinched at its middle, the huge lake shows scalloped coves, evergreen-deciduous shores, and slopes and ledges of white quartzite. Sweet pepperbush, azalea, and mountain and sheep laurel braid together in a showy understory display.

At 4.1 miles bypass a rangers cabin, staying above shore for overlooks and cross-lake views, but no lake access. At 4.9 miles, an open flat with an old foundation and broken bricks and glass hints at a bygone time. At junctions, keep to the black carriageway.

At 5.25 miles the Long Path briefly shares the route; soon after, tour closer to shore. Monstrous hemlocks, pockets of sheep laurel, scenic pines, and lakeside outcrops add to the journey; side paths travel the small peninsulas. Past the foot trail to Spruce Glen and Murray Hill, find the swimming area with its lakeward white outcrop, bumpy with quartz and dotted by pines.

Stay on the black carriageway, drifting into woods at 6.4 miles. At 6.7 miles a spur leads to a ledge overlooking Lake Awosting; now turn away from the lake for good. At the upcoming junction go right on the blue carriageway, now hiking toward Hamilton and Castle Point carriageways.

The trail alternately tours mixed woods interlaced with mountain laurel and stands of small bizarre-shaped pines accompanied by sheep laurel and berry bushes. Periodic outcrops offer views. Glimpses of the white-gray cliff of Castle Point precede to the junction at 7.5 miles. Go left on shale-surfaced Castle Point Carriageway, staying the blue markers.

Pass beneath jutting overhangs and ledges for views spanning a deciduous-filled drainage to scenic Battlement Terrace. Ahead, top Castle Point Terrace, reaching Castle Point at 8.2 miles for a spectacular 180- to 200-degree vista sweeping west and south with Hamilton Point, Gertrudes Nose, Lake Awosting, the wooded rims and swells of the park, and distant Hudson Valley.

With the descent, perspectives shift east, adding views of Sky Tower in the nearby Mohonks. Where the trail passes under a powerline, it drifts from the escarpment edge, touring a more varied woods. Top Kempton Ledge (10.5 miles), for overlooks of Palmaghatt Kill, the Hudson Valley, and an isolated outcrop of fluted cliffs. A pale green lichen blotches the smooth white stone, and deep fissures invade the terrace.

Follow the blue carriageway downhill, avoiding a spur turning right to Hamilton Carriageway. An open grassy area presents a Catskill's view. Upon reaching Lakeshore Drive (the red carriageway rounding Lake Minnewaska), turn left to close the loop at the swimming area (11.7 miles), and return to the picnic area (11.8 miles).

Half the size of Lake Awosting, picturesque blue-green Lake Minnewaska reflects a partial shoreline of abrupt white cliffs with a talus base. Atop the white-cliff terrace sits the attractive stone building of the park office. Hemlock and pine interlace the deciduous trees of shore. Autumn's brush puts a special flourish on this closing image of the tour.

Overview

At this 2,175-acre wildlife management area (WMA), more than half comprised of freshwater wetland, a former railway rolls out an avenue to relaxation and nature discovery. On the west side of Bashakill Marsh, snatches of the historic Delaware and Hudson Canal (1828 to 1898) offer additional exploration. A blockade halting soft-coal shipments from England gave rise to this 108-mile canal linking the domestic coal fields of Pennsylvania with Hudson River ports. A premier bird-watching site, the WMA attracts birders year-round and invites daylight and evening watches.

General description: Part of the greater Long Path, traversing New York State, this rail-to-trail travels the eastern edge of Bashakill Marsh, offering wildlife observation.
General location: Just south of Wurtsboro.
Special attractions: Largest freshwater marsh in southeastern New York; spring-nesting waterfowl and warblers, brooding summer birds, and fall migrants; wetland and upland woods; observation towers; spring flora.
Length: 13 miles round trip.
Elevation: The trail is virtually flat.

Birch-lined rail-trail, Bashakill Wildlife Management Area.

Difficulty: Easy.

Maps: Bashakill Wildlife Management Area brochure.

Special requirements: No amenities available; bring water. Expect some soggy stretches, and avoid during hunting season.

Season and hours: Year-round, 24 hours. In winter, expect snow and unplowed lots to limit access. Although the WMA prohibits camping, night fishing, owl watching, and star gazing are acceptable nighttime activities at the refuge.

For information: New York State Department of Environmental Conservation, Region 3.

Finding the trailhead: From New York 17, take exit 113 and go south on U.S. Highway 209 for 5.2 miles, turning left on Sullivan County 163/ Orange County 61 for Otisville. Go 0.4 mile and turn left to round the WMA's east shore. In 0.1 mile find a fishing access; in 0.2 mile find the southern trailhead for the WMA's rail trail. Find its north end at the southeast outskirts of Wurtsboro.

The hike: From the southernmost access, the rail trail dead-ends to the south in 0.2 mile; the primary tour travels north, edging the marsh. In the morning, songbirds regale travelers, and dew bejewels the vegetation. Woody vines droop between the trees that shape a thin border between the trail and wetland flat.

A wetland often claims both sides of the rail levee. Duckweed, lily pads, loosestrife, clumps of arrowhead, algae, and flooded stumps and snags variously characterize the marsh. Cross-beams and footbridges ease drainage crossings.

Columbine, wild strawberry, wild geranium, violet, and more sprinkle color to the tour. Open sites offer fine marsh vantages and fishing access. In places, the old rail ties ripple the trailbed or lie discarded to its side.

Oriole, warbler, scarlet tanager, bluebird, green heron, grouse, osprey, vulture, and a wide variety of waterfowl lengthen the list of bird sightings. Woodchuck, muskrat, beaver, and white-tailed deer top the one for mammals.

At 0.5 mile find a junction and the second trailhead; with five interim trailheads off South Road, the rail trail readily welcomes hopscotch or car-shuttle travel. To the right a footbridge leads to the parking lot, a nature trail heads left, and curving between the two lies an overgrown segment of the rail trail. Veer left for the nature trail and observation tower; this spur rejoins the rail trail farther north, where it again clears for easier travel.

The nature trail shows a confusion of splits. At the first split, the left fork dead-ends at a fishing access; the right fork advances the nature trail. Upon turning left for Station 1, the trail again splits, with the left fork leading to a marshy point; the right one pursuing the nature trail numbers to the tower (Station 9). White pines and oaks frame the single-story platform, which overlooks open water, treed islands, arrowhead, and lily pads; Canada geese navigate faint channels amid the vegetation.

BASHAKILL WILDLIFE MANAGEMENT AREA

From the tower, continue north along the marsh and bear left at the fork to return to the rail trail (1.2 miles); a right continues the nature trail. Pine, hemlock, oak, mountain laurel, and azalea dress the return to the rail trail; a few yellow disks mark the way. Back on the rail trail and Long Path, find a scenic aisle of white birch. Crossing a gap-toothed boardwalk and an area of embedded ties, reach the next parking area and a launch site at 1.6 miles.

Ties again ripple the trailbed to the north, as birch form a scenic arborway. At times, red-winged blackbirds fiercely defend their nests, bombing any geese that swim past. A vast field of loosestrife claims the marsh to the right, while arrowhead dominates the main marsh. The woody stems of the loosestrife provide natural perches for the blackbirds. Atop a snag sits an osprey nest, as another woodland tour begins.

Prior to an old gnarled maple at 2.25 miles, look for the overgrown path heading left to a second tower; beware, poison ivy intermingles with the grasses. Reach the tower in 200 yards for another overlook of the marsh mosaic. The northbound tour resumes with a bridge crossing. Skunk cabbage and false hellebore line the brook and riddle the wetland woods, as the trail alternates between woods and marsh.

At 3.7 miles cross Haven Road, travel the gravel access road through the parking lot, and round the gate to the north. This is the most popular access to the WMA and often overflows with birders's vehicles.

Pockets of horsetail reed now dot the trail. Bypassing a scenic multi-trunked pine find a spur ascending a steep incline to the left labeled "side trail to lookout." Along it, tags identify some of the tree species. Here the tower view overlooks the meandering course of Bashakill. Hook past the tower, returning to the rail trail and soon bypassing a footboard crossing to the next parking area.

Ahead, swampy passages mar the woods tour. At 5.3 miles pass below an area of private, abandoned houses. Footbridges over the split flow of Bashakill next mark off distance.

Sounds of NY 17 precede the underpass (6 miles), where Virginia creeper scales the tunnel's concrete walls. The rail corridor ahead shows an open cathedral, and turtles plop from the banks as hikers pass. At 6.5 miles the trail comes out opposite Walker Lane in southeast Wurtsboro. While the Long Path continues north, return as you came.

HUDSON VALLEY

This New York region celebrates the Hudson River, a vital transportation and recreation corridor, past and present. Rising above the broad water to the south find the striking Hudson Highlands and Bear Mountain/Harriman complex. The Appalachian Trail spends much of its 95-mile New York sojourn snaking through this region.

At the northeast extent of the region, the attractive Taconic skyline separates New York from Massachusetts and Connecticut. Tucked away at the Connecticut border find the nation's first Registered Natural Historical Landmark.

The Hudson Valley Landscape is one of ridges, peaks, and valleys. Multi-state vistas reward travelers. Mountain laurel, dogwood, and azalea endorse spring tours.

Overview

Snug in the southern Taconic Mountain Range, abutting 11 miles of the Massachusetts and Connecticut border, this New York state park hosts trails that blur state lines. Bash Bish Falls annually brings 100,000 visitors to the park but actually lies in Massachusetts, best reached by a New York trail. The park's prized skyline route, the South Taconic Trail, meanders in and out of New York and Massachusetts with an equal disregard to borders.

General description: Three hikes of varying difficulty begin at Bash Bish Trailhead: an easy round-trip falls hike, a demanding full-day (or overnight) skyline hike, and a peak hike of average difficulty that may be car-shuttled.
General location: East of Copake Falls, New York.
Special attractions: Bash Bish Falls, mid-June to early July azalea and mountain laurel blooms, skyline vistas of three states, overlooks of the Taconic Mountains autumn-painted terrain.
Length: Bash Bish Falls Trail, 1.5 miles round trip; South Taconic Trail (South), 16.2 miles round trip; South Taconic Trail (North), a 4.2-mile shuttle or 7.4 miles round trip.
Elevation: All start at 800 feet. Bash Bish Falls Trail climbs 400 feet, ending at the falls. South Taconic Trail (South) tops Alander Mountain at 2,250 feet, then rolls between 1,500 and 2,300 feet, tagging Brace Mountain (2,311 feet). South Taconic Trail (North) climbs 1,100 feet to Prospect Hill.
Difficulty: Bash Bish Falls Trail, easy; South Taconic Trail (South) strenuous; South Taconic Trail (North), moderate.
Maps: Park trail flier (map not to scale); New York-New Jersey Trail Conference map, South Taconic Trail (has contour lines).
Special requirements: While the New York state park prohibits trailside camping, within reach of the South Taconic Trail (South), Massachusetts has a first-come, first-served cabin and fifteen backcountry campsites (fee and permit required; contact Mount Washington State Forest, East Street, Mount Washington, MA).
Season and hours: Spring through fall, dawn to dusk; state park campground: May 10 to October 31.
For information: New York State Parks, Taconic Region.
Finding the trailhead: From Copake Falls, go 0.7 mile east on New York 344 to reach Bash Bish Trailhead on the right.

To spot a vehicle for the South Taconic Trail (North), take Cemetery Road north from Copake Falls and continue north on North Mountain Road. Go 1.4 miles from the Cemetery-North Mountain roads intersection and turn right on unmarked Sunset Rock Road, a seasonally maintained single-lane gravel road. Reach trailhead parking on the right in 1.1 miles.

Bash Bish Falls, Mount Washington State Forest (Massachusetts)

The hikes: One best appreciates **Bash Bish Falls Trail** in the quiet off-season or in the early morning hours midweek. Follow the closed service road east upstream above Bash Bish Brook for early overlooks of the sparkling stream coursing over bedrock. Hemlock and maples overlace the trail, while boulders and rock slabs punctuate shore and waterway. Although deep pools invite, swimming is not allowed. At 0.75 mile, stairs descend to a boot-polished schist outcrop offering an unobstructed view of the falls.

Bash Bish Falls, a split-character forked falls, spills in an energetic rush around a skyward-pointing rock wedge. An emerald pool enclosed by a crescent cliff and a bouldery outlet capture the water. The right fork shows a tiered veil broadening at the base, the left fork a showery drop ending in a water slide. Downstream, the gorge holds an exciting union of rock and water. Return as you came.

White blazes mark the entire length of the South Taconic Trail.

Hike the **South Taconic Trail (South)**, following white markers along the limited-access road that angles downhill to the cabins, west of Bash Bish Trailhead. Cross the bridge and go past the cabins before entering the wilds on a foot trail. A contouring ascent through mountain laurel, a sharp climb through a stand of 1- to 3-foot-diameter hemlocks, and a tour of a high-canopy maple forest and pine-oak area lead to a ridge junction at 1.1 miles.

Here a 0.2-mile round trip detour via a blue spur trail finds a 180-degree western perspective with Washburn Mountain. The white South Taconic Trail continues its ascent amid oak woodland and later a hemlock grove, soon bypassing a second blue trail. Save for a notch at 3 miles, the trail hugs the ridge. Pines appear now and again, and views flip to the east.

At 3.5 miles, prior to an old lookout site on Alander Ridge, look for a faintly painted blue marker atop a flat exposed outcrop. For the South Taconic Trail alone, continue straight ahead, staying with the white blazes.

For an Alander Mountain summit detour, descend left on the blue trail, coming to a saddle where an old but highly liveable cabin sits. The cabin offers a dry overnight wayside on a first-come, first-served basis; early summer azalea and laurel fancy it up. The blue fork descending past the cabin passes through Massachusetts's Mount Washington State Forest, eventually reaching the backpacker campsites; the blue fork ascending east tags Alander summit in 0.3 mile for a view.

Beyond the junction at 3.5 miles, the South Taconic Trail dishes up a fine 270-degree view with Massachusetts's Alander Mountain and Mount Frissell, Connecticut's Round Mountain, and New York's Brace Mountain and the westward stretching valley and foothills. An outcrop of wavy patterned schist provides the vantage.

The trail, shaded by mixed oaks, maple, and beech, now drops away, sometimes steeply. Where it comes out at a former woods road, follow the woods road left, dipping to a drainage, ascending, and bypassing an overgrown blue trail on the left.

A few white pines tower trailside, near the junction with the red-blazed Robert Brook Trail (5.2 miles). An occasional rock wall or waist-high ostrich

TACONIC STATE PARK

To Hillsdale

To Hillsdale

To Catamount Ski Area

Prospect Hill 1,919 ft.

22

Sunset Rock

Sunset Rock Road

To South Egremont

Taconic State Park

Cedar Brook

Town of Copake Falls

0   0.5   1

Miles

344

To Millerton

Bash Bish Creek

Bash Bish Falls

To South Egremont

N

Alander Mountain 2,250 ft.

Robert Brook Trail

Ashley Hill Trail

New York

Mount Frissell 2,453 ft.

Massachusetts

Connecticut

Brace Mountain 2,311 ft.

To Whitehouse Crossing

fern next decorates the South Taconic Trail. When the mountain laurels close ranks, a splendid floral aisle ushers hikers skyward in early summer.

At 6.7 miles a foot trail veers right traversing a ridge outcrop for a western vantage, before returning once more to the woods road and bypassing the Ashley Hill Trail. After the grade has eased at 7.6 miles, a red trail descends left toward Mount Frissell and Tri-state Point. The South Taconic Trail continues on the old woods road to Brace Mountain; go right where the roadbed forks.

A shrubby, open complex houses this moderate-grade route. At 8.2 miles a foot trail heads left topping Brace Mountain, where a cairn 5 feet tall puts an exclamation mark on the tour. Views sweep the tri-state area. Return as you came, or continue south to Whitehouse Crossing.

The **South Taconic Trail (North)** angles west across NY 344, following white blazes up a wooded slope to the left of Cedar Brook drainage. (A blue-blazed trail along the brook offers an alternative start, but requires low water for fordings; it joins the description at 1.7 miles). At 0.2 mile turn left on a wide woods road and watch for the white markers pointing hikers uphill through a tight conifer stand.

At 0.5 mile join the red trail, ascending a much smaller woods road. From here to where the Cedar Brook Trail arrives at 1.7 miles, a series of color-coded trails arrive and exit; stay with the white blazes. Tall pine and maple offer shade, but with each burst of ascent, the trail opens up. The added sun brings out the park's earliest mountain laurel blooms. The upper reaches of the ridge again present a fuller forest of oak and maple.

At 2.5 miles exit a shrub corridor to find an unmarked spur leading left to Sunset Rock; the continuation of the South Taconic Trail follows the faint jeep track straight ahead. The side spur reaches westward-facing Sunset Rock, a humped-back rock (elevation 1,788 feet) in 0.1 mile. Views pan the immediate valley farmland, with the Catskills and Hudson Valley some 50 miles distant.

Northbound, the South Taconic Trail flattens as it follows the grassy jeep track through an arborway of oak, pine, and thick mountain laurel. At 3 miles turn left for a mild descent along a neatly narrow woods path that comes out at Sunset Rock Road and the shuttle parking area at 3.2 miles.

For Prospect Hill, angle downhill across Sunset Rock Road and pass a springhouse ruins for a comfortable forest ascent through oak-maple woodland and a pine-shrub complex. Outcrops offer views west of farmland, east of mounts Everett and Darby, and south of Bash Bish and Alander mountains.

Prior to a New York-Massachusetts boundary marker, turn left topping Prospect Hill (elevation 1,919 feet) at 3.7 miles, bettering the view from Sunset Rock. Return as you came or to your shuttle vehicle.

General description: This 2,155-mile national scenic trail from Maine to Georgia cuts across the southeast corner of New York State, rolling along ridges and dipping to roads. The New York leg takes an average of seven to ten days to complete.

General location: The trail swings between the Connecticut and New Jersey state lines.

Special attractions: Vistas, side trails, low-elevation mixed forests, historic stone walls, wildflowers, fall foliage.

Length: 95.2 miles one way, with the northern 7.2 miles of trail slipping in and out of Connecticut.

Elevation: In New York, the trail travels between a low point of 125 feet along the Hudson River and a high point of 1,433 feet at Prospect Rock on Bellvale Mountain.

Difficulty: Strenuous.

Maps: Appalachian Trail Conference (ATC), Appalachian Trail maps.

Special requirements: Hikers need to work out the logistics of carrying and obtaining adequate food and supplies, plan what to do in case of an emergency, and arrange for transportation at the end of the trail. Expect rocky, difficult conditions; strong map and compass skills ease travel.

Season and hours: Spring through fall.

For information: Appalachian Trail Conference.

Finding the trailhead: The Appalachian Trail crosses many New York state and county routes and traverses Fahnestock, Hudson Highlands, and Bear Mountain-Harriman state parks. New York State through-hikers will find the northernmost road access to the Appalachian Trail at the New York/Connecticut 55 - Hoyt Road intersection. Find the southernmost road access along New York 17A near Greenwood Lake.

The hike: The first trail in the nation to win national scenic trail distinction, the Appalachian Trail (AT) salutes the mountain wilds of fourteen eastern states. Conceived in the early 1920s, this hiker filament rolls atop the ancient Appalachia Mountains, dipping to cross the important eastern river valleys. Most of the AT greenway has received permanent public protection; some four thousand volunteers along with two hundred public agencies maintain and oversee the trail.

For 95 miles through southeastern New York, the rolling tour passes through low-elevation deciduous woods and hemlock forests, traveling the state's low, rugged ridges and hilltops. The AT dips to cross brooks and drainages (often at road crossings), rounds lakes and ponds but with limited access, and rings up grand views, including looks at the Hudson River Valley, the Taconics, the Catskills, the Shawangunks, the Hudson Highlands, and Manhattan city skyline.

Open to foot travel only, the white-blazed AT advances primarily via foot trail, with some sections of abandoned woods road. The trail does travel developed roads where it descends to cross Bear Mountain Bridge over the Hudson River. The trail can be rocky and steep; expect to use your hands from time to time for steadying, climbing, and easing yourself over rocks. Beware of rattlesnakes. Tight passages such as the "Lemon Squeezer" in Harriman State Park add interest to the tour. As the protected greenway itself can be narrow, keep to the trail to avoid straying onto private land.

While some fifteen lean-tos lie along or just off the trail, a tent remains standard equipment. As these first-come, first-served waysides cannot be reserved, chancing that you will be the first to arrive and claim a lean-to for the night is both unwise and an unnecessary wilderness risk. When pitching a tent, camp in an established site to minimize the environmental harm to the route.

On a north-south tour, the AT sashays between New York and Connecticut for the first 7.2 miles, before committing to New York's watch for the next 88 miles. As it travels the rich hardwood forests of Hammersley Ridge in Pawling Nature Reserve (owned by The Nature Conservancy), a few marshy sites mark the tour. Early views feature the rolling countryside of Dutchess County.

The 7-mile leg between New York 22 and New York 55 finds an open view from West Mountain. Much of the way, large oaks and fields characterize the tour. The southern 2 miles of this segment travel within a quarter mile of a nuclear-fuel testing site, now cleaned up and cleared for unrestricted use. But for hikers who feel uneasy about the land's past, an alternate blue trail travels a roadway, avoiding this woods walk.

After crossing Interstate 84, the AT gathers open views from Depot Hill, traversing rock ledges while rolling along the wooded ridge. The undulating trail remains along ridge or slope, topping Stormville and Hosner Mountains for views of the Catskills, Shawangunks, and Hudson Highlands. Historic stone walls recall an earlier time.

South of the Taconic Parkway, cross Shenandoah Mountain, entering Clarence Fahnestock Memorial State Park. An overlook applauds the shimmery platter of Canopus Lake, before the trail descends to round the wooded slope and ridge of the west shore. The AT only reaches Canopus Lake level, where the trail crosses New York 301.

Ahead, briefly follow the bed of an 1862 narrow-gauge railroad used to transport ore. Hemlock groves, swamps, and ridgetop views advance and vary the trek. Blueberry patches and mountain laurel bring seasonal flourish.

At Denning Hill, the New York City skyline assumes its place in the panoramic view. While traversing the Hudson Highlands, enjoy spectacular Hudson River views. The tour is rugged, but the rewards great. A steep, grueling descent leads to Bear Mountain Bridge, for the Hudson River crossing.

APPALACHIAN TRAIL

The popular Bear Mountain-Harriman State Park recreation complex next hosts the tour. It was here in 1923 that the first section of newly built Appalachian Trail was christened and opened to walking. Within the park complex, interlocking trails present day-hike loops and sample tours of the AT.

Pass through the developed area of Bear Mountain Park with its Trailside Museum and Zoo, picnic area, swimming pool, and lake. A hearty ascent follows, topping Bear Mountain at Perkins Memorial Tower (1,305 feet). Travelers secure vistas from Bear, West, and Black mountains, before skirting Island Pond. The terrain remains steep and rugged, as the trail continues to collect peaks and vistas.

About 10 miles north of the New Jersey state line, Fitzgerald Falls, a hemlock-shaded 25-foot waterfall spilling down a rocky cleft, wins its share of admirers. New York's send-off to the AT comes at Bellvale Mountain, where frequent ledges reward with views of Greenwood Lake and Ramapo Hills.

As spatial constraints necessarily limit the detail of this description, thru-trail travelers and hikers planning short excursions along the AT should contact the ATC (see Appendix D) for its official maps and detailed guides. Entire books have been devoted to this premier hiking trail and to the New York-New Jersey trail component alone; consult the bookshelves of your local library, bookstore, or backpacker/outfitter store.

65 BREAKNECK RIDGE TRAIL

General description: In Hudson Highlands State Park, this trail makes a rugged ascent from near river-level to roll along a knobby ridge, gathering vistas and reaching a lookout.

General location: East side of the Hudson River, 4 miles south of Beacon.

Special attractions: Hudson River, Shawangunk, and Catskill Mountains vistas; old fire lookout tower; mixed forest; mountain laurel and spring and summer wildflowers.

Length: 9.6 miles round trip.

Elevation: The trail shows a 1,500-foot elevation change, with the high point atop South Beacon Mountain.

Difficulty: Strenuous.

Maps: New York-New Jersey Trail Conference map, East Hudson trails.

Special requirements: Expect some hand-over-hand rock scrambles and wear boots that protect ankles. High winds and rain increase risk of the rocky ascent.

Season and hours: Spring through fall.

For information: New York State Parks, Taconic Region.

Finding the trailhead: From the New York 301/New York 9D junction in Cold Spring (8.5 miles north of Bear mountain Bridge), go north on NY 9D for 2 miles to find the trailhead and parking for two vehicles just north of the tunnel on the west side of the highway. Find additional parking 0.1 mile north on the left and the Breakneck Bypass trailhead 0.2 mile north on the right. As this state park corridor is minimally marked, be alert for paint blazes signaling the trail starts.

The hike: For a northbound ridge tour, follow the white-blazed trail southwest, passing through a narrow tree corridor at the north end of the NY 9D tunnel. Almost immediately the trail reveals a "go-for-it" character with a rigorous rocky ascent of the tunnel embankment and the steep west flank of Breakneck Ridge. Sumac, birch, viburnum, and grasses intersperse the rock, though may go unnoticed, as the climb takes utmost attention. Initially, beer cans, bottles, and graffiti mar the stage.

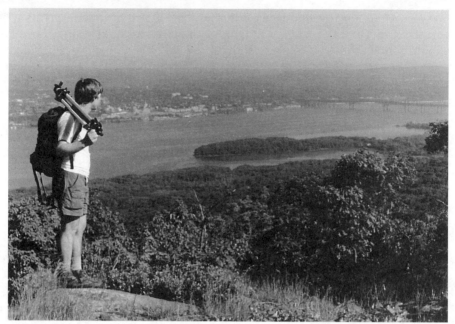

Hudson River from Breakneck Ridge, Hudson Highlands State Park.

With a few directional changes, attain the rocky shoulder of the ridge for views of the river, Pollepel Island, Storm King Mountain across the way, and Palisades Interstate Park to the south. The ascent now follows the ridgeline, adding looks at the steep drainage shaped by Breakneck Ridge and Mount Taurus.

For the next spurt of ascent, hikers have the option of following the white "X" alternative route, which adds a few steps by rounding versus scaling the imposing rocks ahead. At a mile comes the first vista knoll, as the trail rolls from bump to bump traversing the ridge north. Oaks, maple, ash, and birch comprise the woods.

The passage between knobs varies from relatively flat to steep notch descents. A fuller woods claims the dips, and grouse and deer may disrupt one's reverie. Views build as the trail progresses.

At 1.5 miles the red Breakneck Bypass Trail descends left, offering a saner return to the trailhead, but first continue the trek north. The next rise holds a 360-degree view of the Hudson River, the valley communities, the Interstate 84 bridge, and South and North Beacon mountains. Upon descent, the blue trail arrives on the right to share the route ahead. Patches of mountain laurel interlace the mixed forest.

At 3.2 miles the blue trail departs left as the white trail enters a brief forested ascent, tagging Sunset Point—a rock outcrop ringed by low oaks.

BREAKNECK RIDGE TRAIL

0   0.5   1
Miles

South Beacon Mountain

Trail

Wilkinson

Squirrel Hollow Brook

Sunset Point

To Beacon

Sugarloaf Mountain

Trail

Breakneck Ridge Trail

9D

Wilkinson

Breakneck Bypass Trail

N

P

Hudson River

To Cold Spring and Peekskill

A flatter tour follows before a sharp descent to Squirrel Hollow Brook, which generally carries enough water to dampen a bandanna.

Cross the brook and briefly merge with the yellow Wilkinson Trail (4.1 miles), a woods road. Follow it right for a short distance and then break away left for a steep ascent of Devils Ladder; white arrows point the way up this steep rocky slope. A past fire swept this site; young birch and big-toothed aspen lead the succession of reclaiming vegetation. The trail then grades into woods before emerging in the open at South Beacon Tower (4.7 miles).

Whether one chooses to mount the old lookout tower or not, the view atop the breezy ridge rewards, trumping all previous ones. Looks pan the river, the ridge, and the nearby peaks, as well as the distant flat ridge of the Shawangunks and more ragged outline of the Catskills.

While the white trail continues north, retrace your steps to the Breakneck Bypass at 7.9 miles and follow its red-blazed route down the deciduous-wooded west flank. Mountain laurel gains a stronghold, while viburnum and huckleberry weave a complement. At times the descent is markedly steep. After following a thin seasonal drainage, reach an outcrop (8.4 miles) with limited river views and a good look at Sugarloaf Mountain.

Before long, meet the woods road of the yellow-marked Wilkinson Trail, and bear left following it downhill to NY 9D. Big tulip trees and dogwoods decorate the lower slope. The trail comes out on the east side of the highway at 9.4 miles; turn left (south) to reach the additional trail parking in 0.1 mile and to close the loop at the tunnel in 0.2 mile.

General description: A demanding all-day or overnight loop rolls through steep wooded terrain, topping Bear and West mountains, offering views of the Lower Hudson River area.

General location: The northeast corner of the Bear Mountain-Harriman State Park complex, 18 miles south of Newburgh.

Special attractions: Vistas, Perkins Tower, lean-to, historic area, mountain laurel and dogwood blooms, fall foliage.

Length: 9.7-mile loop.

Elevation: The trail shows a 1,100-foot elevation change, with the high point atop Bear Mountain 1,305 feet.

Difficulty: Strenuous.

Maps: State park flier; New York-New Jersey Trail Conference map, Harriman Park-North Half.

Special requirements: Fee parking.

Season and hours: Spring through fall.

For information: New York State Parks, Palisades Region.

Finding the trailhead: From the Bear Mountain Toll Bridge over the Hudson River, go south on U.S. Highway 9W for 0.4 mile and turn right to reach the fee parking lot at Bear Mountain Inn.

The hike: This counterclockwise loop samples several prized trails: the Major Welch (red), the Appalachian and 1777 (both white), Timp-Torne (blue), and Suffern-Bear Mountain (yellow).

From the south side of Bear Mountain Inn, head west to reach and follow the Major Welch Trail north, along an asphalt path on the west shore of developed Hessian Lake. The popular path serves walker and jogger, as well as hiker. A rich forest shades the route, while an outcrop offers a lake overlook. Near the north end of the lake, follow the red-marked footpath to the left, ascending the north flank of Bear Mountain.

With steep spurts, the trail climbs and contours the maple-oak clad slope; rocks and roots sometimes foul footing. After a mile the trail charges straight up, takes a switchback, and finds a host of mountain laurel. The trail now travels on or along granitic outcrops, soon overlooking the wooded hills to the Hudson River. Views build north and east, including an up-river look at Bear Mountain Bridge.

Cross Perkins Drive and continue climbing and topping outcrops. Amid an oak and laurel picnic grove, cross a paved lane to again reach Perkins Drive near the summit; turn right for Perkins Tower (2.2 miles)— an attractive five-story stone tower built in the 1930s and still staffed.

Next follow the red trail, descending the outcrop ledges to the southeast below the tower. This rugged, vista-packed tour enwraps the oak-huckleberry slope, rolling between terraces of granite ledges and tilted outcrops, adding views south and west.

West Mountain trail shelter, Harriman State Park.

At 3 miles cross the road and follow the white-blazed Appalachian Trail (AT) left, staying along the road shoulder for the next 0.5 mile. Turn right, touring an open woods of maple, oak, and box elder. Grasses claim the forest floor.

At 3.8 miles an outcrop offers looks at West Mountain, the next destination. The AT then descends steeply through rock-studded woods to cross Seven Lakes Drive (4.2 miles) and follow the historic 1777 Trail for 0.1 mile. The 1777 Trail retraces the path taken by the British when they stunned the Americans by overtaking two crucial forts along the Hudson River, a strategic supply line during the Revolutionary War.

Turn right at a pine plantation to ascend amid a tall, full forest parted by snags. Follow a woods road left for 0.2 mile to pick up the foot trail on the right, for a more serious ascent. Over-the-shoulder looks find Bear Mountain and the Hudson, as snags and young trees claim the upper slope. Atop West Mountain, outcrops invite travelers to catch their breath, measure their accomplishment, and take in the view.

Angle left atop the summit ridge to merge with the blue Timp-Torne Trail for a rolling tour, tagging the high point at 5.1 miles. Where the trail dips to the other side of the ridge, find a 180-degree view west. An old fire zone claims the upper reaches of West Mountain, with young birch leading the plant succession. Over time, a healthy recovered forest will reclaim much of the view; meanwhile, hikers enjoy vistas every 0.1 mile or so.

BEAR MOUNTAIN LOOP

To Highland Falls

9W

6

To Peekskill

Perkins Drive

Major Welch Trail

Hessian Lake

Hudson River

To Palisades Interstate Parkway

P

Bear Mountain 1,305 ft.

Bear Mountain Inn

P

Seven Lakes Drive

1777 Trail

Appalachian Trail

West Mountain

Timp-Torne Trail

Doodletown Brook

To Stony Point

Suffern-Bear Mountain Trail

N

0   0.5   1

Miles

After attaining a grand 270-degree vista, featuring Black Mountain, West Mountain ridge, Bear Mountain, and the river, stay on the blue trail, which bears left, leaving the AT at 5.8 miles. Soon, the yellow Suffern-Bear Mountain Trail merges, and the joint blue/yellow trail rolls across the ridge, passing from regenerating forest to one of small-stature oak.

Where the route bends left (6.3 miles), the blue and yellow trail part company. A detour right on the blue trail finds an attractive stone lean-to atop an outcrop in 0.1 mile. It serves up a spectacular view of the Hudson River, The Timp, High and Little Tor, and the Manhattan skyline on clear days.

The yellow trail continues the loop, with a rolling descent amid laurel. After topping a bump on the flank of West Mountain, the trail descends steeply to cross and parallel Doodletown Brook downstream; birch and beech line the brook. At 7.7 miles turn left on a woods road bypassing a marshy bottomed forest. Then turn right, still following the yellow blazes, as the route crosses a small rise and side brook.

At the woods road at 8.1 miles, turn right, following the 1777 Trail only to take a quick left on a second woods road for a beautiful tour amid mature woods resplendent with dogwood blooms in the spring. Magnificent, big tulip trees, entangling vines, and Japanese barberry also define the tour.

At 8.6 miles, follow the earthen trail striking uphill to cross Seven Lakes Drive. The tour now follows a shady woods road paralleling an unobtrusive utility line. Mountain laurel replaces the dogwood, as the route descends and contours, once again meeting the white AT. Continue forward following the yellow/white blaze scheme, contouring on a broken asphalt path above the skating rink and administration building. At 9.7 miles, close the loop at the southwest corner of Hessian Lake.

67 PINE MEADOW LAKE LOOP

General description: This rolling, meandering circuit travels the milder reaches of Harriman State Park, touring woodland, topping hills, and skirting brook, lake, and swamp.

General location: 5 miles north of Suffern.

Special attractions: Mixed woods, rock features and ledge vistas, historic ruins, bird watching, mountain laurel and azalea blooms, fall foliage.

Length: 13.2 miles round trip.

Elevation: The trail travels between 500 and 1,200 feet in elevation, with the high point atop Diamond Mountain.

Difficulty: Moderate.

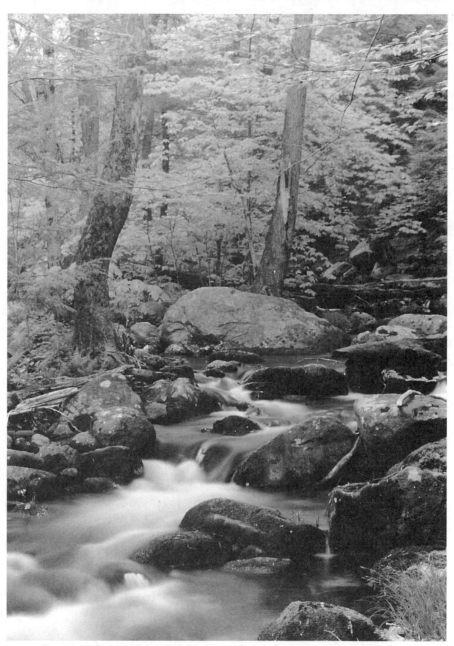

Stony Brook, Harriman State Park.

Maps: New York-New Jersey Trail Conference map, Harriman Park-South Half.

Special requirements: Expect muddy passages, especially in early spring and following rains. A precarious rocky descent off Diamond Mountain, requires caution and the use of hands.

Season and hours: Spring through fall. Reeves Meadow Visitor Center (and restroom): Memorial Day through Labor Day.

For information: New York State Parks, Palisades Region.

Finding the trailhead: From New York State Thruway Interstate 87, take exit 15 and go north on New York 17 for 2.1 miles, passing through Sloatsburg. Turn right on Seven Lakes Drive and go 1.5 miles to find Reeves Meadow Visitor Center on the right and additional parking 500 feet past it on the left.

The hike: On the east side of the visitor center, hike north past the water spigot to pick up an old woods road entering the woods on the right. A red-on-white blazing pattern marks the rocky Pine Meadow Trail as it parallels Stony Brook upstream. Hemlock, oaks, maple, birch, and beech weave a rich canopy, while leaf mat and moss comprise the forest floor. Morning hikers may spook a deer drinking at the rushing brook. Stony Brook is an attractive bouldery waterway, edged by moss-covered rocks, overlaced by branches, and accented by cascades and pools.

At 0.4 mile the trail bears right uphill through forest, remaining on a wide rocky trail, threaded by small drainages. On the slope, mountain laurel contributes to a full midstory. At 1.2 miles a white-blazed trail briefly shares the route; 500 feet ahead, bear left at the fork.

Tulip trees and box elder appear helterskelter amid the forest, as the trail now continues upstream along quiet-spilling Pine Meadow Brook, a headwater fork of Stony Brook. Where the trail grows soggy, rocks become allies instead of obstacles, and violets sprinkle color. Where the blue Seven Hills Trail merges from the right, find a small fireplace.

Cross the Pine Meadow Brook footbridge at 1.6 miles. On the opposite shore, the red and blue trails divide, forming the loop. Stay with the red Pine Meadow Trail, following it upstream (right) to Pine Meadow Lake for a counterclockwise tour. The trail bypasses a scenic moss-and-fern dressed boulder, before reaching trailside Ga-Nus-Quah (Giant Stones) Rock, a room-sized boulder overlooking Pine Meadow Brook where it pours through an outcrop and boulder gorge.

At 2.2 miles a side loop to the left finds a stone foundation with a rusting pipe. Ahead, where the red trail travels the wooded north shore of Pine Meadow Lake, remnant pipeline and an old holding pond echo back to the days of the Civilian Conservation Corps camps.

Upon reaching Pine Meadow Lake hikers may choose first to detour right 200 feet to the dam for an open lake vista, as thick mountain laurel isolates the red trail from the boxy boulder shore. In unlike ways, azalea

PINE MEADOW LAKE LOOP

or a free-swinging brier draws attention as the lake trail bypasses the ruins of Conklin Cabin, which dates back to 1778. At 3.3 miles swing left away from Pine Meadow Lake prior to the inlet for a meandering tour through maple-oak woodland; red blazes continue to point the way.

With a brook crossing, find swampy stretches that again suggest hopscotch travel from rock to rock. Azaleas favor these moist reaches. At 4.7 miles the Pine Meadow Trail halts at the yellow Suffern-Bear Mountain Trail; follow the latter left to continue the loop. A steep descent precedes the ascent of Panther Mountain, a scooped hilltop with twin peaks. Outcrops along the first summit provide the lone views east and south. The quiet terrain rolling away from the hill offers no clue that New York City lies but 30 miles away.

Descend from the second summit and enter a full forest, rich with mountain laurel. Oriole, grouse, turkey, towhee, blue jay, and tanager add to a roster of bird sightings. The trail rolls from rise to brook, coming out at an overgrown woods road, the red-blazed Tuxedo-Mount Ivy Trail. Again an old fireplace marks the junction; go left for the loop.

The trail now skirts Squirrel and Big Green swamps, with only filtered looks at the shrub-filled bottomlands. Where the trail meets a woods road between the two swamps, bear right, cross a footbridge and continue left amid a mountain laurel showcase in June. Be alert for the red blazes.

At the junction in 8 miles with the white Breakneck Mountain Trail, stay the red trail as it curves left. Off the hilltops, the forest shows little change. Cross a gravel road and look over the lower end of Big Green Swamp, which shows areas of phragmites (feathery headed marsh grasses) and open water. The trail then climbs, traveling the flat rock outcrops of a small rise. As this section of the hike receives less foot traffic, watch for markers.

At 9.9 miles, beyond a woods road, find the blue Seven Hills Trail and follow it left for the close of the loop; the trail is again better defined. With a brief woods road link, the rolling foot trail passes through woods, overlooks the watery-arm profile of Lake Sebago, and resumes straight ahead at a junction with the yellow trail (10.5 miles). Soon after, a white trail merges and shares the way, traversing Diamond Mountain with its striated granites and scrub trees.

Stay the blue trail to complete the tour; brief complicated descents lead to and from an open outcrop ledge offering a grand view across the treetops and out Pine Meadow Brook drainage. Think through each descent, be watchful of the thin ledges, and use your hands as needed, but look before you reach, as snakes do exist in this park.

Where the trail comes out at Pine Meadow Brook, turn left (upstream) to close the loop (11.6 miles). Cross the footbridge and turn right, retracing the initial 1.6 miles back to Reeves Meadow Visitor Center.

Overview

Unlike the awe-striking sandstone-shale gorges of New York State's Finger Lakes Region, the steep ravine of the Mianus River Gorge captivates with a dark-woods enchantment. Spared the fate of the axe because of its steep character, the preserve boasts one of the few intact stands of old-growth forest in the East.

This 621-acre preserve represents a pioneer land project of The Nature Conservancy (TNC), now managed by an independent organization affiliated with TNC. The site bears the distinction of being the nation's first Registered Natural Historic Landmark.

General description: A carefree stroll travels downstream along the Mianus River, exploring gorge and rim.

General location: On the New York-Connecticut border, 10 miles southeast of Mount Kisco, New York.

Special attractions: 350-year-old hemlocks, cascades, wooded gorge (ravine), historic quartz-feldspar quarry.

Length: 6-mile loop, including all side spurs.

Elevation: The trail shows about a 200-foot elevation change.

Difficulty: Easy.

Maps: Preserve trail guide.

Special requirements: Donation suggested; no pets, smoking, or picnicking. Obey all posted rules and closures.

Season and hours: April through November, 9:30 a.m. to 5 p.m.

For information: The Nature Conservancy, Lower Hudson Chapter.

Finding the trailhead: From the Bedford Village green, go 0.8 mile east on New York 172 (Pound Ridge Road) and turn right on Stamford/Long Ridge Road. In 0.5 miles turn right on Miller's Mill Road, cross the bridge in 300 feet, and turn left on Mianus River Road. Find the trailhead on the left in 0.6 mile.

From the Merritt Parkway (Connecticut 15) in Connecticut, take exit 34, go north on Connecticut 104 (Long Ridge/Stamford Road) for 7.2 miles, and turn left on Miller's Mill Road, crossing the bridge and turning left for the preserve.

The hike: Round the left side of the information shelter to follow the red Brink of the Gorge Trail east toward the river. Soon, the well-marked 3-foot-wide trail skirts a memorial bench overlooking the shallow, quiet-spilling 20-foot-wide Mianus River—more brooklike than river in character.

MIANUS RIVER GORGE WILDLIFE
REFUGE AND BOTANICAL PRESERVE

To Bedford

P

Safford
Cascade

Hemlock
Cathedral

Mianus River Road

Hobby Hill
Quarry

To
Stanwich,
CT

N

Mianus River

0   0.25   0.5

Miles

Havemeyer
Falls

S.J. Bargh Reservoir

Hugging the shore, the trail tours amid a leafy hollow of beech, birch, maple, hazel, fern, poison ivy, skunk cabbage, and false hellebore. Painted, snapping, and spotted turtles may be spied along the river, box tortoises amid the woods.

A huge white pine stands guard where the trail ascends. Oaks, maple, hickory, pine, and snags dress the higher slope, and a rock-slab footbridge crosses a drainage brimming with skunk cabbage. At the first signed junction, continue straight on the "outgoing" red trail. At 0.5 mile go left to tour closer to the river and visit Safford Cascade.

Downstream from Safford Cascade (0.7 mile), stone-step across the brook. The split lacy stream spills around and over scenic moss-capped rocks. Even when reduced to a mere weep, the mossy site retains its charm. The trail then parallels the brook upstream reaching junction A; bear left to resume the red tour. The blue trail presents opportunities to shorten the loop and return to the trailhead.

A colonial rock wall rests above the trail as it contours the slope, soon overlooking the narrowest point of the gorge. Orange-and-black beetles feed on conchs, while ferns flourish where the sunlight penetrates the forest. With an ascent, the trail enters the majestic beauty of Hemlock Cathedral, with its 100-foot-tall, 350-year-old monarchs. Beech, maple, and tulip trees fill out the forest.

Past the plaque honoring preservationist Gloria Hollister Anable, find junction B (1.1 miles); stay left to travel to the end of the preserve. Ahead, a 0.2-mile round-trip detour leads left to Hobby Hill Quarry, mined by using mule carts in the 1800s and excavated by Native Americans some four thousand years ago. Sparkles of mica and bits of quartz precede the quarry, which shows but a small depression in the slope, time-softened by moss, lichen, and fern; no collecting.

The downstream tour resumes, traversing 250 feet above the river, overlooking the steep gorge slope. Beautiful big beech and tulip trees and more of the colonial rock walls add to the tour. At 2.25 miles the trail bypasses a vernal pool giving life to Royal Fern Glen. After which, a spur to the left leads to a rock outcrop and leaf-framed view of S.J. Bargh Reservoir, a long widening of the river with a scalloped shore. Mountain laurel accents the vista site.

Back on the red trail, cross the stone bridge over the tributary of Havemeyer Falls and take an immediate left to descend to this attractive 15-foot waterfall. Its waters spill to a pool the color of dark ale before racing downhill to the awaiting reservoir. An island of moss and fern isolates the lacy streamers.

The red trail halts along the bank of Bargh Reservoir (3.5 miles); private lands lie to the south. Return following the blue trail, which shares portions of the red trail but clings to the upper wooded slope, smoothing out the dips. The tour again passes amid regal hemlocks and big tulip trees before coming out near the restrooms (6 miles).

LONG ISLAND

Completing the lineup of New York regions, this island domain at the southeast extreme serves up its own prescription for outdoor fun. Stretching from Gateway National Recreation Area to Montauk Point, Long Island brings together rare pine barren habitat; seaward, Long Island Sound, and bay-shore beaches; ghost forests; dune and swale habitats; spring-fed rivers; and a rare pine swamp. At-risk piping plovers and least terns nest on the island's barrier and bay beaches. Fox, deer, owl, osprey, may also enliven a tour. Despite its proximity to Manhattan, the island boasts a surprising wealth of natural discovery.

69 *WEST POND TRAIL*

General description: At Gateway National Recreation Area, this simple interpretive loop within the Jamaica Bay Wildlife Refuge introduces the wildlife and natural habitat of West Pond, Jamaica Bay, and the island's outwash plain.

General location: In New York City, southwest of John F. Kennedy International Airport.

Special attractions: Three hundred bird species with warbler migration (April/May), shorebirds (July/August), raptor migration (September through November), and winter waterfowl (March through early April); outstanding New York City vistas; nesting terrapins (July); flowering shrubs and wildflowers.

Length: 1.75-mile loop for West Pond Trail alone; 2.2-mile loop for a West Pond-Terrapin Trail tour.

Elevation: The trail is flat.

Difficulty: Easy.

Maps: Gateway National Recreation Area brochure.

Special requirements: Hikers are required to carry a free visitors pass while touring the refuge trails, regardless of the hour of their visit. Contact the visitor center to secure a pass. Hikers planning an early morning visit should arrange for the pass on the preceding day.

Season and hours: Year-round, sunrise to sunset. Visitor Center: 8:30 a.m. to 5 p.m. daily.

For information: Jamaica Bay Wildlife Refuge.

Finding the trailhead: From the Belt Parkway in New York City (Brooklyn), take exit 17S and go south on Cross Bay Boulevard for Gateway National Recreation Area. In 3.5 miles turn right for the visitor center and trailhead.

The hike: Protected by the peninsular gateway that lends Gateway National Recreation Area its name, the islands forming Jamaica Bay Wildlife Refuge

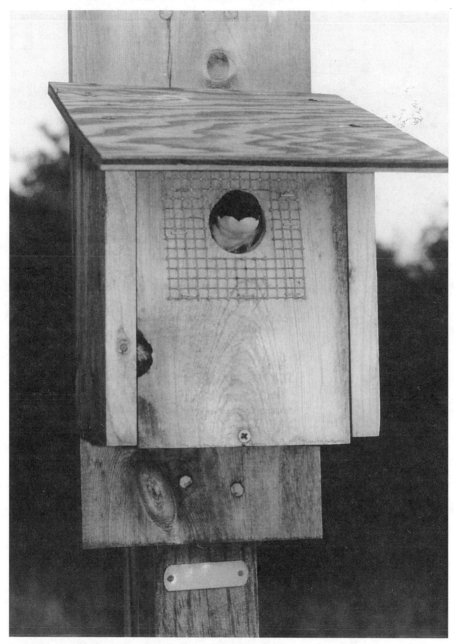

Swallow birdhouse, Jamaica Bay Wildlife Refuge.

WEST POND TRAIL

make up a vital habitat and sanctuary for native and migratory wildlife. West Pond Trail encircles one of the impoundment ponds protected originally as a New York City park, now as part of the national park system.

From the back door of the visitor center near a registry for bird sightings, hike the wide gravel path heading left; the one to the right is the Upland Nature Trail. A flowering shrub and vine thicket borders the trail; beware of poison ivy.

The occasional interpretive sign, bird and bat nesting boxes, osprey nesting platforms, and frequent benches add to a tour. The circuit gradually dishes up views of Jamaica Bay with its mudflats, saltwater marsh, and open water and views of West Pond with its dense rim and crooked-arm peninsula of phragmites (tall marsh grass), and areas of reeds and rushes. Cross-bay views feature the Manhattan skyline and cross-pond views of the World Trade Center. The refuge is an enigma, a natural island in an oh-so urban wild.

With the change of seasons comes a change in residents. Warblers claim spring, snowy egrets occupy the refuge June through August, shorebirds dominate in July and August, and snow geese and migrating raptors reign in October/November. Throughout the year, a vibrant harmony of melodic and raucous notes rides the coastal breeze, with trills, honks, squawks, pipings, and plaintive screeches. Kestrel, ibis, red-winged blackbird, tern, gull, goose, duck, heron, cormorant, vireo, and thrush suggest repeat visits.

The shrub corridors grow more broken, as an outwash plain hosts the tour. Its desert soils give rise to cactus and yucca, which blossom in June. At 0.5 mile find the Terrapin Trail, closed during nesting season June 1 through August 1; opt for this tour only when appropriate. Its sandy path passes between a shrub border and the outwash plain overlooking the riprap bank of a mudflat toward low estuary islands. At times, a frenzy of shorebirds crisscross the productive mudflat in search of food.

This side tour also adds views of the Empire State Building and World Trade Center, before overlooking a closed beach and pretty bay curvature; keep to the trail. At 1 mile rejoin the West Pond Trail at a bench overlooking the pond; go left to continue the clockwise tour. Near shore snags overlay the water, providing cormorants a convenient drying post.

The periodic roar of an airplane amplifies the serenity of the refuge. In spring, Canada geese waddle the paths with their young. Occasionally, the guarded parent will urge hikers on their way with a hostile hiss. By 1.5 miles the broad, channeled estuarine marsh distances the trail from the open-water bay, as the tour alternates between shrub and plain.

Bypass the barn owl box, keeping to the main track of the loop. As the trail approaches Cross Bay Boulevard, side paths branch from it. At 1.75 mile turn right on the gravel lane to return to the visitor center; a double-track heads left.

This last section of trail holds the first shade of the tour. Bypass a drinking fountain, a birder's blind, and a plant identification garden to complete the loop back at the visitor center (2.2 miles). Evening primrose, bouncing bet, and mugwort grow along the route.

---

70 ROCKY POINT NATURAL RESOURCES MANAGEMENT AREA

Overview

For the price of one dollar, New York State purchased this 5,100-acre pine barren and oak-wooded parcel formerly used by Radio Corporation of America (RCA) for transatlantic broadcasting. Now, only the concrete footings of the transmission towers remain. The northern reaches of this natural resources management area (NRMA) mildly roll, while the southern extent stretches out flat. Rocky Point Road severs the preserve into cast-west halves.

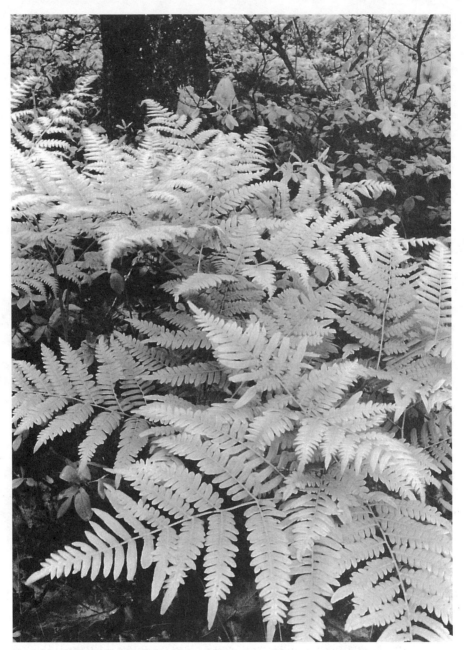

Fern forest floor, Rocky Point Natural Resources Management Area.

The color-coded hiking trails crisscross sandy woods roads and fire breaks, some of which serve as mountain bike or horse trail. Independent trail systems serve each user.

General description: A relaxing circuit explores the NRMA's pine barren and oak woodland habitats.
General location: Rocky Point, Long Island.
Special attractions: Pine barrens; spring wildflowers; wildlife sightings of deer, songbird, woodpecker, box turtle.
Length: 10.8-mile loop.
Elevation: The trail shows a 100-foot elevation change.
Difficulty: Easy.
Maps: Rocky Point Natural Resources Management Area trail map.
Special requirements: Access by permit only; for free permit and map, request in person or in writing (two weeks in advance) from New York State Department of Environmental Conservation in Stony Brook. In written requests, state your name, address, intended activity, and specify Rocky Point NRMA.
Season and hours: Year-round, best to avoid during hunting season (November through the January deer season).
For information: New York State Department of Environmental Conservation, Region 1 (Stony Brook Office).
Finding the trailhead: From the junction of Rocky Point Road (Suffolk County 21) and New York 25A in Rocky Point, go south on Rocky Point Road for 2.5 miles, and turn east on Whiskey Road. In 1.1 miles, turn north to enter the trail parking lot.

The hike: Cross the stair stile entering the NRMA and follow the footpath north into a pine barren; initially, red trail markers and Paumanok Path symbols mark the way. Within 100 feet, oaks and huckleberry fill out the forest. At 0.5 mile lies the loop junction; bear right for a counter-clockwise tour, staying along the red trail. The blue trail concludes the tour.

The loop now parts company with the Paumanok Path (a burgeoning 100-mile-long trail traversing Long Island's pine barrens from Rocky Point to Montauk Point). The flatness of the tour and the sameness of the forest lull one into a relaxed, trancelike state. Crossing over woods roads and passing firebreak clearings, the trail reaches and ascends Sand Hill, topping it at 2.9 miles.

The hill likely owes its start to a stream that flowed over a glacier, depositing silt over time. When the glacier receded at the end of the Ice Age, this modest hill remained.

Curve left over the sandy summit, absent of views, to again find the red trail. It descends steeply for 0.1 mile and then turns left. A few American chestnuts, sassafras, and sweetfern contribute to the tour. The yellow trail straight ahead rolls over the next rise to reach a trailhead on NY 25A.

ROCKY POINT NATURAL RESOURCES
MANAGEMENT AREA

The well-marked loop continues through oak woodland, crossing fire grades and woods roads, with pines once more winning a place in the forest. Throughout the tract, bountiful ferns announce recently burned areas. While fire regenerates the pine forest, a fearful, encroaching civilization looks unkindly upon fire as a renewing life force. With this being the case, setting aside large intact tracts of pine barren becomes key to the habitat's survival. Pine barrens once covered 250,000 acres of Long Island; now only a third of the barrens remain.

At 4.5 miles a narrow foot path leads to the crossing of Rocky Point Road and the western half of the preserve, where oak woods and huckleberry bushes claim the tour. At the junction at 4.6 miles, continue straight on the red trail.

The gently rolling tour passes through firebreak field and pine-oak woods nearing the NRMA boundary, coming out at an open flat with concrete walks and roads, an old foundation, and untamed border of maple, chokecherry, dogwood, and poison ivy. Skirt the site, following the paved route to the right.

At 5.4 miles where the abandoned avenue forks, go left for the loop, once again finding the white blazes of the Paumanok Path. To the right lies NY 25A with its fast food eateries, should hikers want to grab a burger or soft drink. Rounding the foundation flat, keep an eye out for the blue-blazed path on the right; it continues the loop.

The trail now passes through a varied woods of red cedar, ash, cherry, oak, and pine, with an understory of grass, Virginia creeper, fern, and poison ivy. At 5.6 miles find a pair of rocks, identified as "Sitting Rock" on the NRMA map. The lone rocks for the tour, they do indeed suggest a seat.

At 5.9 miles, a 0.5-mile yellow trail journeys left to Lookout Point, for an uninspired woods view overlooking a firebreak corridor. The loop follows the blue trail, ringing up still more road and trail crossings. Ant mounds riddle the forest.

Where the trail bottoms out, it again travels a pine barren, with an open cathedral and only patchy shade. Long straightaways characterize travel. Scarlet tanagers capture attention with their brilliant color, while cinquefoil and violet dot spring to the porous sand. After 8.3 miles, taller oaks fill out the forest. At the junction in 8.7 miles stay on the blue trail as it crosses back over Rocky Point Road.

The trail continues much as it has through pine barren, returning to the loop junction at 10.4 miles. Turn right on the red trail, retracing the 0.5-mile spur back to Whiskey Road.

---

71 DAVID A. SARNOFF PINE BARRENS PRESERVE

Overview

This 2,056-acre preserve features classic pine barrens, wetlands, and kettle depressions. Suffolk County 104 divides the preserve into east-west tracts, with the largest barren located west of the highway.

General description: A loop trail explores each of the pine barren tracts. Discoveries include the subtle changes in pine-oak mix, size, canopy, and tightness of forest.
General location: Long Island, just south of Riverhead.

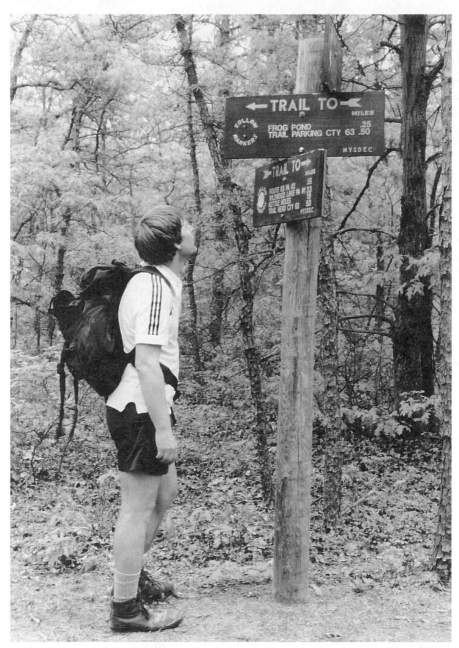

Trail sign, David A. Sarnoff Pine Barrens Preserve.

Special attractions: Pine barrens, arid meadows, wildlife ponds, kettle depressions, and bird watching.
Length: Western Loop, 5.4 miles round trip; Eastern Loop, 3.6 miles round trip.
Elevation: Trails show less than 100 feet in elevation change.
Difficulty: Easy.
Maps: David A. Sarnoff Pine Barrens Preserve trail map.
Special requirements: Access by permit only; for free permit and map, request in person or in writing (two weeks in advance) from New York State Department of Environmental Conservation in Stony Brook. In written requests, state your name, address, intended activity, and specify David A. Sarnoff Pine Barrens.
Season and hours: Year-round, best to avoid during hunting season (November through January).
For information: New York State Department of Environmental Conservation, Region 1 (Stony Brook Office).
Finding the trailhead: For the Western Loop, from the New York 24 rotary in South Riverhead, take Suffolk County 63 south for 0.2 mile, finding off-road parking on the east side of County 63. For the Eastern Loop, from the NY 24 rotary, go south on County 104 for 2.2 miles, finding off-road parking on the west side of the highway.

The hikes: Both loops aptly present the natural features and aesthetic qualities of the pine barren preserve.

The **Western Loop** (red trail) bears right, edging an open, paved flat, and stays right traveling an oak-huckleberry complex toward Frog Pond (0.2 mile), an oval water adorned by lily pads and overhung by red maples. Bullfrogs serenade in raucous harmony, while a flicker may betray its hole.

A tight order of pines next claims the way. Disk markers appear at regular intervals, with signs at key junctions. At 0.5 mile lies the loop junction, go left for a clockwise tour, traveling a pine-oak woods, with bearberry and the occasional lady slipper calling attention to the porous sand floor.

After a mild incline the trail turns left at 0.75 mile, passing through an area of small-diameter pines, not more than 20 feet high. By 1 mile the open trail travels the northern edge of an arid wildflower meadow to cross a paved road. Angle slightly right, keeping toward the woods rim of the meadow. Swallows emerge from the bird houses, darting after insects.

At 1.2 miles turn left re-entering woods. Oaks come and go from the mix, while open flats, crossroads, and concrete footings and cables from abandoned antennae mark the tour.

At 2 miles the loop turns right, as a yellow access trail heads left toward County 104. At 2.25 miles turn left on a sandy woods road; follow that up by taking a second left on a smaller woods lane. At 2.5 miles the loop follows a foot trail to the right, skirting a kettle depression barely visible beyond the trees and shrubs. Amid the kettle, gray birch appear.

DAVID A. SARNOFF
PINE BARRENS PRESERVE

At the remains of an antenna at 3.2 miles, go left, still rounding the kettle depression to the left. Descending at 3.4 miles, be alert for where the loop turns right onto a narrow, overgrown foot trail vaguely marked by a melted trail disk in 1995. As the DEC reposts its trails every two to three years, the problem should be remedied in the near future; meanwhile, stay alert.

The trail now ventures into a second kettle depression, touring a complex of tall shrubs, highbush blueberry, laurel, and azalea. At the 3.5-mile junction, continue straight for the loop. The trail mildly rolls and sashays, drawing out of the moist kettle habitat to sign-off the tour amid classic pine barren. Bear right at 4.6 miles and again at 4.8 miles to close the loop at 4.9 miles. Retrace the first 0.5 mile to return to the vehicle.

The **Eastern Loop** begins on the west side on County 104, rounding to the right of an old foundation and heading north through an open area, following white blazes and yellow disks. At 0.1 mile follow the footpath to the right through pine woods that recently burned, leaving behind a few downfalls and a trail less tracked. By next year, the sole evidence will be a more vibrant understory and new growth. At 0.2 mile bear left passing through head-high scrub oak and scattered pines to cross County 104 at 0.3 mile; exercise caution in crossing.

Now, the straight-arrow tour passes through pine barren, showing an undertangle of blueberry, huckleberry, sweetfern, and bearberry. At 0.8 mile go left to reach the loop; the white-blazed Pine Barrens Trail (part of the long-distance Paumanok Path from Rocky Point to Montauk Point) continues straight. At the loop junction at 0.9 mile, go left, following the blue markers for a clockwise tour.

At the start, lush, elbow-high huckleberry and tall pines and oaks crowd the trail. Gradually, the lush stand yields to a drier, more open pine barren. At 1.5 miles cross an avenue of broken pavement to follow another straight-arrow lane.

Be alert, approaching a seasonal wetland pond rimmed by dense vegetation at 1.7 miles, as here the trail turns right off the woods lane. Although marked, the blue disk sits inside the woods some 30 feet from the trail, and is easily missed.

The trail now skirts the southern wooded edge of the pond, bypasses and overlooks a second pond, and then edges a third one. Scrub oak fills out the midstory; dwarfed laurel appear in the mix. Past a small open pine flat, bear left at the trail junction. Tall oaks ease back into the ranks, but the corridor again opens up as the loop draws to a close at 2.7 miles. Retrace the initial 0.9 mile back to the vehicle.

---

72 CONNETQUOT RIVER STATE PARK PRESERVE

Overview

Color-coded primary and unmarked secondary trails explore this 3,500-acre state park preserve, once a private trout and hunting reservation for an elite sportsman's club, whose membership included such names as Tiffany, Vanderbilt, Belmont, and Carnegie. Distinguished guests included Ulysses S. Grant, Daniel Webster, and General Sherman. A fish hatchery, restored grist mill, and rustic buildings recall the preserve's past. River, pond, hardwood-evergreen forest, and pine barren engage travelers.

General description: A long, lazy loop travels former carriage roads and trails through this unique natural area.

General location: Long Island, west of Oakdale.

Special attractions: Trout fishing; fish hatchery, ponds, and river; historic lodge and restored grist mill; pine barrens; deer, swan, fox, osprey, heron, hawk, and box turtle.

Length: 9.8 miles round trip.

Elevation: The terrain is flat.

Difficulty: Easy.

Maps: State park preserve flier.

Special requirements: Access permits required; request in writing two weeks in advance. Indicate name and address, intended activity (hike, fish, horseback ride), number in the party, and intended date of visit, and include a legal-sized self-addressed envelope. Permit and identification must be in possession while touring the preserve. No smoking, no pets.

Season and hours: Closed Mondays year-round; Mondays and Tuesdays, October through March. Hours: 6 a.m. to sunset.

For information: Connetquot River State Park Preserve.

Finding the trailhead: From Oakdale on New York 27 (Sunrise Highway), go 1.4 miles west and turn north entering the park. Eastbound traffic must make a U-turn in Oakdale, as there is only westbound access.

Main Pond, Connetquot River State Park.

The hike: This tour links the red, blue, and green trails swinging a north-south loop the length of the preserve.

From the entrance station, hike northeast along the park road coming to a barricade. To the left lie the yellow and green trails; the road straight ahead launches both the red and blue trails. Follow the red/blue markers past the rustic shingle-sided buildings, including the Main House, an 1820s tavern that served as the clubhouse from 1866 to 1973; bear right passing between Main and Lower ponds. Above the spillway sits the restored Nicoll Grist Mill, circa 1760.

Canada geese graze the lawns and ply the ponds alive with fish. No wonder anglers covet the preserve's thirty-two allotted fishing sites; do not intrude on their designated spaces. An osprey grasping a large trout struggled to get airborne—another satisfied sportsman.

The ponds show an attractive mixed-deciduous rim, with pine trees overlooking the leafy tops. Brook Road (a dirt road) continues the loop, touring a wetland woods of oak, red maple, sweet pepperbush, poison ivy, and jack-in-the-pulpit. Pungent skunk cabbage invades the standing water. From the east shore of Main Pond, cross-pond views reflect the grist mill.

At 0.5 mile the red and blue trails part company, following parallel routes. With the red trail touring closer to Main Pond and the river, follow it. Tall pitch pines brush the blue sky, and highbush blueberry borders the trail. By fishing site 8, detect the river's influence on upper Main Pond. Like the three other major rivers draining Long Island (the Nissequogue, Carmans, and Peconic), the Connetquot springs from an aquifer beneath the pine barrens, a habitat decimated by development.

Keep to the red trail. Deer, garter snake, red fox, and hawk commonly divert the eyes. According to preserve regulars, fox have grown comfortable with their preserve immunity and commonly venture forth in the daylight.

At 1.6 miles, bypass wells bringing water to the surface. As the red trail nears the fish hatchery, arrows point travelers clockwise on a brief interpretive trail; plaques explain the natural history. Cross the river below the hatchery. Water starwort thickens the water, while a black-crowned heron may wing to safety. At the hatchery, restrooms, a drinking fountain, and picnic table serve travelers.

The loop now follows the blue trail north along shore for a short distance to cross a pair of bridges over the river and the lower end of Deep Water Pond. At Brook Road (2.3 miles), turn left (north), touring amid an oak woodland.

Opposite a closed area at 3 miles, continue straight ahead now on the green trail, part of the Greater Greenbelt Trail that traverses Long Island. At Collins Junction (4.3 miles), bear right, following the green markers toward the noise of Veterans Highway and the park's east boundary. Here the Greenbelt Trail leaves the park; turn right on the blue trail for the loop.

A younger, congested woods with low-growing shrubs frames this sunny southbound tour; Veterans Highway lies but 100 yards away. At 5.5

CONNETQUOT RIVER
STATE PARK PRESERVE

miles turn right, following Cordwood Road through the preserve's pine barrens—woody thickets of scrub oak, runty pitch pine, and dense shrub—a veritable tinderbox. The wide, shadeless roads suggest firebreaks; carry water, and wear sunglasses and a hat. At junctions, keep to Cordwood Road and the blue trail.

After 6.4 miles the barrens show full-sized oaks versus scrub oak and gradually lose the thicket midstory. At the crossroads with Mud Hole Road (8.2 miles), continue straight ahead, returning to a full mixed deciduous-pine woods. At 8.6 and 8.8 miles bear right keeping to Cordwood Road. A detour left at 8.8 miles finds Slade Pond in 100 feet. Water starwort riddles the pond, coloring it green; trees and shrubs crowd the rim. At 9.2 miles, bear left passing through a wetland woods to close the loop at Main Pond within sight of the grist mill; retrace your steps to the parking lot (9.8 miles).

---

73 *FIRE ISLAND NATIONAL SEASHORE*

Overview

This circuit travels between Smith Point and Watch Hill, exploring a 7-mile stretch of Fire Island—a 32-mile-long barrier island protecting Long Island's south shore from the punishing Atlantic. The toe of the seaward dune attracts nesting piping plover and least terns April through August; maintain a respectful distance. The back bay and dune swale comprise Otis Pike Wilderness Area, the only federally designated wilderness in New York State. Flowering beach plum, beach heather, and wild rose accent a springtime return through the dunes.

General description: An all-day loop explores the sandy beach of the national seashore and the back bay and dune swale of Otis Pike Wilderness Area. When starting the hike at Smith Point Ranger Station, find the end of the loop along the site's 0.8-mile boardwalk interpretive trail.
General location: Fire Island, off the south shore of Long Island.
Special attractions: Nesting piping plovers and least terns; migrating waterfowl, songbirds, raptors, and butterflies; deer, rabbit, and fox; primary dunes, blowouts, swales, thickets, and salt marsh; beach plum and beach heather; Atlantic Ocean and Great South Bay views; interpretive trail; visitor centers.
Length: 14.2-mile loop, with opportunities to shorten the tour at the established boardwalk crossings.
Elevation: The beach portion is flat; the back-bay return shows less than a 100-foot elevation change.
Difficulty: Moderate.
Maps: Fire Island National Seashore brochure.

Special requirements: Rangers recommend wilderness area hikers register at the Smith Point Ranger Station, alerting the staff to their presence in this little used area. Heed closures for nesting piping plovers and terns, and be sensitive of the primary dunes, crossing only at designated sites with stairways and boardwalks. As mosquitos are common, carry repellent. Amid vegetation, be attentive to the presence of poison ivy and deer ticks (Lyme disease carriers). These ticks may exist year-round, so take precautions. Find drinking water at Smith Point and Watch Hill only.

Season and hours: Year-round. Smith Point Ranger Station, year-round. Watch Hill Visitor Center, July and August.

For information: Fire Island National Seashore.

Finding the trailhead: On Long Island at Shirley, take exit 58S from New York 27 (Sunrise Highway) and go south on New York 46 (William Floyd Parkway) for 5 miles, crossing over the bridge to reach Fire Island National Seashore and Smith Point Suffolk County Park. As the national seashore offers parking for handicapped users only, park at Smith Point County Park, a fee area. A ferry operating out of Patchogue, New York, accesses the Watch Hill area for an alternative approach to the national seashore.

The hike: For an east-to-west beach stroll, descend the seaward-stretching boardwalk at Smith Point Ranger Station and turn right on the 150-foot-wide strand. A fine, light-colored crystalline sand tosses back the sun, as thunderous waves break in long strings close to shore. Energy spreading

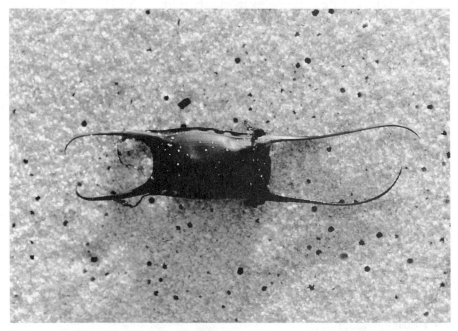

Skate case, Fire Island National Seashore.

along the wave's crest and the churned foam sliding up the beach hold travelers transfixed.

As the official wilderness area only extends from the toe of the primary dune north to Great South Bay, the ocean beach falls outside the protective designation, leaving it open to some beach driving. Generally, expect to see tire tracks, save for the last week in May and during the entire month of June, when the National Park Service closes the beach to all vehicles for the protection of the nesting birds.

Along the beach, staggered posts mark off the nesting sites; grant the birds a wide margin, so as not to interfere with nesting. The lower beach typically offers easier walking with tide-compressed sand; where walkable, the upper beach holds discoveries of wind patterns, lacy insect signatures, and bird chirps. At a mile, a gap in the primary dune offers a glimpse north at Great South Bay.

At 2 miles a stairway leads to Old Inlet, offering the first opportunity to shorten the loop. Here, hikers find a boardwalk linking beach and bay, an attractive T-shaped dock on the bay, and seasonally-open toilets and showers.

For a full day's hike, continue west along the beach. To shorten the loop to about 4 miles, hike north on the Old Inlet boardwalk. Part way, find the faint track of Burma Road (a nature-reclaimed jeep road that predates the wilderness) as it intersects the boardwalk. Hike east on Burma Road, traveling at the back side of the dune, returning to Smith Point.

Along the ocean front, clam shells, skate cases, sea-polished pebbles, and horseshoe crabs being toyed with by gulls call to beachcombers. The cant to the ocean grows more pronounced, tiring calf muscles. The dunes now fluctuate from a few feet high to 20 feet high.

Atop the dunes at 3.6 miles, a slat-roofed deck overlooks the beach. Owned by the village of Bellport, this site offers travelers a shady resting stop and another turnaround point. Follow the boardwalk toward the bay to find the dune trail as it bisects the boardwalk. Turn right to return to Smith Point, touring back bay and dune swale.

Continue west along the beach for the full loop; terns swoop the waves. At 7.1 miles find the boardwalk that crosses the primary dunes to the Watch Hill area and campground, both hidden by the rise. A slat-roof lean-to for shade, a restroom/changing facility, showers, phone, drinking fountain, and snack bar serve travelers. In July and August, lifeguards oversee the beach.

From the campground boardwalk, find sandy Burma Road at the base of the seaward dune and follow it east away from camp to close the loop. The trail alternately tours loose sand or overgrown track, passing through a shrub swale with beach plum, beach grass, sweet pepperbush, salt-spray rose, and poison ivy. Springtime brings a blush of color.

At the 7.8-mile fork, bear left continuing east across the dune-protected area. Caches of tall, feathery headed phragmites, springtime puddles pulsing with toads, and a lush, green estuary characterize the trek.

FIRE ISLAND NATIONAL SEASHORE

After 8 miles, dip into a sandy bowl, then top its rim for a bay overlook and the merest peek at the ocean. The trail then levels, traversing areas of beach grass and beach heather, sandy plains, and pockets of pitch pine; beware of poison ivy and brier, which commonly grow beneath the pines.

Where the trail curves toward the beach at 10 miles, it travels the loose sand of a secondary dune, skirting blown-out depressions. Wooden debris, an old cable route, and seashells are possible sightings, but the shifting sand frequently alters the canvas.

At 10.7 miles an old well feeds a circle of green. At 11 miles, bypass the picnic shelter owned by Bellport Village, crossing over its boardwalk. The sandy track now rolls up rims and through bowls, soon traversing a broad coastal plain; the small bay island and cottage off Old Inlet command the view. At 12.6 miles, cross over the boardwalk at Old Inlet.

The track becomes more grassy, and shrubs reappear, as the trail draws a straight shadeless line back to Smith Point Ranger Station. It arrives at the boardwalk interpretive trail near post 12 (midway); go either way to end at the ranger station (14.2 miles).

74 *MASHOMACK PRESERVE*

Overview

Covering the southeastern third of Shelter Island, this 2,000-acre preserve of The Nature Conservancy (TNC) encompasses a maritime environment of tidal creeks, woodlands, fields, swamps, freshwater ponds, and 10 miles of stirring but inaccessible coastline. Four interlocking color-coded trails and a short barrier-free Braille trail tour the site. A fine nature garden introduces some of the common vegetations.

General description: A 12-mile round-trip tour travels each of the four loops in their entirety, backtracking on itself only once, the 0.75-mile stretch between junctions 3 and 4.
General location: East End Long Island.
Special attractions: Natural osprey nesting colony, a rare pine swamp, dogwood blooms, vistas, colorful fall foliage.
Length: 12 miles round trip.
Elevation: Despite a modest elevation change, the rolling tour rings up a sizable cumulative elevation, 10 to 20 feet at a time.
Difficulty: Easy.
Maps: Preserve trail map (available at visitor center).
Special requirements: Reached by ferry service. Suggested donation to TNC; keep to the trail and obey posted rules. As TNC has marked the trails for only one direction of travel, follow the flow pattern indicated on the preserve map to avoid losing your way.
Season and hours: Year-round, daily except Tuesdays. Hours: 9 a.m. to 5 p.m. (9 a.m. to 4 p.m. October through March). Visitor center: summers and weekends only.
For information: Mashomack Preserve or The Nature Conservancy, South Fork-Shelter Island Chapter.
Finding the trailhead: From North Haven, take the South Ferry to Shelter Island and go 1 mile north on New York 114, turning east to enter the preserve. Arriving from the North Ferry out of Greenport, follow NY 114 south 3 miles to the entrance.

The hike: All trails share a common start near the Trail House (the preserve visitor center). The 0.2-mile barrier-free boardwalk tours the native plant garden, woods, and a freshwater kettle, while the color-coded trails head east off the entry road into a rich woodland of mixed oaks, red maple, hickory, beech, dogwood, and black locust.

A rare pine swamp, recognized for its uniqueness by the New York State Department of Environmental Quality, occupies the western edge of the preserve. Rimmed by swamp azalea, water willow, and highbush blueberry, the site's pines spring from a floating mat of sphagnum moss.

Nearing a service road at 0.3 mile, bear right per the red arrow. The trail then merges with a wide woods lane, rounding to a gazebo overlooking Miss Annie's Creek—a tidal marsh bay with sandy strands and a treed island. Views pan south across Shelter Island Sound and the South Ferry crossing.

At junction 1 (0.8 mile), bear right for the yellow, green, and blue trails; the red trail hooks left returning to the visitor center. A boardwalk continues the tour, crossing a salt meadow extension of the marsh; keep an eye out for the osprey nesting platform. After crossing a management road, tour amid twisted oaks and an open field before descending to junction 2 (1.25 miles). Here the yellow trail heads left to close its loop, the blue trail heads straight, and the green trail bears right.

Follow the blue-marked trail through field to explore the largest of the preserve loops, soon entering a shady beech-climax woods. At 2.25 miles bear left per the markers and again bear left in another 0.1 mile. At 2.6 miles the blue trail turns right, following a semi-shaded woods road as it curves east toward the bluff rim for a sunnier tour.

At 3.1 miles a bench overlooks Gardiners Bay and Island, and at 4.1 miles, a triple-trunked beech presides trailside. As the blue trail travels the outskirts of Great Swamp, dense with phragmites (tall feathery marsh grass), a foot trail briefly replaces the woods road; keep to the rim. Bullbrier entangles the woods, as the open trail rolls south, trading looks at Gardiners Bay for looks at Northwest Harbor. Dogwoods accent the tour.

Shelter Island beach, Mashomack Preserve.

MASHOMACK PRESERVE

At 4.4 miles, reach the Northwest Harbor overlook, with Plum Pond sometimes visible beyond the leafy shroud. The trail then rounds above a kettle depression, bearing right, coming to a birder's blind. Set back in the woods and camouflaged by phragmites, the blind overlooks the upper estuary of Bass Creek. From inside the blind, look left for a sapsucker-drilled trunk; holes ring the circumference every few inches.

Where the blue trail tags the green loop at junction 4 (5.4 miles), bear right to stay on the marked trail and follow the flow pattern indicated on the preserve map. The trail passes through mixed woods and crosses a service road to reach junction 3 (the head of the green trail loop) at 6.15 miles.

Bear left to add the green loop; going right returns to the visitor center. The green loop passes through a diverse woodland, overlooks the blue waters of Smith Cove, and at 8.4 miles reaches a blind looking out at Log Cabin Creek.

Ahead, turn right on the management road, passing through the staff residence area, with its wood-shingled buildings, groomed lawns, shade trees, tidal ponds, and freshwater Sanctuary Pond. The road becomes a doubletrack as it re-enters the woods at 9.2 miles, skirting the Bass Creek estuary. With an upland woods ascent, the tour returns to junction 4 at 9.65 miles. Go left, retracing the tour between junctions 4 and 3.

Once again at junction 3, follow the green trail, ascending the steps to the right to return to the visitor center. Scenic oaks shade a bench and suggest a pause, as the trail traverses a coastal bluff. Below the trail lies a pristine, thin pebble beach reserved for wildlife (off-limits to the public). Upon crossing the management road, pass through woods and fields to reach junction 2 (10.4 miles).

Take the right fork of the yellow trail, tracking the yellow and red arrows back to the Trail House. Soon after crossing the management road at 10.9 miles, bear right on the wood shavings path of the red trail. It quickly turns left on a closed roadway for the return to the visitor center; plaques identify the diverse roadside vegetation.

75 HITHER HILLS STATE PARK

Overview

On Long Island's east end, this 1,755-acre state park brings together a superb line-up of offerings: walking dunes and "phantom forests"; a pristine mile of Atlantic beach; the cobbly, remote Napeague Bay shore; Goff Point, where piping plover, tern, and oyster-catcher nest; and an interior region of pine barrens, dune heath, and maritime grassland. Semi-formal trails explore beach, bay, spit, and dune. For hikes through the woods and barrens, consider joining a guided walk led by a local hiking club.

General description: Informal hikes introduce and explore the park's unique habitats; customize the lengths to fit your interest and time constraints.
General location: 7 miles east of Amagansett.
Special attractions: 40-foot dunes, buried forests, seashells, a native cranberry bog, wild plums, bird watching.
Length: Atlantic Beach Walk, 2 miles round trip; Walking Dunes Trail, 1-mile loop; Napeague Shoreline Hike, 15 miles round trip (13 miles when nesting season closes off Goff Point).
Elevation: Beach and shoreline trails, flat; Walking Dunes Trail, 40-foot elevation change.
Difficulty: Atlantic Beach Walk, easy; Walking Dunes Trail and Napeague Shoreline Hike, easy to moderate.
Maps: State park map (request at campground).
Special requirements: Obey posted closures; best to avoid Goff Point during nesting season. Expect some beach driving along Napeague shore (access by special permit in designated areas).
Season and hours: Year-round. Hot and humid hiking in summer.
For information: New York State Parks, Long Island Region.
Finding the trailhead: From Amagansett, go 6 miles east on New York 27 (Montauk Highway) and turn north on Napeague Harbor Road to reach the trailhead for Walking Dunes and Napeague Shoreline in 0.7 mile; sand drifts limit parking to a handful of vehicles. Be careful not to block the vehicle access to the beach. For Atlantic beach access, from Amagansett

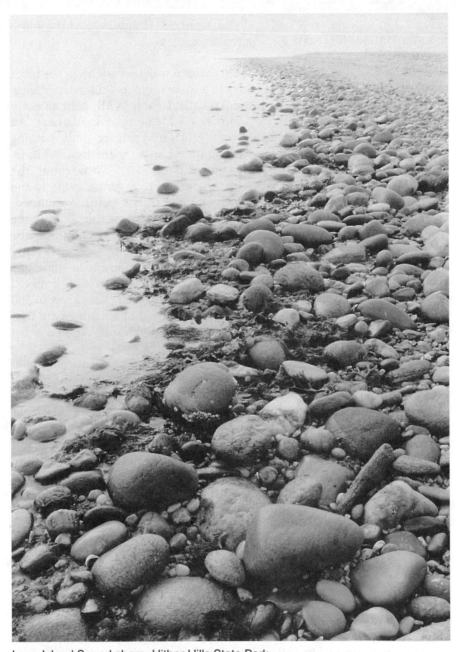

Long Island Sound shore, Hither Hills State Park.

drive 7.2 miles east on NY 27 and Old Montauk Highway, turning south to enter Hither Hills State Park, a fee area.

The hikes: The Atlantic shore holds the park's developed offerings; the hikes off Napeague Harbor Road treat hikers to a more remote, wilder experience.

For maximum enjoyment of the **Atlantic Beach Walk** plan an early morning or off-season stroll, as summers find legions of sunbathers. An east-to-west tour shuns the neighboring resorts and private lands, passing below the developed campground and day-use area for the first 0.3 mile. The final 0.7 mile travels the undeveloped park shore. Throughout, the mile-long beach shows a broad, clean strand with a gentle slope to the ocean. At its back, low, flattened grass-topped dunes build to rounded, rolling ones at the park's west end. Marked paths traverse the dunes to the beach; cross only at these designated sites. Admire, but do not trample the sensitive dunes.

For the **Walking Dunes Trail,** head east (right) off the end of Napeague Harbor Road, following a sandy path into a maritime corridor of mixed oaks, beach grass, beach plum, pitch pine, bearberry, and poison ivy. In 100 feet, an interpretive sign introduces this rare zone of shifting sand that "walks" over trees 30 feet tall. Again, the sensitive landscape calls for respectful appreciation; no dune play.

At a three-prong fork, take the central path passing through an oak-fringed blowout. At 0.1 mile, where the trail again forks, go right for the prescribed counterclockwise loop, avoiding the well-tracked assault on the dune straight ahead. Notice how only the crowns of the nearby oaks clear the burying sand. With a gust of wind, the sands again go walking.

The trail contours and gradually ascends the dunes, with first forest and then wetland sweeping away to the right. Minerals can streak the dunes purple or black, while beach grass and beach heather vegetate the tops. As the dune curves noticeably northwest, angle to the top of the dune for a grand Walking Dunes-Hither Hills State Park overview, with Napeague Harbor and Bay, the sandy spit of Goff Point, and Gardiners Island.

The trail then descends to the western bowl, reaching a sign for "phantom forest;" survey the bowl for snags recording past forests overtaken and ultimately killed by the sand. Next up, the counterclockwise tour rounds a native cranberry bog; stay to its left. Passing through bayberry, aim for the wide sand track ahead and follow it over a rise and into the next bowl to reach the harbor beach (0.8 mile). Turn left to return to the vehicle and close the loop.

This **Napeague Shoreline Hike** explores Napeague Harbor, Goff Point, and the Napeague Bay shore east as far as Rocky Point. In places, tire tracks may steal from the harbor and bayshore wildness, but generally the tour does not disappoint. Late May through June, hikers should forgo rounding Goff Point and instead, cross to the bay at the neck of the spit at 1.2 miles.

HITHER HILLS STATE PARK

From the end of Napeague Harbor Road, follow the Napeague Harbor shoreline north, traveling an avenue of pinkish-orange sand and cobbles. Terns, gulls, herons, and egrets suggest one bring binoculars. A scattering of open-hinged scallops may record the recent passing of a turnstone.

At the neck of Goff Point (1.2 miles), a broad flat draws feeding piping plover and resting terns; sit quietly and watch their antics. Water spouts betray the presence of clams. When appropriate, continue north around the spit, but keep below the high-tide line as oyster-catcher, piping plover, and tern have nesting territories; netted enclosures protect the plover nests.

By 1.5 miles, round the sand and pebble shore at the head of Goff Point, where gulls congregate, cormorants string off shore, and slipper and orange jingle shells collect in long deposits. The tour leaves the spit of Goff Point opposite Skonk Hole, a wet depression at 2.2 miles.

At the start of the bay tour, a breach in the dune offers a look south at a maritime grassland of beard and switch grass, with beach plum adorning the dunetop in showy spring finery. Rounded cobbles and shells form a crunchy thoroughfare. Again, slipper shells abound, with caps of pink, white, and green seaweed.

Before long, looks east find the pilings of a shellfish bed and distant Rocky Point. By 3.6 miles, the beach shows more sand; over-the-shoulder views admire the curve of Goff Point. Gradually, the dune gives way to a 25-foot bluff with an abrupt slip face; colonies of swallows nest in the solid seams.

At 4.3 and 4.7 miles, boulders scatter the beach, suggesting a dry seat. As the tour rounds Rocky Point at 5.9 miles, cobbles once again dominate the strand, and a cliff rises above the beach. Eastern views of Fort Pond Bay and Culloden Point signal the turnaround at 7.5 miles. Return as you came.

During nesting season, high tides, or strong winds, a jeep trail paralleling the Napeague Bay shore offers an alternative approach or return. The jeep trail veers east at the northern edge of the Walking Dunes (0.2 mile north of the end of Napeague Harbor Road) and remains within 0.1 mile of the bay shore for much of the way. Breaches in the dune suggest natural passageways between the jeep trail and bayshore. When starting on the jeep trail, find the first bay access at 1.2 miles, just east of Goff Point.

APPENDIX A — HIKER'S CHECKLIST

Not every item on the following checklist will be needed for every trip, so customize the list, taking into account your needs and comforts, the duration of the outing, weather, and the unexpected. Use this list as an organizing tool for planning, packing, and minimizing oversights. Feel free to pencil in items that you find critical to a successful trip.

Ten Essentials
- [ ] extra food
- [ ] extra clothing
- [ ] sunglasses
- [ ] knife
- [ ] firestarter
- [ ] matches in waterproof container
- [ ] first-aid kit and manual
- [ ] flashlight
- [ ] map(s) for the trail
- [ ] compass

Clothing
- [ ] light-weight underwear
- [ ] longjohns
- [ ] under socks
- [ ] wool boot socks
- [ ] long pants
- [ ] shorts
- [ ] long-sleeve shirt
- [ ] T-shirts
- [ ] wool sweater or shirt
- [ ] wool hat and gloves
- [ ] visor or cap
- [ ] raingear
- [ ] warm coat or parka
- [ ] belt
- [ ] bandanna
- [ ] swimsuit or trunks
- [ ] hiking boots
- [ ] sneakers or camp shoes

Personal Items
- [ ] contacts or eyeglasses
- [ ] comb
- [ ] toothpaste and brush
- [ ] biodegradable soap/towelettes
- [ ] towel
- [ ] nail clipper and tweezers
- [ ] facial tissue or handkerchief

- [ ] toilet paper and trowel
- [ ] sunscreen and lip balm
- [ ] insect repellent
- [ ] wallet and keys
- [ ] emergency medical information
- [ ] watch

Gear

- [ ] water bottles
- [ ] pack(s)
- [ ] tent, with required poles and pegs
- [ ] ground cloth
- [ ] sleeping bag and foam pad
- [ ] stove and fuel
- [ ] pots and eating utensils
- [ ] can opener
- [ ] rope
- [ ] stuff bags
- [ ] large trash bags for emergency shelter for self or gear
- [ ] plastic bags for trash
- [ ] zip-seal bags for foodstuffs
- [ ] aluminum foil

Food

- [ ] three meals, plus snacks for each day out
- [ ] extra food for delays
- [ ] salt/pepper
- [ ] vegetable oil
- [ ] drink mixes

Health and Safety Items

- [ ] medications
- [ ] emergency blanket
- [ ] water pump or purification tablets
- [ ] whistle
- [ ] pencil and paper
- [ ] picture wire for emergency repairs

Miscellaneous

- [ ] mosquito netting
- [ ] binoculars
- [ ] camera and film
- [ ] guidebooks
- [ ] identification books
- [ ] fishing gear and valid license

APPENDIX B — FURTHER READING

Appalachian Hiker II by Ed Garvey. Appalachian Books.

Backpacking One Step at a Time, Fourth Edition by Harvey Manning. Random House.

The Basic Essentials of Map and Compass by Cliff Jacobson. ICS Books.

Be Expert with Map and Compass by Bjorn Kjellstrom. Charles Scribner's Sons.

A Child's Introduction to the Outdoors by David Richey. Pagurian Press Limited.

The Complete Walker III by Colin Fletcher. Alfred A. Knopf.

Country Walks Near New York by William B. Scheller. Appalachian Mountain Club.

A Field Guide to the Birds by Roger Tory Peterson. Houghton Mifflin Co.

Fifty Hikes in Central New York by William P. Ehling. Backcountry Publications.

Fifty Hikes in the Hudson Valley by Peter Kick, Barbara McMartin, and James M. Long. Backcountry Publications.

Fifty Hikes in Western New York by William P. Ehling. Backcountry Publications.

Finding Your Way in the Outdoors by Robert L. Mooers Jr. E.P. Hutton Co., Inc.

Guide to Adirondack Trails: Central Region by Bruce C. Wadsworth. Adirondack Mountain Club, Inc.

Guide to Adirondack Trails: Eastern Region by Betsy Tisdale. Adirondack Mountain Club, Inc.

Guide to Adirondack Trails: High Peaks Region edited by Tony Goodwin. Adirondack Mountain Club, Inc.

Guide to Adirondack Trails: Northern Region by Peter V. O'Shea. Adirondack Mountain Club, Inc.

Guide to Adirondack Trails: Northville-Placid Trail by Bruce Wadsworth. Adirondack Mountain Club, Inc.

Guide to Adirondack Trails: Southern Region by Linda Laing. Adirondack Mountain Club, Inc.

Guide to Adirondack Trails: West-Central Region by Arthur W. Haberl. Adirondack Mountain Club, Inc.

A Guide to Field Identification: Wildflowers of North America by Frank D. Venning. Golden Press.

Guide to the National Wildlife Refuges by Laura and William Riley. Collier Books.

Mountaineering First Aid, Third Edition by Martha J. Lentz, Steven C. Macdonald, and Jan D. Carline. The Mountaineers.

Mountaineering Medicine by Fred T. Darvill. Wilderness Press.

Natural New York by Bill and Phyllis Thomas. Holt, Rinehart and Winston.

New York Walk Book, Fifth Edition by the New York-New Jersey Trail Conference. Anchor Books, Doubleday.

Official Guide to the Appalachian Trail in New York and New Jersey by the New York-New Jersey Trail Conference. The Appalachian Trail Conference.

Rock Scenery of the Hudson Highlands and Palisades by Jerome Wyckoff. Adirondack Mountain Club.

Short Nature Walks on Long Island, Third Edition by Rodney and Priscilla Albright. The Globe Pequot Press.

The Shrub Identification Book by George W.D. Symonds. William Morrow and Company.

Travel Light Handbook by Judy Keene. Contemporary Books.

Wild Country Companion: The Ultimate Guide to No-trace Outdoor Recreation and Wilderness Safety by Will Harmon. Falcon Press Publishing Co., Inc.

Wilderness Basics: The Complete Handbook for Hikers and Backpackers, Second Edition by the San Diego Chapter of the Sierra Club. The Mountaineers.

APPENDIX C — WHERE TO FIND MAPS

For trail maps produced by the managing agencies, contact the information source indicated in the trail summary table; find the complete address and phone number in Appendix D.

For copies of United States Geological Survey topographic quadrangles (USGS quads), check at libraries, at most backpacking and mountaineering stores, or at specialty maps and publications stores. A state index will help you identify the name of the quad(s) that cover the area you are seeking.

Or contact the United States Geological Survey Map Distribution Center, Box 25286 Federal Center, Building 41, Denver, CO 80225, for a New York State index and a price list for the maps.

For information on how to acquire New York State Department of Transportation (DOT) maps, contact the Map Information Unit, New York State Department of Transportation, State Campus, Building 4, Room 105, Albany, NY 12232.

Maps produced by the New York-New Jersey Trail Conference, Adirondack Mountain Club, or Appalachian Mountain Club typically are available at backpacker and mountaineering stores or for direct order from the organization. For an order blank and price list, contact the respective organization:

New York-New Jersey Trail Conference, 232 Madison Avenue, New York, NY 10016; 212-685-9699.

Adirondack Mountain Club, Rural Route 3, Box 3055, Lake George, NY 12845-9523; 518-668-4447.

Appalachian Mountain Club, 202 East 39th Street, New York, NY 10016; 212-986-1430. Or the Appalachian Trail Conference, P.O. Box 807, Harpers Ferry, WV 25425-0807.

For information on ordering the Finger Lakes Trail Conference maps, contact the Finger Lakes Trail Conference, P.O. Box 18048, Rochester, NY 14618-0048; 716-288-7191. These simple line-drawing maps show the trail, key routes, towns, public lands, and landmarks; paired with each is a point-to-point description, indicating the progressive mileage.

APPENDIX D — LAND MANAGEMENT LISTINGS

Adirondack Nature Conservancy
P.O. Box 65
Keene Valley, NY 12943
518-576-2082

Adirondack Trail Improvement Society
P.O. Box 565
Keene Valley, NY 12943
no phone number for general information

Appalachian Trail Conference
P.O. Box 807
Washington and Jackson Streets
Harpers Ferry, WV 25425-0807
304-535-6331

Beaver Lake Nature Center
8477 East Mud Lake Road
Baldwinsville, NY 13027
315-638-2519

Chautauqua County Visitors Bureau
4 North Erie Street
Mayville, NY 14757
716-753-4304 or 1-800-242-4569

Connetquot River State Park Preserve
P.O. Box 505
Oakdale, NY 11769-0505
516-581-1005

Erie County Parks
Recreation and Forestry Department
Genessee Road
East Concord, NY 14055
716-496-7410

Finger Lakes National Forest
Hector Ranger District
5216 Star Route 414
Hector, NY 14841
607-546-4470

Finger Lakes Trail Conference
P.O. Box 18048
Rochester, NY 14618-0048
716-288-7191

Fire Island National Seashore
120 Laurel Street
Patchogue, NY 11772
516-289-4810

Five Rivers Environmental Education Center
New York State Department of Environmental Conservation
56 Game Farm Road
Delmar, NY 12054
518-475-0291

Iroquois National Wildlife Refuge
P.O. Box 517
1101 Casey Road
Alabama, NY 14003
716-948-9154

Jamaica Bay Wildlife Refuge
Floyd Bennett Field
Building 69
Brooklyn, NY 11234
718-318-4340

Mashomack Preserve
P.O. Box 850
Shelter Island, NY 11964
516-749-1001

Mohonk Mountain House
Lake Mohonk
New Paltz, NY 12561
1-800-772-6646

Mohonk Preserve
1000 Mountain Rest Road, Mohonk Lake
New Paltz, NY 12561
914-255-0919

The Nature Conservancy
Central and Western New York Office
315 Alexander Street
Rochester, NY 14604
716-546-8030

The Nature Conservancy
Lower Hudson Chapter
41 South Moger Avenue
Mount Kisco, NY 10549
914-244-3271

The Nature Conservancy
South Fork-Shelter Island Chapter
P.O. Box 5125
East Hampton, NY 11937
516-329-7689

New York State Canal Corporation
200 Southern Boulevard
P.O. Box 189
Albany, NY 12201-0189
1-800-422-6254

New York State Department of Environmental Conservation, Region 1
Building 40 SUNY
Stony Brook, NY 11790-2356
516-444-0345

New York State Department of Environmental Conservation, Region 2,
1 Hunters Point Plaza
4740 21st Street
Long Island City, NY 11101
718-482-4900

New York State Department of Environmental Conservation, Region 3
21 South Putt Corners Road
New Paltz, NY 12561-1696
914-256-3000.
For Forest Preserve information only: 914-256-3083

New York State Department of Environmental Conservation, Region 4
1150 North Westcott Road
Schenectady, NY 12306
518-357-2066

New York State Department of Environmental Conservation, Region 5
Route 86
P.O. Box 296
Ray Brook, NY 12977-0296
518-897-1200

New York State Department of Environmental Conservation, Region 6
State Office Building
317 Washington Street
Watertown, NY 13601-3787
315-785-2239

New York State Department of Environmental Conservation, Region 7
1285 Fisher Avenue
Cortland, NY 13045
607-753-3095

New York State Department of Environmental Conservation, Region 8
6274 East Avon-Lima Road
Avon, NY 14414
716-226-2466

New York State Parks, Allegany Region
2373 ASP Route 1
Suite 3
Salamanca, NY 14779-9756
716-354-9101

New York State Parks, Central Region
6105 East Seneca Turnpike
Jamesville, NY 13078
315-492-1756

New York State Parks, Finger Lakes Region
P.O. Box 1055
2221 Taughannock Park Road
Trumansburg, NY 14886
607-387-7041

New York State Parks, Genesee Region
1 Letchworth State Park
Castile, NY 14427
716-493-3600

New York State Parks, Long Island Region
P.O. Box 247
Babylon, NY 11702
516-669-1000

New York State Parks, Palisades Region
Administration Headquarters
Bear Mountain, NY 10911
914-786-2701

New York State Parks, Saratoga-Capital Region
19 Roosevelt Drive
Saratoga Springs, NY 12866
518-584-2000

New York State Parks, Taconic Region
Staatsburg, NY 12580
914-889-4100

New York State Parks, Thousand Islands Region
P.O. Box 247
Alexandria Bay, NY 13607
315-482-2593

Paul Smiths Visitor Interpretive Center
P.O. Box 3000
Route 30
Paul Smiths, NY 12970
518-327-3000

Saint Lawrence County Planning Office
48 Court Street
Canton, NY 13617-1194
315-379-2292 (weekdays only)

Saratoga National Historic Park
648 Route 32
Stillwater, NY 12170
518-664-9821

Tifft Nature Preserve
1200 Fuhrmann Boulevard
Buffalo, NY 14203
716-896-5200

GLOSSARY

Car-shuttle hikes. Typically, these are linear routes for one-way travel that allow for a drop-off and pick-up arrangement or for the spotting of a second vehicle at the trail's end.

Woods roads. These dirt, grass, or rocky roads or faint road depressions represent old logging, mining, or farm routes that through time have fallen into disuse. Reclaimed for trails, most are closed to vehicle travel, although some may allow snowmobile or mountain bike use. We have attempted to alert readers to where vehicle use or illegal vehicle use occurs on these routes.

Truck trails. These maintained dirt roads are intended for and do receive vehicle travel; most allow a maximum speed limit of only 25 miles per hour.

Service roads. These routes hold minimal traffic, allowing official vehicles only.

Forest lanes. These routes typically are narrower than a woods road, yet wider than a trail, serving foot and horse traveler.

Carriageways or cart paths. In the past these well-groomed, well-graded routes offered comfortable travel for guests staying at the state's historic nineteenth-century mountain inns. Today, closed to vehicles, these routes may serve foot, horse, and/or bike travel; prior to a visit, check with the managing agency for acceptable use.

Jeep trails. These doubletrack routes typically serve foot and horse travelers. Most are no longer drivable.

Corduroy. This side-by-side alignment of logs, boards, or branches provides dry passage over soggy trail segments or delicate meadow sites.

ABOUT THE AUTHORS

Over the past fifteen years, the Ostertags, Rhonda (a writer) and George (a photographer), have collaborated on four western outdoor guidebooks; sold hundreds of articles on topics of nature, travel, and outdoor recreation; and participated in environmental impact studies. They now have turned their boots east, with *Hiking New York* being the first of three books presently on their slate.

George was born and raised in Connecticut and brings to the book his childhood enthusiasm tempered by a reflective eye. Find the passion he holds for the region reflected in his photography. Rhonda, harking from Oregon by way of Montana, brings the fresh perspective of a Western-eyed newcomer.

After logging 2,000 miles of trail and going through two pair of hiking boots, this couple knows New York and speaks from the trail. Other titles by this team include *California State Parks: A Complete Recreation Guide (1995)* and *100 Hikes in Oregon* (1992).

American Hiking Society

American Hiking Society is the only national nonprofit organization dedicated to establishing, protecting and maintaining foot trails in America.

Establishing...

American Hiking Society establishes hiking trails with the AHS National Trails Endowment, providing grants for grassroots organizations to purchase trail lands, construct and maintain trails, and preserve hiking trails' scenic values. The AHS affiliate club program, called the Congress of Hiking Organizations, brings trail clubs together to share information, collaborate on public policy, and advocate legislation and policies that protect hiking trails.

Protecting...

American Hiking Society protects hiking trails through highly focused public policy efforts in the nation's capital. AHS affects federal legislation, shapes public lands policy, collaborates with grassroots trail organizations, and partners with federal land managers to protect the hiking experience. Members become active with letter-writing campaigns and by attending the annual AHS Trails Advocacy Week.

Maintaining...

American Hiking Society maintains hiking trails by sending volunteers to national parks, forests and recreation lands; organizing volunteer teams to help affiliated hiking clubs; and publishing national volunteer directories. AHS members get involved, get dirty and get inspired by participating in AHS programs like National Trails Day, America's largest celebration of the outdoors; and Volunteer Vacations—week-long work trips to beautiful, wild places.

Join American Hiking Society...

Be a part of the organization dedicated to protecting and preserving the nation's footpaths, our footpaths, the ones in our backyards and our backcountry. Visit American Hiking Society's website or call to find out more about membership. When you join, Falcon Publishing will send you a FREE guide as a special thank you for contributing to the efforts of American Hiking Society.

American Hiking Society
1422 Fenwick Lane
Silver Spring, MD 20910
OR CALL: (888) 766-HIKE ext. 1
OR VISIT: www.americanhiking.org

FALCON GUIDES ® Leading the way™

FalconGuides® are available for where-to-go hiking, mountain biking, rock climbing, walking, scenic driving, fishing, rockhounding, paddling, birding, wildlife viewing, and camping. We also have FalconGuides on essential outdoor skills and subjects and field identification. The following titles are currently available, but this list grows every year. For a free catalog with a complete list of titles, call FALCON toll-free at 1-800-582-2665.

BIRDING GUIDES

Birding Georgia
Birding Illinois
Birding Minnesota
Birding Montana
Birding Northern California
Birding Texas
Birding Utah

PADDLING GUIDES

Paddling Minnesota
Paddling Montana
Paddling Okefenokee
Paddling Oregon
Paddling Yellowstone & Grand
  Teton National Parks

WALKING

Walking Colorado Springs
Walking Denver
Walking Portland
Walking Seattle
Walking St. Louis
Walking San Francisco
Walking Virginia Beach

CAMPING GUIDES

Camping Arizona
Camping California's
  National Forests
Camping Colorado
Camping Oregon
Camping Southern California
Camping Washington
Recreation Guide to Washington
  National Forests

FIELD GUIDES

Bitterroot: Montana State Flower
Canyon Country Wildflowers
Central Rocky Mountain
  Wildflowers
Chihuahuan Desert Wildflowers
Great Lakes Berry Book
New England Berry Book
Ozark Wildflowers
Pacific Northwest Berry Book
Plants of Arizona
Rare Plants of Colorado
Rocky Mountain Berry Book
Scats & Tracks of the Pacific
  Coast States
Scats & Tracks of the Rocky Mtns.
Sierra Nevada Wildflowers
Southern Rocky Mountain
  Wildflowers
Tallgrass Prairie Wildflowers
Western Trees

ROCKHOUNDING GUIDES

Rockhounding Arizona
Rockhounding California
Rockhounding Colorado
Rockhounding Montana
Rockhounding Nevada
Rockhounding New Mexico
Rockhounding Texas
Rockhounding Utah
Rockhounding Wyoming

HOW-TO GUIDES

Avalanche Aware
Backpacking Tips
Bear Aware
Desert Hiking Tips
Hiking with Dogs
Hiking with Kids
Mountain Lion Alert
Reading Weather
Route Finding
Using GPS
Wild Country Companion
Wilderness First Aid
Wilderness Survival

MORE GUIDEBOOKS

Backcountry Horseman's
  Guide to Washington
Family Fun in Montana
Family Fun in Yellowstone
Exploring Canyonlands & Arches
  National Parks
Exploring Hawaii's Parklands
Exploring Mount Helena
Exploring Southern California
  Beaches
Hiking Hot Springs of the Pacific
  Northwest
Touring Arizona Hot Springs
Touring California & Nevada
  Hot Springs
Touring Colorado Hot Springs
Touring Montana and Wyoming
  Hot Springs
Trail Riding Western Montana
Wilderness Directory
Wild Montana
Wild Utah
Wild Virginia

■ *To order any of these books, check with your local bookseller
or call FALCON ® at 1-800-582-2665.
Visit us on the world wide web at:
www.Falcon.com*

FALCON®